Richard P. Coleman

Bernice L. Neugarten

SOCIAL
STATUS
IN THE
CITY

Jossey-Bass Inc., Publishers
615 Montgomery Street · San Francisco · 1971

SOCIAL STATUS IN THE CITY
Richard P. Coleman and Bernice L. Neugarten

Copyright © 1971 by Jossey-Bass, Inc., Publishers

Jossey-Bass, Inc., Publishers
615 Montgomery Street
San Francisco, California 94111

Library of Congress Catalog Card Number 70-132820

International Standard Book Number ISBN 0-87589-081-4

Manufactured in the United States of America
Composed and printed by York Composition Company, Inc.
Bound by Chas. H. Bohn & Co., Inc.

JACKET DESIGN BY WILLI BAUM, SAN FRANCISCO

FIRST EDITION

Code 7102

The Jossey-Bass
Behavioral Science Series

General Editors

WILLIAM E. HENRY, *University of Chicago*

NEVITT SANFORD, *Wright Institute, Berkeley*

Preface

*T*he basic purpose of *Social Status in the City* is to present a method for measuring social status in large urban settings, the Index of Urban Status (IUS). By describing the procedures used in studying the social structure of a particular midwestern city some fifteen years ago, we show how the index was originally derived and the concepts of status on which it is based. The IUS has been modified several times by the senior author as he has employed it in commercial research studies of social class phenomena in many American cities. The current version of the IUS is presented here in some detail, together with guidelines for its use by other investigators. In this connection, the book should be seen in the context of the sociologist's concerns with problems of urban stratification, the characteristics of various social class groups, and the ways these groups change over time. In this context, the book is intended to make a contribution to method.

Another purpose is to present sufficient data regarding Kansas City, Missouri, so that the substantive findings will provide a benchmark description of the status hierarchy of a large American city in the mid-1950s. Here we have followed in the tradition of W. Lloyd Warner and others who have attempted to understand the status structures of whole communities. In this second context, the novelty of *Social Status in the City* lies in the fact that we have focused upon a single community that is larger in size and more complex in organization than any previously described.

The analysis of the social structure of a large city was originally undertaken in connection with the Kansas City Studies of Adult Life, two interrelated sets of studies carried out under the auspices of the Committee on Human Development of the University of Chicago in the period from 1952 to 1962. The first set of those investigations was focused on middle age and the variations that occur in life styles and in social-psychological patterns of behavior with age, sex, and social status. The studies were financed by a grant from the Carnegie Corporation and were conducted by a research team of which Robert J. Havighurst was chairman. The second group of those investigations focused on changes that occurred over time in a panel of middle-aged and older persons followed over a six-year period. They were financed by a grant from the Professional Services Branch, National Institute of Mental Health (#M9082), and were under the direction of William E. Henry, Robert J. Havighurst, and Bernice L. Neugarten. A large number of publications based on the Kansas City Studies have appeared within the past several years, dealing with various topics: social role performance of middle-aged persons, leisure patterns, age status, personality changes, adaptational patterns, the disengagement theory of aging, and the subsequent modifications of that theory. Publication of the data regarding the social structure of Kansas City has, however, been delayed until now.

Kansas City was chosen as the site for those investigations of adult life for a number of reasons. Varieties of behavior were to be viewed in an urban setting, and, to understand that setting, studies of the community itself—especially its social structure—were planned from the outset. Thus a site was needed which would be urban in character yet not so large or complex as to preclude completing a study of the community as a first phase of the research. Another important factor was that a cooperative arrangement had been made with Community Studies, Inc., of Kansas City, a local social science research organization which had already gathered much of the basic data needed for a project of this scope. The staff of Community Studies offered to act as hosts to the University of Chicago investigators.

The study of the social structure of Kansas City was motivated, however, by more than the need to understand the community setting as the context for viewing middle age and aging. Members of the research team—notably W. Lloyd Warner, Robert

J. Havighurst, and we—were interested in adapting the methods used earlier in studying small communities to the problems of studying the large city and in evaluating the extent to which a large city could be accurately described as a hierarchical status structure. Warner and his associates had previously studied small towns in New England and in the Midwest with populations less than twenty thousand, then a Midwest community of 95,000. They wished next to consider a large city, in this instance, one of some 850,000. As an outgrowth of those research interests in the status structures of American communities, we hope that our findings regarding Kansas City in the 1950s will have implications for the American urban scene beyond the borders of Kansas City and beyond the 1950s.

Methods and findings are always intertwined. To pick but one example—special attention was given to the role played by wives in influencing the social status of their families, a phenomenon often overlooked in previous studies. One of our findings in Kansas City was that a woman's educational background correlated more highly than did her husband's with family income and with the family's social class position. Education of wife was thereafter included as one dimension in the multidimensional Index of Urban Status.

Because of the intricate relationship between methods and findings, the exposition to follow must, at least to some extent, deal simultaneously with both. For the reader who is interested in one more than the other, a brief overview of *Social Status in the City* may be helpful. The first three chapters describe how we studied Kansas City, adapting the methods used in small communities to the problems of studying the large community; how we identified the dimensions of status perceived by Kansas Citians; and how we weighed the importance of neighborhood, housing, occupation, education, ethnic identity, religious affiliation, and community participation in assessing the status of Kansas City families.

The fourth chapter describes how we delineated the status structure and presents a statistical summary of the characteristics of each of the social classes based on data gathered from a representative sample of persons aged forty to sixty-nine. Some of the complexities of an urban community are reflected in discussions of the differences in social characteristics, in life styles, and in community reputation that distinguished the thirteen strata that composed the social hierarchy, of the problems involved in equating Negro and white status groups, and of how, after further analysis, the thirteen strata produced a coherent picture of the social structure as a basic five-class structure.

In Chapter Five we pursue the problem of measurement and describe the Index of Urban Status (IUS) as it evolved from the earlier index used in Kansas City and as it has been elaborated in subsequent studies carried out by the senior author. The several components of the IUS have been scaled to reflect the evaluations placed upon them by residents of the various communities studied. Thus the IUS represents an approach that stands midway between, on the one hand, the evaluated participation techniques used by Warner and his associates in studying small towns and, on the other, the socioeconomic indices more often used by other sociologists.

Chapters Six through Ten present discursive accounts of the social class groups in Kansas City and reflect something of the variety of life patterns included at each level. For example, Chapter Six shows how the upper class was itself a complicated status pyramid and how the position of any given family was determined by a complex interweaving of various qualifications and social connections rather than by any single criterion such as lineage. Together with the data of Chapter Four, these five chapters show how a group of Americans born in the period 1885 to 1914 were distributed in the status hierarchy by the time they had reached middle age. The descriptions present the patterning of social characteristics to be found in families who, within a given social class, represented elite, core, or marginal status positions. The upper and the lower classes are treated here in somewhat more detail than in other books that have dealt with class phenomena, for it is with regard to these two classes that major differences occur between the large city and the small town. The upper class has merited special attention not only because its members wield power disproportionate to their numbers but also because it is a more heterogeneous group than might have been assumed from earlier studies. The lower class is also a more varied group in the city than in the small community and contains within it more than one subculture.

Chapter Eleven is a study of social mobility among Kansas Citians and of the factors relating to intergenerational mobility as well as to mobility that occurs from one to another period in adulthood. If these data are representative of what has prevailed in other cities, the American status system is a very open system. Over half these men and women experienced a change of social class identification, moving up or down a class or two from the level of their parents.

In Chapter Twelve an attempt has been made to compare the social class groups which emerged in Kansas City with those described by investigators who had studied other communities and also to see how various local status systems fit together to constitute a nationwide status hierarchy.

Finally, in Chapter Thirteen, we comment briefly upon the changing status system of contemporary America and raise the question, as have others before us, of whether the growth of a large middle-majority together with other forms of social change is producing a three- rather than a five-class social structure over the country at large.

We are indebted to many persons. Foremost is our intellectual debt to W. Lloyd Warner, whose earlier studies of social stratification were the foundation for this one. We are indebted also to Robert J. Havighurst, who provided continuing guidance and assistance; to Martin B. Loeb, who was for a time field director of the Kansas City Studies and who played an important role in helping to clarify our views of the status structure; to Warren A. Peterson, who made important contributions particularly to the development of the Index of Kansas City Status; to Elijah White, who assisted in setting up the sampling design; to John Scott, who played a central role in the study of social mobility reported in Chapter Eleven; and to David Riesman and Betty Orr for assistance in interviewing upper-status people.

William D. Bryant, who was director of Community Studies, Inc., and host to the Chicago research team, was unsparing of his time and encouragement. A brief history of Kansas City prepared by Bryant appears as Appendix A. Homer Wadsworth, executive director of the Kansas City Association of Trusts and Foundations, helped the Chicago team maintain good community relations and was instrumental in making a special fellowship available to the senior author.

Finally, we are indebted to several persons who worked later in Chicago to help prepare the manuscript for publication: Jacqueline Falk, James Gorney, Elizabeth Garber, and, in particular, Grace Lieberman. A special acknowledgment also must be made to Lee Rainwater for his assistance and encouragement to the senior author, who completed the final draft and editorial work on the manuscript while employed at the Joint Center for Urban Studies of Massachusetts Institute of Technology and Harvard University on NIMH Grant #1-PO-MH-15567.

Cambridge   RICHARD P. COLEMAN
Chicago   BERNICE L. NEUGARTEN
October 1970

Contents

Social Status
in the
City

Part One

Studying an Urban Status Structure

Chapter 1

Overview of Research Procedures

No published account of social class structures in large American cities had yet appeared when this study of social class in Kansas City was begun in 1952, although a number of community studies had been conducted in small towns or small cities. The proposition that American communities comprise social class structures had been formally set forth by W. Lloyd Warner and his associates in 1941 with the publication of the first volume of the Yankee City series (Warner and Lunt, 1941). Warner proposed, on the basis of his research in a New England community of seventeen thousand, that there were six social classes in the United States. This six-class division coincided closely with a description of American community life that had appeared four years earlier in Lynd and Lynd, *Middletown in Transition* (1937). Although the Lynds described five classes rather than six, the similarity was striking in that four of the five classes were identical in occupational and other characteristics with those identified by Warner in Yankee City.

By the end of the 1940s the social class structures of several other American communities had been examined, notably in the Allison Davis, Burleigh Gardner, and Mary Gardner study of Deep South—a Mississippi river town of thirteen thousand, and in W. Lloyd Warner's study of Jonesville—a county seat in central Illinois

3

with a population of six thousand (Davis, Gardner, and Gardner, 1941; Warner et al., 1949).[1] Although these studies corroborated the earlier sets of observations, they did not help to determine whether the concept of social class was meaningful in understanding the social life of a large city.

Since 1952, social class phenomena have been studied in urban settings. August B. Hollingshead's study of New Haven and the Harold M. Hodges, Jr., study of the San Francisco-San Jose area are the best documented (Hollingshead and Redlich, 1958; Hodges, 1963).[2] These studies differed from the Kansas City study because those investigators transferred to the city scene the assumptions regarding social class which had been developed in small towns without investigating the perceptions of city dwellers regarding the dimensions of status that characterized their communities.

Although the vast outpouring of theoretical papers and empirical studies regarding social stratification continues, no recent full-scale community studies are aimed at delineating the social class structure for a number of reasons, among them the controversy that developed among sociologists in the 1940s and 1950s about the value of further work along these lines. The validity of some of the concepts when applied to a large urban or metropolitan community has been questioned; and the issue of whether a national social class structure could be generalized from studies of individual communities has not been resolved[3]

The present research included an extensive investigation into the ways Kansas Citians described the class structure of their com-

---

[1] Studies of small towns and rural communities published in the 1940s include, among many others: Dollard (1949); Form (1945); Stendler (1949); and West (1945). Studies completed after 1950 include: Bailey (1953); McCall (1954); Vidich and Bensman (1958); and Gallaher (1961).

[2] Two studies of suburban sectors of major American cities are described in Dobriner (1963) and in Laumann (1967).

[3] For critiques of Warner's social class analysis of American society, the best single source is Bendix and Lipset (1953 and 1966), especially the papers by Hyman, Kornhauser, and Parsons. Other significant articles include Gross (1949), Pfautz and Duncan (1950), Lenski (1952), Stone and Form (1953), Tumin (1953), and Hodge and Treiman (1968). See also Thernstrom (1964), and Thernstrom (1965).

Among major books on social class are: Kahl (1957), Gordon (1958), Reissman (1959), Hodges (1964), Lasswell (1965), and Roach, Gross, and Gursslin (1969).

munity and the dimensions of status they perceived to be important. Scales for measuring status were built upon these evaluations and were thus tailored to Kansas City rather than borrowed from previous studies of social class in smaller communities. (These scales have since been generalized to apply to other cities, as described in Chapter Five.)

Nature of Social Class

In Warner's terms, a social class is essentially a group of people who are judged by members of the community as equal to one another in social prestige and, in turn, believed to be superior or inferior in prestige and acceptability to other groups who constitute the social classes below or above them. A society containing social classes is one in which there are

> two or more orders of people who are believed to be, and are accordingly ranked by the members of the community, in socially superior and inferior positions. Members of a class tend to marry within their own order, but the values of the society permit marriage up and down. A class system also provides that children are born into the same status as their parents. A class society distributes rights and privileges, duties and obligations, unequally among its inferior and superior grades. A system of classes, unlike a system of castes, provides by its own values for movement up and down the social ladder. In common parlance, this is social climbing, or in technical terms, social mobility.[4]

By this definition, Yankee City, Deep South, Jonesville, Kansas City—and presumably every community in the United States—can be described as social class systems.

The number of social classes identified by investigators has varied from four to six, presumably because of the differences among communities in age, geographic location, population size, and ethnic composition. In all these communities the correlation between occupational status and social class groupings is marked. Yet the most important observation about social classes in small communities is that they do not represent merely similar occupational groups or income levels. Instead, social classes are categories of persons whose educational backgrounds are similar, who share patterns of community participation and social interaction, whose

[4] Warner and Lunt (1941).

life styles and value systems are remarkably similar, and whose similarities sometimes transcend differences in occupation or income. Above all, the members of a social class regard each other as social equals.

A principal question of the present research was whether a social class system similar to that observed in smaller communities was present in a city as large, and presumably heterogeneous, as Greater Kansas City, Missouri. That is, do the citizens of a large city make judgments about each other's social standing similar to those made by residents of smaller communities? Do they perceive their city as composed of distinct social strata? And if so, what are the dimensions of status in the city?

Methods for Studying Status

In order to study the characteristics of the class system in a large urban setting, the development of new methods was necessary. It was obviously impossible to study social classes by the same technique of evaluated social participation used in small cities.[5] Yankee City, Deep South, and Jonesville were all small enough so that the research teams were able to observe and document many of the socially evaluated interactions occurring in the daily lives of the citizens. Informal clique behavior could be observed, membership rosters for every club could be obtained, and participation within the clubs could be examined. In short, it was possible to obtain a full set of facts on who associated with whom. The placement of a particular person in the social structure could be made by using this information. The major lines of social stratification were ascertained. Names were obtained of a few persons whom interviewees agreed upon as occupying given positions in the hierarchy. It was then noted with whom these persons associated in informal social cliques, social clubs, service clubs, church associations, and so on. Other persons were then placed in relation to the original group, and eventually the majority of the community could be placed on the social map.

Along with examination of patterns of social interaction, the research teams in Yankee City, Deep South, and Jonesville conducted hundreds of interviews to learn how townspeople described

[5] For a full description of evaluated participation, see Warner, Meeker, and Eells (1949).

the social divisions in their communities and what social rankings they applied to one another. These two types of data—observation of participation (formal and informal) and social rankings—were then combined, and a master diagram of the community status structure was drawn up. Warner spoke of this type of diagram as representing "the major social groupings perceived, experienced, and described by the citizens themselves."[6] It represented a composite portrait of what the researcher learned, not the picture offered by any single citizen but the consensus of residents' perceptions.

The researchers in Yankee City, Deep South, and Jonesville produced social class descriptions based on rich observational data. In so doing, they went beyond the direct verbal statements of informants into an area of social reality which at least some residents preferred to deny. They learned that while Americans talk a great deal about some of the phenomena of status and rank, they do not readily acknowledge the existence of social classes as such—even in the light of evidence that social participation patterns demonstrated consistent status differentiations.

Obviously the phenomena of social class and the placement of individuals cannot be studied in the same way in a large urban setting. The sheer size of a big city makes it impossible for a research team to observe and chart patterns of social interaction for the whole city or to examine more than a sampling of clubs and associations. Moreover, the residents of a large city do not know any more than a tiny fraction of the other residents. On the other hand, citizens in large cities from diverse walks of life can be interviewed to ascertain their general picture of social divisions in the community and their perceptions of the significance of various status dimensions. Procedures such as participant-observation, analysis of social interaction networks, and analysis of status rankings of all organizations or persons with whom an informant is acquainted can be applied to a sample population. Further, the distribution of class members and the characteristics of each social class can be established by sampling.

These considerations led to the sequence of research procedures listed below. The foregoing exposition of problems related

[6] *Ibid.*

to method indicates why the authors feel that a main contribution of this research has been the tailoring of procedures to fit the conditions of an urban scene. The methods adopted derive much, of course, from the approach developed by Warner and his students in their researches on small towns. The basic principles are still applied: the status hierarchy as described must reflect a consensus of the views held by members of the community; and placements of individuals within this hierarchy must be made on the same basis and must reflect the same values as the residents themselves use in evaluating each other.

Research Procedures

The research procedures used in studying Kansas City can be summarized as ten steps, each elaborated later in this book.

First, to determine the degree of status consciousness among Kansas Citians, a series of pilot interviews were obtained. These were designed to elicit the type and degree of class consciousness felt by informants and the social divisions recognized in the community.

Second, to obtain the prevailing perceptions of status factors, a cross-section of over two hundred Kansas Citians was interviewed regarding their impressions of the relative ranking of various social clubs, neighborhoods, churches, occupations, educational levels, and ethnic identifications. This procedure can be seen as an urban equivalent of the procedure of asking people in small towns to rate one another directly. In cities people rate their fellow citizens by superficial evidence and by symbols such as residential address, occupational titles, and club memberships. Individuals are only vaguely aware of people at social levels far removed from their own, and they deal with such people mainly in symbolic terms.

Third, to utilize the observations of particularly sensitive observers, a group of Kansas Citians who occupied civic, social, or professional leadership positions were interviewed regarding their observations of status distinctions and of participation patterns in clubs, organizations, and informal social relationships. Kansas City newspapers were carefully monitored, also, for reports of participation, club life, and individual social achievements, as well as for the status imagery implied in descriptions of neighborhoods, community activities, and social events of various types. This procedure was substituted for the direct participant-observation used by social scientists who studied small towns.

Fourth, upon completion of the first three steps, a first attempt was made to draw a diagram of the Kansas City class structure. This delineation represented a set of working hypotheses based on the data at hand and opened the way for further research steps.

Fifth, a representative sample of 462 Kansas Citians aged forty to sixty-nine, were interviewed about their social participation, occupations, incomes, religious affiliations, educational backgrounds, and other pertinent aspects of their life histories and current styles of life. These interviews were used to provide evidence—about actual characteristics and social behavior—against which the prevailing Kansas Citian *perceptions* and our own preliminary view of the social structure could be checked. They also provided the quantitative data on which subsequent characterizations of each social class were based.

Sixth, an Index of Kansas City Status (IKCS) was developed to assess the status of individuals and families. The various dimensions of status which had emerged as important—occupation, income, housing, neighborhood, club membership, community participation, ethnic identity, educational background, and church affiliation—were scaled independently and then combined into the index.

Seventh, tentative class placements were made for each of the several hundred members of the sample.

Eighth, the preliminary delineation of the social structure was then reexamined. Boundaries between classes and subgroups and linkages between status levels were studied by examining participation patterns in relation to rankings on the dimensions of status.

Ninth, a final delineation of the status structure was drawn up, in which five main social classes and thirteen substrata were identified. All members of the sample of 462 were classified into one of these thirteen status groups.

Tenth, the distribution within status groups of the total middle-aged population of Kansas City was then estimated from the sample, and the characteristics of each group relative to all nine dimensions of status were described (see Table 2 in Chapter Four).

Two additional researches were undertaken that were related to this study of the Kansas City social status system. The first was a study in depth of the higher status levels in Kansas City and the roles of higher status persons in community affairs. For this study, one hundred men and women at or near the top of the prestige hierarchy were interviewed at length, and detailed information was obtained from a variety of sources regarding the social characteristics of some six thousand high status families. Data on these six thousand upper status families have been combined with data obtained from interviews of the sample of 462 to produce Table 2 in Chapter Four. That table shows the social characteristics of Kansas City's thirteen strata. The second study was of the intergenerational social mobility that characterized middle-aged Kansas Citians and of patterns of mobility in relation to age, class of origin, and other factors. These data are reported in Chapter Eleven.

Once these studies of Kansas City had been completed, there remained the problems of generalizing both our findings and our methods. As already indicated in the preface and as evident from the table of contents of this book, we undertook additional research steps. We compared our findings from Kansas City with the findings of other investigators in pursuing the broader questions of social classes in American communities and the extent to which a nationwide social hierarchy can be said to exist. Finally, making use of other sets of data gathered subsequently in other cities, we transformed the Index of Kansas City Status (IKCS) into the Index of Urban Status (IUS); and utilizing various sets of census data, we have from time to time altered the scale values to keep the IUS a current working tool for the study of large or small American cities in the 1960s and now in the 1970s.

Chapter 2

Class Consciousness
in the City

Kansas City in the Mid-Fifties

*K*ansas City, in the 1950s, could surely qualify as a metropolitan center. The population of the metropolitan area was 815,000 according to the 1950 census, and by 1955, when the field work for this study was completed, the population had passed the nine hundred thousand mark. This pattern of growth was average for a metropolitan center and indicates that Kansas City was neither a boom town in this postwar period—like many cities in California, Texas, or Florida—nor a static or declining city.

In the 1950s Kansas City, Missouri, and its environs, was most nearly comparable in size to Milwaukee, Cincinnati, Houston, and Seattle and not much smaller than Cleveland, Washington, St. Louis, or Baltimore. At the same time it was not too much larger or markedly different from cities like Toledo, Memphis, Rochester, Indianapolis, Denver, and San Antonio, which had populations ranging down to half that of Kansas City. With respect to size, then, Kansas City appeared to be an ideal representative of the American city.

All or parts of five counties constituted the Kansas City metropolitan area as defined both by residents and census officials:

11

Jackson, Clay, and Platte counties in Missouri, and Wyandotte and Johnson counties in Kansas. This area encompassed the satellite cities of Kansas City, Kansas (with a population of 130,000), and Independence, Missouri (with a population of 45,000), as well as the principal city of Kansas City, Missouri, whose population was approximately 465,000. The area also contained county towns of a few thousand, and crossroads hamlets of a few hundred. Some of the residents of these towns and hamlets worked in Kansas City; others were traditional townspeople who went to the central city only occasionally for shopping or entertainment.

Suburban housing developments spread out from the center city, embracing the satellite cities of Independence on the east, Kansas City, Kansas, on the west, and almost reaching the county towns to the north, south, and southwest. Almost all the population growth between 1950 and 1955 had occurred in the suburbs. In this respect, Kansas City was typical of the thriving metropolitan areas of the United States; the suburbs, not the cities, grew rapidly in the 1950s. Finally, there were areas of open country and farm land within the boundaries of the metropolitan area; some of this land was occupied by city farmers, who worked at part-time jobs in the city, but most of it was occupied by families engaged solely in farming.

All these persons—city dwellers, suburbanites, city farmers, real farmers, exurbanites, small town people, and inhabitants of the satellite communities—were drawn into the research sample in numbers approximately representative of their proportion in the metropolitan population. Accordingly, this is a study of people living within the boundaries of a metropolitan area rather than a study of city dwellers only.

Ethnically and racially, Kansas City was probably as representative of American cities in the mid-1950s as any single city could be. The people living there liked to call their city the "Heart of America" and to think of it as typical of the whole country. The population was predominantly native born—the proportion of foreign born (only 3 per cent) was half that of Chicago and only a third that of New York City—and to a certain extent was thereby not really typical; as one Kansas Citian expressed it, this made it "more American than America itself."

Negroes constituted about the same proportion of the population of Kansas City as of the United States as a whole. In-migration of Negroes had begun in the 1930s and reached a high level during the immediate postwar years. In the mid-1950s the Negro population in the Kansas City area was approximately 13 per cent of the total.

The proportion of Catholics in Kansas City was about 20 per cent, below average for larger cities. The proportion of Jews— only 3 per cent—was also below average for cities of comparable size but typical for most places west of the Mississippi. Thus Kansas City was more predominantly Protestant than all but a few other major cities; in addition, its people were perhaps more predominantly of English, Scotch, and North Irish origin than are the people in any other major northern city, except perhaps Denver. These population characteristics are relevant to the perceptions of status among Kansas City residents, and they are also important in considering the class distribution that emerged. Given such a composition of racial, religious, and ethnic groups, Kansas City was a relatively simple city in which to study status phenomena; but by the same token nonethnic factors in the social structure were probably highlighted as compared with other cities.

Interviews about the awareness of status differences were centered in Kansas City, Missouri, and in those suburban areas which were primarily within its sphere of influence. This limit was established early in the research when it became clear that people in Kansas City, Missouri, interacted very little with people in Kansas City, Kansas (except for economic transactions), and that the metropolitan area was divided into at least three independent social systems—one dominated by the central city, the other two dominated respectively by Kansas City, Kansas, and Independence, Missouri. In addition, each of the county towns and townships comprised a somewhat separate social system, although suburban growth was pulling more and more of these county towns into the social orbit of Kansas City, Missouri.

The members of each social system showed themselves quite unaware of finer points in the status imagery of the other systems. They related to one another primarily with remarks and attitudes reflecting good-humored rivalry or jealousy and bitterness. They were aware that class distinctions in other communities paralleled those in their own communities—that the status system in each community had an economic base overlaid with social and personal forms of differentiation.

A Continuum of Gentle Gradations?

Kansas City men and women seemed to have a highly developed awareness of social status, even though they talked more readily about the symbols of status and the relative rank of individuals than about social classes. The individual citizen could easily describe the types of people he regarded as being above him or below him in the social hierarchy.

Status consciousness was focused on specific symbols of status, such as where a person lived, the clubs to which he belonged, the church he attended, and, to a lesser extent, his occupation and his educational level. Men and women who differentiated only a top and a bottom class could nevertheless often rank neighborhoods by as many as seven status levels; similarly, they could readily explain why one social club should be rated higher than another or why one church or school had more social prestige than another.

When asked how many classes there were in Kansas City, only a few informants generalized across the community and described as many as five social levels; a somewhat larger number described four. By far the most common view was one in which only three classes were identified—a top, a bottom, and a middle. The top and bottom classes were usually seen as very small in size and were defined in extreme terms as the richest people and the poorest. This description left the rest as one giant-sized middle, including 80 or 90 per cent of the population.

A young lawyer saw the social levels as a series of "gentle gradations": "I would find it hard to think of classes or strata as separate and distinct entities. I think I would describe Kansas City as a series of continuous gradations from top to bottom. It seems to me that classes are a matter of degree. They blend into one another, and it would be hard to specify how many strata or classes there would be."

Was the Kansas City status system a continuum of gentle gradations? Or did the complexity of the urban environment make it difficult for citizens to recognize social class divisions? These questions were implicit in the remarks of a prominent committeewoman:

All I can say is that Kansas City is just like any other city. There are several different groups which occupy differently regarded social levels; some are on top and some are on the bottom. From the nature and necessity of community life there must be people who are most influential and people who are without influence; people who are wealthy and people who are poor; and then there are all degrees of influence and affluence between these two poles. . . . There are so many varieties and kinds of people here I wouldn't even be able to decide where any lines might be drawn to divide them into classes . . . nor would I be able to say in what kinds of activities people from each of these social levels engage.

The attitude toward status classification reflected in these two statements grew out of a realization that social position in Kansas City was not a simple matter of financial affluence or any other single factor but was influenced by several different criteria. This awareness of the multiple dimensions of status made it difficult for Kansas City people to draw social class lines as easily as had residents of small towns.

The Top and the Bottom

Even though Kansas Citians found it difficult to specify how many social classes there might be, they found little difficulty in describing the people who constituted the top and the bottom groups. One man said:

There is this top crowd who everyone seems to look up to as leaders. These are the men who are outstanding in the civic and business affairs of Kansas City. They would be regarded by people all over the city as outstanding and prominent persons. I think they have more to recommend them than just money. Of course, they would all be well-to-do executives and the top-ranking professionals. Most of them live there along Ward Parkway. They are the Society of the town. These are the men who are regarded by the average man as a rank or two above [himself]. Then there's the other extreme . . . the lowest classes of people—and this includes whites as well as colored. You generally find them in the areas closest to the downtown district. It's primarily a man's economic position—being down and out, so to speak—that keeps him living in these worst areas. When you get right down to it, it's the common laborers, the people who live in slummy houses, who just wear rags and who never bother with church, the drunkards—it's the people like that who are stamped as being at the bottom of the heap.

A salesclerk furnished this comparison of the two status extremes:

> We have this group of topnotchers here in town which includes
> some people from old, old families with a lot of money, and
> who've had it a long time, like the Galbraiths and Woods, the
> Norcutts, Blankenships, and Kings.[1] They are the families who
> are always being reported in the Society pages of the news-
> papers. . . . The Southwest part of town all around Ward Park-
> way is where you have the center of Society—that moneyed
> group. The North End is the area of all our disreputables . . .
> and the lower class. . . . That's where most of the meanness in
> Kansas City is found. Those Italians are always getting into
> trouble—that gang of Moretti, Rienza, and Fazio. The illiterates
> would also be in the bottom class, along with your underworld.
> The Mexicans would be there on the bottom too. Well . . .
> hmmm . . . I guess [the middle class is] everybody else!

Descriptions like these were repeated with slight variations in
phrasing by people at all levels of Kansas City life. Each person had
his own favorite phrase for people at the top, but the most common
were "the big rich," "the blue bloods," "the bankers and lawyers,"
"people who live in the mansions out Southwest," and "those people
in the elite country clubs."

Quite frequently the name of the most prominent banking
family was used to symbolize the top class, as when people spoke of
"the extreme social world of the Galbraiths." In using this family
as a symbol of Society, people committed the error of characterizing
a group by its most extreme and visible member. Whenever other
names of top families were used, they were of three principal types:
the street-name families, who had played pioneer roles as city
builders and whose real estate holdings had been amassed in the
early periods of Kansas City history; the business rich, whose names
were associated with large commercial or industrial establishments;
and certain leading civic personalities—business executives and important political officials whose names and pictures frequently appeared in the newspapers.

[1] Throughout this book an attempt has been made to preserve the
anonymity of residents of Kansas City but at the same time to make no
more changes in the data than necessary. Accordingly, names of streets and
residential areas have not been changed, nor have the names of associations
that are nationwide in memberships, such as the Masons. Names of individuals and names of purely local clubs and churches have all been changed.

The only other status level to which Kansas Citians frequently attached particular names was the lowest class. Over and over Kansas City people mentioned the names Fazio, Rienza, and Moretti, as symbolic of the racketeering underworld or as examples of "the lowest crowd we've ever had in town." These names had become familiar to the public because they had repeatedly made unfavorable headlines in the Kansas City daily newspapers. Indeed, apart from sports figures or local television and radio personalities, the only names that had conversational currency in Kansas City were those which represented one or another of the social extremes. When people from different status levels talked to one another (such as cabdriver to passenger, beauty operator to customer, or newspaper reporter to his readers), the meaning of these names was understood by all; they had come to signify a status level and a way of life.

The social extremes in Kansas City were also highly visible because both groups were seen as living in residential isolation from the rest of the community. The very rich were perceived as inhabiting great mansions in the southwest corner of the city, along Ward Parkway and in Mission Hills. The very poor were thought to inhabit slums or otherwise socially condemned neighborhoods surrounding the business district in the old North End and West Side areas. As one young woman said: "I think it is really the houses that some of those people live in that make the rest of us think of them as upper class. When you drive around and see those big houses, rows and rows of them all over that Southwest area, you naturally think that the people living in them must be as wonderful as their houses. That's why we call the people out in those big houses our upper class of people."

In parallel fashion, slums and substandard housing suggested to Kansas Citians that the people living in them must be "as awful as their houses." The image of the lowest class was not only a product of their poor living conditions; it was also a product of the need many higher status people had to look down on people below them. Kansas Citians repeatedly spoke of the lower classes in contemptuous phrases such as "public enemies," "the criminal class," "the immoral," "the riff-raff," "the booze hounds," and other strong appellations indicating disapproval of character. When referring to the poverty of this lowest class, they usually attached blame and implied that the poor were responsible for their own condition; thus, the poor were called "incompetents," "shiftless," "people who have never tried to better themselves—they just live in shacks and don't seem to care."

Differences within the middle ranges of the social class hierarchy were much less salient for Kansas Citians; such differences did not evoke strong feelings of envy or contempt. Kansas Citians were by no means oblivious, however, to status inequalities within the middle range. When informants were questioned about this issue, various dividing lines and various dimensions of status were described.

Collar-Color and Political Party Lines

The status distinction most commonly used to divide the vast middle ranges of the status hierarchy was based upon occupation and can be called the *collar-color line*. As one Kansas City woman put it, "people who work in offices and wear white collars generally have more status than people who work in factories, who work with their hands and are what you call blue-collar workers." A second division perceived by many respondents was the *political party line,* based on the notion that "people who vote Republican are generally higher [in social class] than those who vote Democratic."

When the collar-color line was used, it implicitly or explicitly divided Kansas City people into four status categories: "rich people who are the high executives and owners of big businesses"; "all the rest of the people who work in offices—white-collar workers you would call them"; "people who work in factories, who work with their hands—the blue-collar workers—and other people like that who aren't really poor"; and, at the bottom, "the poor," "the criminals," and "people who won't work at all."

Most Kansas City informants who employed the collar-color line felt that it had little more than a broad, general applicability; they made it clear that every white-collar worker was not to be regarded as socially superior to all blue-collar workers. They were careful to acknowledge that even if this division had once been valid, the great gains in economic status experienced by blue-collar workers in the previous two decades had partially erased its importance as a status distinction. In general, the view was that many blue-collar workers from the higher rungs of the blue-collar world had translated their economic gains into social advancement and thus achieved equality with families in the lower ranks of white-collardom.

This collar-color line, while widely shrugged off as no longer important, lingered on very strongly in the feelings of people who had worked themselves up from blue-collar backgrounds into white-collar occupations. They were proud of the gains they had made in social position. It lingered on also in the feelings of men and women who had quit school very young. They had not been able to overcome their resentment at how "people who work all dressed up feel they are better than us who work with our hands and get dirty." Finally it was being perpetuated by the most active participants in labor-management struggles.[2]

The political party line also implicitly or explicitly created four classes: "the top class of rich people who are almost always Republicans"; "other people who vote Republican but aren't rich"; "people who vote Democratic but aren't at the bottom of the barrel"; and "the lowest class—when we have elections around here, those people vote Democratic at least twenty to one."

In the early 1950s the Democratic Party in Kansas City was still commonly identified as the "champion of the underdog" and the Republican Party as the "voice of privilege." Ever since the 1930s, when Democratic Party boss Thomas Pendergast had welded together a powerful political machine composed of Irishmen, Italians, Negroes, and the poor of all races and backgrounds, politics in Kansas City had engendered strong emotions. Long-standing differences between Democrats and Republicans on political issues were compounded by accusations of corruption, vote fraud, and politically inspired murder. During the 1920s and 1930s the Kansas

---

[2] It is likely that the collar-color line was less important in Kansas City than in many other American cities. Given the diversified economy of the city and the absence of heavy industry, unionism was relatively weak. There was no history of labor-management conflict, for instance, nor of dominance by any single union. Furthermore, most blue-collar workers in Kansas City were of North European descent and more often Protestant than Catholic. Unlike other cities where ethnic and religious differences go hand in hand with occupational differences to further the demarcation along the collar-color line, in Kansas City many blue-collar families who were prosperous and who maintained relatively high living standards were readily accepted as social equals by white-collar families.

City *Star* became the most prominent and persistent enemy of the Pendergast machine. In 1940 a nonpartisan reform government led by the *Star* overturned the Pendergast regime, but in the early 1950s the legacy of political conflict was still strong in Kansas City.

Many people seemed to regard this conflict as an important aspect of intergroup rivalry in their community. A number of informants talked at length about the continuing political fight between the "haves" of the southwest corner and the "have-nots" of the northwest corner. They often stated that the leaders of the two political parties were the respective spokesmen for these two extreme social groups. One man said:

> The real fight in this town has always been the "haves" against the "have-nots." It's been the Gold Coast on the southwest side against the dispossessed of the northwest corner and the North End. The Kansas City *Star* is the Republican Party for all practical purposes. In every election for the past thirty years, it has carried with it the eighth, ninth, and tenth wards, which are down in the southwest corner. That's the heartland of Republicanism. The Pendergast machine—that's the Democratic Party —has just as regularly carried the first, second, third, fourth, eleventh, and fourteenth wards in the northwest corner. Those are the Negro wards and the poorest white wards, including the Italian neighborhoods. The main poles of this city, socially speaking, are the old eighth ward—which has now been divided into the eighth, ninth, tenth—and the first ward. The eighth is in the very center of the Southwest, and the further east and north you go away from the old eighth ward, the further people are from the eighth ward social set. The closer you get to the first ward, which is the worst part of the North End, the nearer to the social bottom you are. And the people vote accordingly. The closer the ward is to the old eighth, the more Republican they vote; and the closer to the first ward, the heavier are the Democratic majorities. The real social outcasts of this city are the people who live in the first ward, north and west of the downtown district. They feel separated from the rest of the city, and they feel a powerful resentment against the southwest crowd. This is reflected every time we hold an election around here, by the tremendous margins they build up against whatever it is the Southwest and the Kansas City *Star* stand for. Those people have concentrated their hatred against the Kansas City *Star* because whatever the *Star* says is taken as scripture by the southwest people.

This political party dividing line had a widely recognized geographic parallel in Thirty-first Street, a thoroughfare which crossed the city from east to west and cut it approximately in half. The informant quoted above described this boundary when he went on to say, "Historically Thirty-first Street has been a political dividing line here in Kansas City. . . . The precincts and wards north of Thirty-first Street almost always go Democratic, and south of it, they almost always go Republican." This same street was also frequently cited as the dividing line between the predominantly blue-collar and predominantly white-collar halves of the city. Thus, geographically at least, the political party and collar-color lines coincided in public impression to divide the city socially.

Kansas City informants did not think of these political groupings as social classes, and no one contended that all Kansas City Republicans were socially superior to any of its Democrats. Yet the frequent equation of this political division with a social dividing line indicates that party affiliation often reflected intense emotional reactions to social stratification and to social class discrimination. The choice an individual voter made between identifying himself with the causes of the haves or the have-nots often indicated his view of his own social position and his social and economic aspirations. In this respect political affiliation polarized social classes in Kansas City, pulling them apart according to whether people wished to be associated in spirit and status with those on the top or with those on the bottom.

Skin-Color Line

The presence of a sizeable Negro population in Kansas City offered many residents an easy answer to the question of how many social classes there were and who was in them. Many Kansas City whites simply said, "The only important classes are the white and the black," or, "Social class is the color line—the only difference that really counts is between white and colored." According to this view, Negroes were the lower class and whites the higher class. Although many whites did not make such a quick and easy distinction, the majority considered all Negroes at or near the bottom of the status hierarchy, and if not in a class by themselves then in "the bottom class along with the lowest of the whites."

Only a small number of white Kansas Citians who were interviewed did not subscribe to this blanket placement of Negroes. These few—mostly community leaders or intellectuals—observed, for example, that "a higher class of Negroes—doctors and lawyers—have recently moved into a neighborhood of very fine homes." Or they told of having met a "very fine type of Negro leader" at a civic gathering and admitted that "of course, a Negro like that wouldn't be in the lowest class." Some even spoke of "a middle-class group of Negroes," although they had no idea where such Negroes might fit into the white social status system.

One of the most accurate reflections of the Negro's position in the white perception of the status order was given by a store clerk who remarked, "I'd say the Negroes have just no rating at all." In other words, in the early 1950s, Negroes were perceived by whites as a group totally outside the white social order.

Negro-white interaction was minimal. The public schools were segregated, as were all but one of the restaurants. There were no social clubs with mixed memberships; and among the churches only the Unitarians, a local Unity group, and one Catholic parish had mixed memberships or permitted mixed attendance. While a few leaders of the Negro community served on civic boards and on welfare agency committees, their roles were quite different from those played by whites, for they were considered supplicants for an underprivileged minority; they were included to symbolize the democratic ethos. These handpicked Negroes did not function as donors or decision makers, which were the roles assumed by most of the white members.

In spite of this, many Negroes in Kansas City believed that "the better class of whites really prefer to associate with the better class of Negroes than with the lower class of whites." This may have been true in the abstract, but as of 1954 very few whites had ever demonstrated such a preference. Few would have agreed with the Negro minister who said, "The better class of Negroes is socially equal though segregated." The essential feeling of whites was better summed up by a leading white clergyman who said, "The truth is that Negroes here are totally unequal as well as completely separate."

Ethnic Groups

A further form of status consciousness in Kansas City was evident in the frequent branding of two ethnic groups—the Italians and the Mexicans—as "the lowest class of whites." The perception of Italians as social outcasts occurred in part because they were residentially isolated in the Little Italy of the old North End, but a more important factor was that so many of the Italians who had become well known in Kansas City had come into public view through underworld activities. Throughout the prohibition era of the 1920s, the Italian neighborhood was considered the center of bootlegging. In the 1930s a series of kidnappings and gangland killings was linked to Italians and many of the public enemies named by the police and newspapers had Italian names. In the postwar years the Kansas City public was informed once again by its newspapers that there was a syndicate in Kansas City run by Italians who were reputed to be linked to the mysterious, nationwide Mafia. This reputation led to descriptions of the Italian population as "the criminal and hoodlum element," or "our local underworld." The disrespectful phrases *dago* and *wop* served many Kansas Citians as synonyms for the term *gangster*. The Little Italy neighborhood was often described as looking "very foreign." As one person explained it, "They seem to like having little balconies and the semi-garden kind of yards they were used to having in Italy."

While these images still dominated public thinking in the early 1950s, many citizens had begun to sense that the Italians were unfairly perceived. Discussions of the status of Italians occasionally ended with conciliatory statements. "The Italian district has been rather widely regarded as the breeding place of crime here. . . . However, no more than a small fraction of the Italian element is criminal." "One thing we're facing in our part of town right now is an influx of Italians. I've met some of them, and I've been surprised. They are good, substantial people—and they're trying to prove they are just as good Americans as anybody else." Although some Italians were no longer considered part of the lowest class, it was apparent, as one informant put it, that "the Italians in Kansas City are all prisoners of their descent," unduly handicapped by their names. It was frequently said that Italians found it difficult to obtain white-collar jobs. As one newspaper reporter described it:

> The Italians are held in social confinement. An Italian worker has virtually no chance to rise in some companies. He doesn't have his choice of occupations. Many businesses here wouldn't think of hiring an Italian girl as a secretary. An Italian girl has a difficult time being anything but a waitress or an elevator

operator. The men are pretty nearly excluded from the white-collar world. And that's why they've gone into liquor and night-club businesses, which aren't too respectable.

Although a considerable number of Italian men had done very well in businesses such as wholesale produce, contracting, funeral homes, and insurance, social exclusion was still the rule. A prominent Catholic remarked:

> Even when an Italian does make good—like Ted Francisco—he can buy the biggest marble palace in the whole Country Club District, but he's still strictly a social zero. Francisco is a steel contractor, but his father was what we'd call a "junk dealer." Francisco has assembled one of the biggest fortunes in town these last few years, but he is socially ignored by everyone. His money is too new, even though others with new money have crashed the big time socially. What's wrong in Francisco's case is that he has risen from the very worst part of town, as wrong a side of the tracks as you could find, the Italian North End.

In 1952 not one Italian had gained admission to a high status country club or an elite downtown men's club or had ever been asked to serve on an important civic board or commission. By 1955, however, a man of Italian descent who owned a large chain of liquor stores was elected to membership on the board of directors of the Kansas City Philharmonic Orchestra, one of the most prestigious directorates in the city. Thus, opportunities for social advancement were increasing for Italians—they were no longer at the bottom in social fact nearly so much as in image and reputation.

The attitudes Kansas Citians exhibited toward the Mexicans were more nearly ones of pity than hostility because the Mexican community appeared to be a harmless, though hopelessly poverty-stricken, group: "Pity the poor Mexicans. Nobody ever thinks of them as even being here. They're over there to themselves on the West Side . . . and they don't bother anybody." "I suppose the Mexicans on the West Side are at the bottom socially—but nobody ever hears about them or pays any attention to them."

The Mexicans lived in an isolated enclave. Their neighborhood of about twenty city blocks was located at the bottom of a steep hill and was hemmed in by railroad tracks. There was little reason for most people to pay attention to or know anything about the Mexicans because, as one civic leader said, "When a Mexican commits a crime, it's just petty thievery, not grand larceny or murder, like it is with the Italians." No Mexican family was known to have achieved financial success in the same manner as had some of the Italians. Were any to have done so, it was clear from prevalent attitudes that they would have faced great barriers in translating economic advance into social acceptance.

A third group who were often singled out as "part of the lowest class of white Kansas Citians" were the "Arkies," or "hillbillies." These people had migrated to Kansas City during the war and postwar period from the Ozark mountain regions of Missouri and Arkansas and from the hills of Kentucky, Tennessee, and Alabama. This group was most noticeable to school administrators and social workers, who were concerned with the problems these people encountered as they attempted to adjust to urban living. They had entered the Kansas City labor market as unskilled workers and had thus far remained at the same occupational level. Most had records of job instability; their educational level was low; and their families were large. They lived either in converted apartments at the edge of the business district or in shack areas along the Blue River.

No other ethnic or special groups in Kansas City were described as occupying a particular place in the social status hierarchy. Only fifteen thousand of the 456,000 people residing within the city limits of Kansas City, Missouri, were foreign born, and only a slightly larger group were first generation. The rest of the white population was at least second generation, almost entirely of English, Scotch, Irish, German, or Scandinavian ancestry. Among the foreign born and first generation residents, Italians constituted the largest single group, and Jews of Russian and Polish origin ranked second. Aside from these two groups, Mexicans were the only group in Kansas City which included more than a thousand foreign born.

This characteristic of the population was a source of considerable pride to most residents. They frequently expressed pleasure in this homogeneity, saying that their city had been spared many of the intergroup antagonisms found in other communities. A school administrator remarked: "Our neighborhood isn't much different from the rest of the city. We have a cross section of American types. Almost all of our kids come from real American families. You can pronounce every one of their names. . . . They are very much the fair-skinned all-American youngster."

Kansas Citians looked rather fondly upon their city as a crossroads or as a melting pot for families from all parts of the United States, for Yankees and Confederates, for ex-Ohioans and ex-Tennesseans, for small town Missourians and former Kansas farmers. As a lawyer whose family had lived in Kansas City since before the Civil War explained:

> I'm a native Kansas Citian, but very few of my friends are. This is why we have had a dynamic city. We have been continuously invaded by energetic, ambitious people leaving their home communities to find opportunity. We have many people who came here from the East. We have a large part of our population from both the North Central and Southern parts of the United States, also. The southern groups moved here shortly after the Civil War. They are predominantly second and third generation Kentucky and Virginia families, and this probably accounts for the Negroes here being completely segregated in the schools. Counterbalancing this has been a strong influence of people from Iowa, Wisconsin, Illinois, and Indiana, and the whole area from the Dakotas over to Pennsylvania. Kansas City has always been a crossroads city, as Americans moved west and southwest.

Recognizing this characteristic of the population, another informant observed: "Most of our factory workers here are old Americans, and I would say they are too deeply entrenched a part of this country's Anglo-Saxon heritage to be called a lower class."

Members of the Protestant majority sometimes betrayed thinly disguised prejudice or animosity toward Irish Catholics and Jews, especially as they commented on rivalries for economic and political power. But these attitudes had not resulted in more than a slight handicap to the status aspirations of persons who were Irish-Catholic or Jewish; more nearly, the impact was that Protestants, Irish-Catholics, and Jews tended to move in separate social circles, with the Protestant circles at any given income bracket regarded by all as slightly superior. (We have more to say about religious differences in Chapter Three.)

City Line

Residents of Kansas City, Missouri, expressed hostile attitudes toward Kansas City, Kansas, the smaller satellite city across the Kaw River, attitudes which suggest that class consciousness would have been more related to ethnic factors had there been more ethnic groups in the Missouri community. The Missouri-side people often spoke deprecatingly of Kansas City, Kansas, for having "a heavy foreign element." One respondent volunteered these impressions: "They have a large representation of foreign born over there in Kansas City, Kansas, people who have come from countries like Poland, Russia, Hungary, and Yugoslavia. In that respect Kansas City, Kansas, almost seems like a dirty factory city on the East Coast. It is a lot more polyglot than Kansas City, Missouri." Another informant expressed much the same view: "The lowest class of regularly employed factory workers live over in Kansas City, Kansas. They are Polish and Croatian. They are definitely on the lower edge of the working class in Kansas City. They live mostly in a place we call Balkan Hill that has a real foreign flavor to it. You'll even see foreign language signs on the shops. They are employed in the packing houses and the low-skill jobs on the railroads."

The inferior status assigned to Kansas City, Kansas, also reflected a difference in occupational distribution between the two communities. Almost 80 per cent of the men in Kansas City, Kansas, worked at blue-collar jobs, as compared with 50 per cent in Kansas City, Missouri; and this distribution led many to think of Kansas City, Kansas, as "a proletarian type community" or "a lower class place." As one business leader put it: "A lot of people who employ all those foreign-born factory workers in Kansas City, Kansas, live over here in Missouri or in Johnson County, so you have a pattern of the employers living this side of the Kaw River, while the workers live on the other side."

In one sense, the residents of Kansas City, Kansas, were the largest disadvantaged minority group in the metropolitan area. The Missouri-side and Johnson County (Kansas) residents felt superior even to Kansas City, Kansas, people of their own economic level. They felt proud of being residents of the "better city," and believed that somehow to be a part of the Kansas City, Missouri, world was sophisticated and up-to-date. One newspaper man remarked: "We here in Kansas City, Missouri, think of Kansas City, Kansas, about like Manhattan people think of the Bronx or Brooklyn. It's a place you wouldn't live in if you could help it."

Informants from Kansas City, Kansas, acknowledged the difference in character of the two cities and were apologetic for the inferior status of their own community. One woman, the wife of a railroad union leader from Kansas City, Kansas, spoke without defensiveness: "We're not too proud of this town. Men are always telling my husband we ought to move out of here, but he feels very strongly that it would be wrong to live in a different neighborhood from the men he represents." A newcomer bitterly remarked: "There are three kinds of people in Kansas City, Kansas. First, there are the Polish and the colored, who don't amount to anything. Then there are the people who were born and raised in Kansas City, Kansas, and whose grandparents also lived here; they stay on because they like its small town atmosphere. Then there are fools like me who moved in because we didn't know any better."

The other satellite, Independence, Missouri, was viewed quite differently. It was often described as a "typical Missouri courthouse town," and Kansas Citians spoke enviously of its "different pace of life, much slower, friendlier—more like a small town." The top families of Independence were regarded with considerable respect, partly because several were "old Missouri aristocracy" and partly because one of these families, the Wallaces, produced the wife of a United States president—Bess Truman. A socially prominent Kansas City woman stated: "Independence aristocrats are more aristocratic than Kansas City's aristocrats. . . . They've had their money for a longer time, though they don't compare in wealth with the wealthiest families in Kansas City. On the other hand, their family trees are just as good [as], if not better than, any that Kansas City can boast."

The main body of citizens in Independence were also well regarded. A number were Latter Day Saints (Reorganized), a branch of the Utah Mormons, and were noted for their habits of thrift and hard work. Kansas City Missourians described this group as "an unusually decent lot—hardworking, sound, and sober," and "much more in the mainstream of our nation's Anglo-Saxon heritage than many of Kansas City, Kansas' factory and railroad workers."

From the beginning of this research, a number of important differences were noted in the way the social structure was described by residents of Kansas City as compared with the way it was described by the residents of small towns. In small communities, status hierarchies have been described primarily in terms of evaluated social interaction—who associates with whom—and only secondarily in terms of socioeconomic indices such as area of residence, occupation, or education. In the city, relatively few persons are known to one another, and—with the exception of a few highly visible families—patterns of social interaction are inferred more than observed. Thus the manifest symbols of status—the social geography of the city, the collar-color line, and the skin-color line— necessarily were given precedence in the eyes of community members over the evaluation of observed interaction.

Chapter 3

The Dimensions
of Status

*A*s noted early in Chapter Two, the people of Kansas City were highly conscious of status symbols. Every neighborhood in the city and surrounding suburbs was perceived as having a rank in relation to every other, and agreement about these ranks was very high; even streets and blocks were sometimes separately ranked. Religious denominations and, often, individual churches within these denominations were perceived as having social ratings, as were the many town and country clubs, women's associations, and men's fraternal organizations. Also ranked were occupations, schools, houses, clothing, stores, and cars. All these things were considered when Kansas Citians ranked people as above, equal to, or beneath themselves in the status hierarchy.

Residential Address

Whenever Kansas City people talked about stratification systems more complex than those based on wealth, collar-color lines, or ethnic grouping, they almost invariably turned to residential geography. Most persons identified at least five levels of neighborhoods, and many identified six or seven. Residential address was considered the quickest index to a family's social status—the foremost sign of the breadwinner's financial competence and his or his

30

wife's social ambitions. Salesclerks located their customers on the social ladder when they asked for the address in writing up sales slips. Strangers, when introduced, tended to inquire, "Where do you live?"

The use of residential address as a primary sign of status was facilitated by the simplicity of Kansas City's social geography. There was a basic north-south gradient of neighborhood desirability, modified by a lesser east-west gradient. One man said, "In general, the further south and west a man lives, the greater his monetary competence."

Many residents of Kansas City could characterize each neighborhood by its typical house style and could estimate the prices of these houses on the real estate market. Many could give detailed descriptions of the occupational groups concentrated in each neighborhood, the kinds of clubs residents belonged to, the general pattern of social activity, and the cultural and educational levels to be found there. They usually predicted accurately the political attitudes of citizens in each area. While many of these impressions were derived secondhand, most of them were correct, as was shown later when a cross section of people from each neighborhood was sampled and interviewed.

Over seventy different neighborhoods in Kansas City, Missouri, and its suburbs were singled out and rated. Those informants most sensitive to nuances in neighborhood status, such as realtors or local political leaders, grouped these neighborhoods into seven status categories. Less informed residents sometimes saw fewer groupings, but there was little disagreement about which neighborhood was better than the other in any comparison. The seven-step ranking system in the researchers' opinions represents the best summation of the social geography of the city and is shown in Figure 1.

Ward Parkway and Mission Hills: The highest-ranked neighborhood was usually spoken of as "the Ward Parkway Gold Coast." It stretched for three miles down the southwest edge of the city along both sides of Ward Parkway and extended west across the state line into the Kansas-side suburb of Mission Hills. The streets leading off Ward Parkway were "lined with mansions" which, in 1952, were believed to sell from $45,000 on up. (The house valuations quoted throughout this chapter are in 1952 dollars,

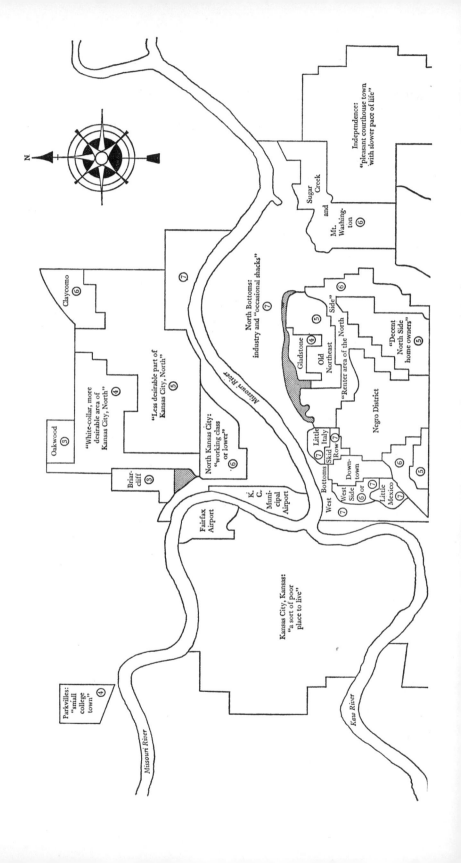

N

Parkville: "small college town" ④

Missouri River

Fairfax Airport

K. C. Municipal Airport

Missouri River

Briarcliff ③

Oakwood ⑤

"White-collar, more desirable area of Kansas City, North" ④

Claycoomo ⑥

"Less desirable part of Kansas City, North" ⑤

⑦

North Kansas City: "working class or lower" ⑥

North Bottoms: industry and "occasional shacks" ⑦

⑦

Sugar Creek and Mt. Washington ⑥

Independence: "pleasant courthouse town with slower pace of life"

Kansas City, Kansas: "a sort of poor place to live"

Kaw River

West Bottoms ⑦

West Side ⑥ or ⑦

Little Italy ⑦

Skid Row ⑦

Down-town ⑥

Little Mexico ⑦

Gladstone ④

⑤

Old Northeast ⑤

Gladstone ⑥

"Renter area of the North" ⑤

"Decent North Side home owners" ⑤

Negro District ⑥

⑤

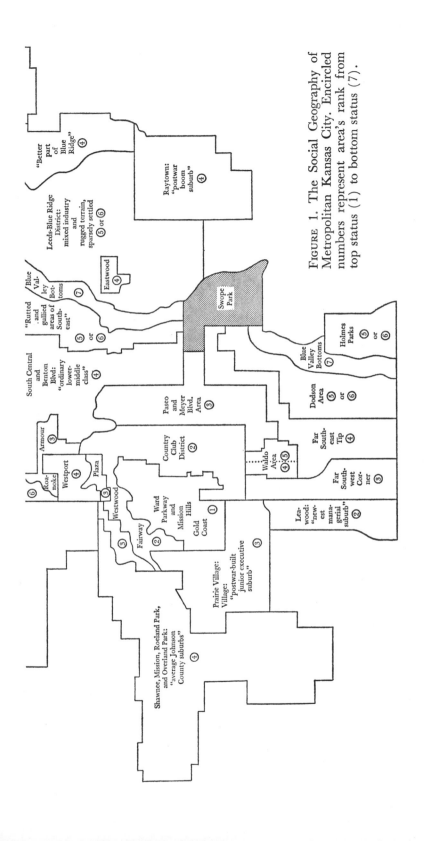

"Better part of Blue Ridge" ④

Leeds-Blue Ridge District: mixed industry and rugged terrain, sparsely settled ⑤ or ⑥

Raytown: "postwar boom suburb" ④

Eastwood ④

Blue Valley Bottoms ⑦

"Rutted and gullied areas of Southeast" ⑤ or ⑥

South Central and Benton Blvd: "ordinary lower-middle class" ④

Swope Park

Blue Valley Bottoms ⑦

Holmes Parks ⑤ or ⑥

Paseo and Meyer Blvd. Area ③

Dodson Area ⑤ or ⑥

Armour ③

Roanoke ⑥

Westport ④

Plaza ③

Country Club District ②

Far Southeast Tip ④

Waldo Area ④-⑤

Far Southwest Corner ③

Westwood ③

Fairway ③

Ward Parkway and Mission Hills ②

Gold Coast ①

Leawood: "newest managerial suburb" ②

Prairie Village: "postwar-built junior executive suburb" ③

Shawnee, Mission, Roeland Park, and Overland Park: "average Johnson County suburbs" ④

FIGURE 1. The Social Geography of Metropolitan Kansas City. Encircled numbers represent area's rank from top status (1) to bottom status (7).

A comparable figure in 1970 dollars would be at least 85 per cent higher.)

The "blue bloods," "the uppercrust," "the Society crowd," and "the topnotchers," were said to live in this area. A man who could afford one of these mansions was assumed to be "one of the big industrialists," "a leading man of commerce," "a well-to-do executive," "a top-ranking lawyer or doctor," or "one of the big shots among the real estate boys and stocks and bonds brokers." This was the area thought to supply most of the members of the elite country clubs, leaders in the Chamber of Commerce, and board members of various cultural institutions. The Gold Coast precincts were said to vote Republican by a nine-to-one majority in election after election.

Country Club District: The second best residential area, the Country Club District, was famous as the first large fully planned residential development built in the United States for upper income families. It surrounded the Ward Parkway Gold Coast on three sides and included the Kansas suburbs of Westwood, Fairway, and Leawood. Its houses were typically seven or eight room brick homes, either ranch style or modified two story Tudor and Colonial structures, ranging in price from eighteen thousand dollars to about forty thousand dollars.

The men who lived in this area were said to be "the more ordinary lawyers and doctors," "other higher-bracket professionals such as engineers, certified public accountants, and dentists," "managerial employees with incomes at the twelve to fifteen thousand dollar a year level," and "successful businessmen who aren't in the really top bracket financially." The families who lived in this area were identified socially as "members of one of the country clubs of suburbia." The men were described as also-rans in the Chamber of Commerce but active in service clubs such as Kiwanis or the Optimists; the women were described as active in the "League of Women Voters and organizations like that" and also as workers (not leaders) in annual fund drives of the Red Cross and Community Chest.

Paseo, Prairie Village, and Armour: Three neighborhoods constituted the third rank, each said to be "better than ordinary, but not as good as the Country Club District." The largest of these was the Paseo district, located along Paseo Street and Meyer Boulevard, east of the Country Club District and south of Forty-seventh Street. A typical house was a six room brick bungalow or seven room, two story frame house built in the late 1920s or 1930s, and valued by realtors at approximately fifteen thousand dollars. Men in the Paseo area were described as teachers, other professionals in a lower financial bracket, accountants, insurance salesmen, owners of small businesses, and other white-collar workers at the eight or nine thousand dollar income level. The organization memberships of the men and women of this neighborhood were viewed as being very different from those of the Country Club District because it was not expected that people at this level could afford a country club membership. It was assumed that the men might be in a businessmen's club but "not in anything as big as the downtown Chamber of Commerce or the big luncheon-service clubs."

A different kind of neighborhood, also third in status rank, was the new suburb of Prairie Village, where the houses were five and six room ranch style or split level houses, on the average not quite as expensive as those in the Paseo district. Prairie Village was seen as the place where young couples with college degrees and good family backgrounds established their first homes. The location of Prairie Village at the western edge of the Gold Coast and Country Club Districts made it ideal as a way station for people who expected to move eventually to these higher-status neighborhoods. It was commonly conceded that the sons and daughters of the blue-stocking families lived in Prairie Village until they could afford to move into "a big house in Mission Hills." Prairie Village men were described as junior executives on their way up or as young doctors and other professonals starting their careers. It was assumed that Prairie Village people were oriented toward Country Club District associations—that the men were in a round of professional organizations as a necessary part of improving their occupational status and that the women, when not kept at home by young children, were taking part in fund raising drives or in college alumni groups.

The third neighborhood at this status level, Armour, was an area of fading aristocracy, where, although the houses were still large and beautiful, there was a suspicion that this external grandeur masked internal decay. A few older aristocrats were said to be staying on amidst the surrounding social ruins of large houses being converted into small apartments, boarding houses, and nursing homes. Kansas City people talked about Armour and another neighborhood, the Roanoke district, in a tone of nostalgia, recalling the glamorous past.

Respected Average Neighborhoods: The fourth ranked neighborhoods took up the rest of the South Side. The heart of this district was the older South Central Kansas City area between Thirty-first and Forty-seventh Streets and east of Troost Avenue; this was the part of the South Side farthest away from Ward Parkway. In addition, Kansas Citians always recognized two small areas north of Thirty-first Street as equal in status to South Central Kansas City. One was the old Gladstone neighborhood, a thin sliver of blocks overlooking the Missouri River valley at the north edge of the city; the other was an urban renewal project of high-rise apartments located west of downtown Kansas City in a neighborhood called Quality Hill (in recognition of its pre-1900 status as the prestige area). A new residential area across the river in the hills of the North Side was also ranked at this fourth level, as were the suburbs of Raytown, Overland Park, Mission, Roeland Park, and Shawnee.

In neighborhoods at this level, houses ranged from six and seven room, two story homes of pre-World War I vintage to well-built five room bungalows constructed right before or after World War II. Their selling price ranged from eight to fourteen thousand dollars. Residents of these neighborhoods were said to be department store salespeople, postal clerks, mailmen, contractors, plumbers, carpenters, railroad conductors and engineers, plant foremen and supervisors, and proprietors of neighborhood businesses such as grocery stores or gasoline stations. The recreational and organizational patterns of people in these neighborhoods were not easily described, but it was believed that they were essentially home and neighborhood people.

Decent Areas of the North Side: Neighborhoods ranked at the fifth level were almost all located in the North Side. Two characteristics of neighborhoods rated at this level were often mentioned: home ownership (as one informant put it, "this is where you have factory workers who own their homes and have a pride in keeping them decent") and distance from the slums, the industrial plants, or the Negro district. These houses were older and smaller than those of the four better neighborhoods. Real estate dealers and residents of these neighborhoods quoted seven to eight thousand dollars as the asking price for the houses.

The men of these neighborhoods were described as skilled workers like brick masons, carpenters, paperhangers, painters; owners of small filling stations and groceries, factory workers, mechanics and store clerks. They were not usually described in terms of associational affiliation or social activites. The typical recreational custom often attributed to the people of these neighborhoods was "the Sunday afternoon drive out into the countryside." Many of the men were said to be avid fishermen and hunters, while the women "stay home, watch the children, and talk over the back fence."

Substandard neighborhoods: The sixth level areas were characterized as neighborhoods "where the homes aren't really slums or shacks but not as well kept as they might be since mostly they're occupied by renters, not owners." In the early 1950s these areas bordered the Negro district and were often close to industrial districts and railroad tracks.

The residents were assumed to be semiskilled workers or low income workers like taxi drivers and truckers. Kansas Citians could say very little about the social lives of these people. The most common impressions were that many of them liked emotional religious services and spent a good deal of time at Assembly of God meetings and churches of similar type and that many of the men, and sometimes the women, frequently spent their evenings at a tavern.

Slums: The lowest ranked neighborhoods were those labeled as "slums" or "the areas of the disreputables." These were generally near downtown Kansas City or in the most frequently flooded parts of the Blue River Valley on the eastern margin. Five neighborhoods shared bottom status in the eyes of Kansas City people. One, the West Side, was an area of rooming houses and converted apartments whose inhabitants were regarded as "indigents" or "people who've never made anything of themselves." The North End, the Italian neighborhood, was considered the "center of the underworld." A third area, connecting the Italian neighborhood with the West Side, was mentioned as a "skid row area" and "what remains of our red light district." It was castigated as the center of immorality, the home of "winos, booze hounds, and the depraved." A fourth area was the most depressed Negro neighborhood; it provided a locus for public condemnation of "all those colored people on the relief rolls." Finally, there was the Blue River Valley district, several miles to the east, more rural than urban in appearance; it was described as "a straggle of hovels, mud huts, tar-paper shacks, and lean-tos." The people who lived there were referred to as "hill-billies," or "the real white trash, who still live like animals when they move to the city."

It was generally assumed that the people of these slum neighborhoods worked intermittently as common laborers, garbage collectors, "plant workers at the sweeper level," or as other types of unskilled workers. Many of these individuals were imagined to constitute the main bulk of the relief rolls and to fill the ranks of the chronically unemployed.

Implicit in Kansas Citians' rankings and feelings about neighborhoods, as described above, was the notion that families tended to live near others of similar status, an assumption supported by the apparent degree of homogeneity in the houses in each district. In truth, there was a range in the quality of housing within each neighborhood, although the more significant phenomenon was that the sale price of a home in a higher ranked neighborhood was often higher than the price of an identical house in a lower ranked neighborhood.

Part of the social significance of a family's address was the evidence it provided about the social aspiration of that family. For instance, it was often suggested that families who were willing to pay extra money for a house in the Country Club District, "just to get a Southwest address," had shown themselves to be "socially sensitive" or "social climbers." On the other hand, people who could afford homes in the Country Club District but who had chosen to buy elsewhere, in order to "get more house for their money," were characterized as "just not very socially conscious" or as people who "don't care much about keeping up with the Joneses."

Jobs and Dollars

It was quite common for Kansas City people to maintain that the basis of social class in America was financial position, that "classes are all economic," and that "money is the yardstick against which everybody is measured." The average man—taxi driver, salesclerk, factory worker, or housewife—took it as one of the immutable truths of American life that "anyone making forty thousand dollars a year" would be in "the top class."

Kansas Citians pegged each neighborhood by income level: Gold Coast residents were assumed to have incomes of at least twenty-five thousand dollars a year, "before taxes"; Country Club District families were generally believed to have incomes around twelve to fifteen thousand dollars; people in the Paseo and Prairie Village, eight to nine thousand dollars; those in the average South Side neighborhoods, five to six thousand dollars; and in the home-owner working class areas, four to five thousand dollars. (All income figures quoted here are in 1952 dollars. To equate this with 1970 dollars, at least 75 to 80 per cent must be added.) When Kansas Citians guessed at the incomes of those living in the two lowest ranking neighborhoods, they tended to add a qualification: "It isn't really how much they earn in many cases there, but that they don't spend it as wisely as they should." Informants imagined that people living in the "renter working class" neighborhoods either earned less than four thousand dollars or, if they made more, that they managed their money less carefully than those who were homeowners. Similarly, when slum area residents were discussed, they were often labeled "dirt poor" or "on the welfare lists"; but it was recognized that others were living in slum conditions because they had "frittered their money away on drink and foolishness."

More sophisticated Kansas Citians made a similar distinction between patterns of consumption and amount of income at higher levels in the status structure. Often they would compare families who "may not have much more than twenty thousand dollars a year to live on but have the right connections and behave right, so they are in top society" with families who "are social outcasts even though they are easily in the over-fifty-thousand-dollar income group." The average man was not aware of this type of social discrimination at the higher levels of Kansas City life, but it was frequently commented upon by those within those levels.

Hence, it became clear that income itself was not as good an index of social status as was the living standard maintained by a particular family. Kansas Citians rated each other on the appearance of income as manifested in such status symbols as housing and general style of life, not on the actual amount of income. There were other qualifications. For example, dollars earned through white-collar jobs were generally felt to be more respectable than those earned through blue-collar jobs. Similarly, Kansas Citians liked to believe that income acquired in unorthodox ways, through racketeering or political graft, did not entitle the earner to the same status as that of other people of the same income level.

Yet, in the final analysis, Kansas Citians placed far greater emphasis on the amount of money a man earned than on the specific nature of his occupation. When they talked of doctors, they differentiated "the top flight medical men, the high-powered specialists who make over thirty thousand dollars a year," from men who were merely "doing fairly well in their practices, maybe earning around twenty thousand dollars a year, but not top flight"; in turn, they differentiated the latter from men who were "just ordinary family doctors, maybe not even making any more than twelve thousand dollars." The first type of doctor was assumed to be a member of the social and financial elite; the second type, a typical resident of the Country Club District; and the third type, "not up to Country Club par." Similarly, insurance salesmen were graded from "big shots who must make at least $100,000 a year," through those "who are doing pretty well but will never make the big time," down to "guys who are just struggling along and don't make any more than a lot of factory workers do these days."

Distinctions based on financial success were made within all occupations. Business owners were differentially graded as "big wheels," "medium-sized operators," or "small-time operators." Company employees were identified as "top-salaried executives," "semi-executives," "managers," and "junior executives" down to "low-paid white-collar workers." Blue-collar workers were divided into "highly paid foremen," "skilled workmen," and "run-of-the-mill operatives."

In this manner Kansas City people indicated that occupational titles were not precise indicators of status if taken alone. Men in each occupation were recognized as too varied in financial achievement to belong to the same social stratum. The result was that Kansas Citians structured the occupational status ladder primarily in terms of income. They agreed that "it's not so much what a man does that counts but how well he does it—that is, how much money he makes at it." Given this view, the occupational hierarchy is best described as a ramp, not a ladder, or, as a Kansas City bank president put it, "that ladder [of occupational status] would have as many stairs on it as one stretching from earth to heaven."

Elite and Nonelite Clubs

Among the thousands of clubs in Kansas City, fewer than sixty were well known or had widely acknowledged importance in the status structure. A majority of these were prominent because of their reputation for exclusiveness and their identification with the socially elite. Some were prominent because they were large and inclusive; they drew their members from many levels of the status hierarchy, particularly from the ranks of the middle class.

Clubs identified with the elite were of six types: family country clubs, men's downtown clubs, women's town clubs (where members met for lunch or tea and to hear lectures or book reviews), men's business and service organizations such as Rotary or Kiwanis, women's charitable or cultural patronage groups (Junior League, for example), and men's clubs organized for the pursuit of a specific sport such as polo, yachting, or tennis. These clubs were viewed as elite because membership was by invitation only. The public assumed that only the well-to-do could afford the time and money to belong. The average Kansas Citian spoke of these clubs with awe or with respect. He assumed that they were "only for people from the Country Club District or Ward Parkway." To the people of Ward Parkway and the Country Club District, the particular elite club a family belonged to was a more crucial indicator of a family's social standing within the upper strata than income, house size, occupation, or neighborhood.

An intricate ranking system had developed around a few of these clubs, so that they had themselves become the rungs of a finely graded social ladder. A society reporter quipped, "Golfdom's fairways are Kansas City's social stairways"; and all higher status citizens recognized that "anyone in the First Jackson Country Club is automatically top rung and higher up the social ladder than anyone in Missoukana." In turn, Missoukana, the country club ranked second, was widely perceived as enough better than Silver Hills so that "anybody in Silver Hills would quit it in a minute if he were asked to join Missoukana." Silver Hills members were described as "well-to-do," "socially very active," and "almost big wheels but not quite."

The following quotation from a prominent auto dealer illustrates how higher status Kansas Citians ranked the family country clubs:

> The really top part of Society is contained in the First Jackson Country Club. It is the ambition of every Kansas Citian with any social standing at all to be asked to join the First Jackson Country Club. Society with a real capital "S" is centered there. . . . The people at Missoukana Country Club are on the second rung of Kansas City's social ladder. They're doing well, but they're not yet on the top. Silver Hills Country Club is third best and right above Emerald. Back in the 1930s Emerald Hills was quite a good club, but it has faded in recent years and isn't nearly as exclusive as it used to be. Some of its older members probably have as high a social standing, though, as almost anyone at Silver Hills. . . . Below that, all the rest of the clubs are also-rans. Shawnee Woods and Blue View are just ordinary country clubs as far as I know. Then you have those private golf clubs, but I haven't any idea about them at all. I wouldn't think they would stand as high as Shawnee Woods and Blue View, though. Anyone who has the dues can become a member of those golf clubs.

In similar fashion a high ranking advertising executive commented:

> The top country club here is the First Jackson Country Club. Missoukana runs a pretty good second, though. Everyone that really counts in Kansas City is in one of those two. Silver Hills ranks third, and I guess you might give it an "A-minus" rating. The rest of the country clubs—Emerald Hills, Shawnee Woods, and Blue View—are just typical suburbiana. Emerald Hills has an edge on the others because it used to be very popular, and some of the Irish elite still hang out there. The other clubs, like Log Cabin, Arrowhead, and Southcrest, are player's clubs. They're more for golf than social stuff. They aren't family clubs, just private golf courses.

In much the same way the downtown men's clubs, certain women's clubs, and the service organizations served to place their members in this elaborately graded hierarchy.

The average citizens in Kansas City, unlike those of high status, were not aware of these intricate differentiations. This was particularly true of the men and women living north of Thirty-first Street, to whom all elite clubs seemed, to quote one railroad worker, "Hi-falutin' places where people have their meetings and parties and spend pots of money." Among white-collar South Siders, there was some understanding that the elite clubs had different ranks in the eyes of Country Club residents; but the farther away a South Sider was from the Ward Parkway and Country Club social worlds, the less he knew about the specific positions of various clubs, and the less he comprehended that club membership transcended wealth and other visible symbols of status in fixing the social position of the higher-up families.

The most prominent of the nonelite clubs—the American Legion, the Parent-Teachers' Association, and the various Masonic orders—were very large and drew members from all social strata. Less prominent, but still widely known, were the fraternal orders (the Moose, Elks, Woodmen of the World, Oddfellows) and their women's auxiliaries. This group of clubs drew their members almost entirely from the middle layers of the social hierarchy. Rarely did the names of any of these large clubs enter the conversation when Kansas Citians talked about status, even though these clubs were an integral part of the social life of many Kansas Citians. They were primarily thought of as democratic organizations which included people of many different social positions. Membership in them did not place individuals in the status hierarchy. Thus, from the middle levels of the social structure down to the bottom, little importance was assigned to clubs or associational membership in drawing social distinctions. At these levels, area of residence, type of home, occupational status, and ethnic or racial identity were always the prominent indicators of status.

Religious Affiliation

From the manner in which Kansas Citians talked about religious affiliation as a factor in community life, three significant implications for the status structure emerged.[1] First, many Kansas Citians saw their city as divided into three separate social worlds— Protestant, Catholic, and Jewish. Second, Catholics and Jews were thought to be somewhat disadvantaged socially in competition with Protestants. Third, within the Protestant world, a family's denomi-

[1] This material on the role of religious divisions in Kansas City's social order is based on analysis of behavioral data, on material from the city's newspapers, and on historical references, as well as on interviews.

nation and specific church affiliation could enhance or handicap its status.

The distinctions related to religion were talked about at length and seemed to reflect considerable intergroup hostility and rivalry. Their impact on social status was not correspondingly great, however, for it was understood that the social standing of any particular Catholic, Protestant, or Jewish family was determined primarily by factors other than religious identification. The separations were described as essentially vertical, rather than horizontal. Kansas City Protestants, Catholics, and Jews were said to socialize primarily among members of their own group. In the case of the Catholics, this separation reflected some Protestant disapproval of Catholic religious practices and doctrine and was often a subject of humor. Protestants, for example, applied a variety of uncomplimentary nicknames to Catholics, among which *fish eaters* and *micks* were perhaps the most frequent. With reference to Jews, awareness of differences was more extreme and prejudice far greater, causing a noticeable amount of discomfort to the Jewish group.

The Catholic World: The social separateness of Catholics was evident in many ways. The parochial school system kept Catholic and Protestant children apart from kindergarten through high school. This separation continued through college for most middle- and upper-status Catholic youth, who usually attended one of the local Catholic colleges (Rockhurst for men and the College of St. Teresa for women) or else went away to Notre Dame, Marquette, or Marymount. The effect, as Kansas Citians described it, was that Catholics and Protestants rarely established close relationships during childhood and adolescence, and the lack of social contact tended to continue throughout adulthood. Even when Catholics and Protestants shared membership in the same large formal organizations, they tended to separate into informal cliques organized around early friendships.

Politics also played a part in separating the two. Catholics of all social levels supported the Pendergast machine in the 1920s and 1930s, and many wealthy Catholics—along with some of the well-to-do Jewish businessmen—were still known in the 1950s to provide the great bulk of financial support for the Democratic Party.

This behavior, perhaps as much as the religious difference itself, constituted a social handicap for Catholics. To many South Side Republican Protestants, Catholics had been "tainted by the sins of Pendergastism." As one Protestant explained it:

> A lot of Protestants will never quite forgive the Catholics for supporting Pendergast. I think a lot of Catholics didn't like him much better than we did, but he was "one of theirs" and so they stuck by him whenever election time rolled around. And, of course, a lot of them weren't above getting in on the rewards. I guess that's why most Catholics are good Democrats. . . . And even though they've been in Kansas City two or three generations now, a lot of the Irish stick together as if they had just come over on the latest boat.

Catholics were also somewhat separated geographically. Their churches and parochial schools often served as the nuclei for development of neighborhoods predominantly Catholic in composition. Some, established in the North End early in the history of the city, had remained political Irish fiefdoms down to the 1950s. With the passage of years, many of the Irish had prospered and moved to newer, better locations, so that by 1952 most of the well-known Irish Catholic neighborhoods were on the South Side. The most prominent of these was honored by the phrase "the rich Catholics of Rockhill Road." The Catholics who lived on Rockhill occupied houses similar to those of Ward Parkway, and it was widely remarked that they were an inbred group who had little or no contact with wealthy Protestants. The precincts along Rockhill Road were the only ones in the Country Club District which habitually produced Democratic party majorities.

Except for the fraternal orders, Catholics were not socially separated in the private club structure of Kansas City. Membership in Masonic orders is expressly forbidden to Catholics, so they had a comparable brotherhood of their own—the Knights of Columbus (with a women's auxiliary, the Sisters of Isabella). The Knights of Columbus was a very large organization in Kansas City and included men from a wide range of economic and social levels. It was generally thought to provide cohesion among Catholics from different social strata.

No formal rules barred Catholics from membership in any of the downtown men's clubs, the country clubs, or women's clubs.

But it was reported that gentlemen's agreements had sometimes operated in the past to limit Catholic membership in these higher status clubs. By 1952, however, only the First Jackson Country Club was believed to have remained a "solid bastion of Protestantism." In the preceding few years, men of the Catholic group had been elected to the presidency in the Missoukana Country Club, the Kan-Citian Club, and the Tavern and Trail, and an increasing number of Catholic girls were being admitted each year to the Junior League. Using these facts as evidence, Kansas Citians were generally inclined to believe that the status barriers which formerly had impeded Catholics were crumbling.

Kansas Citians generally liked to believe that the status of Catholics had never been as bad in their community as in Boston and cities of the East Coast, where report had it that Catholics were "kept out of the Social Register and things like that." They believed this difference was due primarily to the fact that most of the Catholics in Kansas City were of Irish, German, or French descent instead of southern and eastern European. In other words, it was felt that Catholics and Protestants in Kansas City shared the same cultural and ancestral North European background, minimizing the differences between them. A second factor sometimes cited was the personal popularity of the late Bishop Lillis, who had been head of the Catholic diocese for almost a third of a century. A prominent Protestant clergyman said,

> One of the most beloved men in Kansas City was Bishop Lillis. He was respected by Protestants and Jews as much as by Catholics. His father had been a prominent contractor here around the turn of the century and respected in his own right. Bishop Lillis had several brothers and sisters, who have also been admired and effective people in the community. Bishop Lillis was responsible for keeping the Catholic Church here deeply rooted in the very best of Kansas City's traditions. More than anybody can imagine, he cancelled out much of the bad feeling toward Catholics that Pendergast caused.

The Jewish World: The social separation of the Jewish population was more extreme than that experienced by Catholics. Almost anyone who had a Jewish ancestor was considered Jewish, and the designation therefore included many people who never attended services in a synagogue or temple. Even when such persons joined a Christian church, they were usually still considered by both Jews and non-Jews to be part of the Jewish community. Only in rare instances were they integrated socially into the Gentile community.

Jews were expressly excluded from membership in most of the clubs in the city, especially from the men's downtown clubs, the country clubs, and the women's social service groups. Only three of the larger elite clubs had any Jewish members. One of these, the Tavern and Trail, had admitted four of the most socially prominent Jewish men but was nevertheless considered a closed club by most of the Jewish community. The Midday Woman's Club had allowed itself what one of its members called "a representative number of Jewish women," and usually one Jewish woman was on its board of directors. The Downtown Athletic Club was said to have begun admitting Jews during the Depression, when the club was having financial difficulties; it still had a few Jewish members. Informal social interaction between Jews and non-Jews, such as dinner parties in each other's homes, was described as "not a common occurrence." Marriages between Jews and non-Jews were said to be extremely rare and frowned upon by Jewish parents as well as by Gentiles.

Nevertheless, the two groups interacted in three spheres—in the business world, in educational institutions, and in civic activities. In respect to the first, interaction between Jews and non-Jews occurred to a moderate extent in the many businessmen's associations, the Chamber of Commerce, and all the professional associations. All of the service clubs also provided contact, and each was thought to have a liberal sprinkling of Jewish members. Jews and Protestants interacted more in educational institutions than either did with Catholics. Jewish children were enrolled in the public schools along with Protestant children, and the wealthier among them often attended the elite private schools. It was reported, however, that the children in both private and public schools generally separated into cliques based upon this ethnoreligious distinction; and teen-age social clubs were either Gentile or Jewish in their membership.

Probably the most meaningful interaction between Jews and non-Jews occurred in the realm of civic affairs. Prominent members of the Jewish community were welcomed onto the boards and sponsoring committees of all the cultural and philanthropic institutions. Every important civic organization—from the board of the Philharmonic to the governing committee of the Community Chest—drew at least 10 per cent, and often 15 or 20 per cent of its membership from the Jewish community. This number was impressively high, given that less than 4 per cent of the Kansas City population was Jewish. In some important civic groups, Jews were more numerous than Catholics, although there were over five times as many Catholics in the city. Further evidence of the high status of Jews in civic life was shown at the Jewel Ball, the annual presentation of debutantes, where approximately 10 per cent of the girls each year were from Jewish families.

The most impressive aspect of the Jewish presence in Kansas City, as far as non-Jews were concerned, was their apparent economic well-being. It was widely known that the years from 1939 to 1952 had witnessed a large-scale movement of Jews into the Country Club District and other superior neighborhoods south of Forty-seventh Street. The impression of Jewish prosperity was so dominant that it was almost inconceivable to a Kansas City Gentile that a Jew might be a part of the North Side working class; it was generally assumed that at worst some Jews were only average white-collar workers or small businessmen. This prosperity was viewed with mixed feelings by non-Jews and elicited frequent hostile remarks—disparagement of foreign accents, for example, or comments suggesting that some Jews had achieved financial success by "being pushy" or by "hard bargaining" and that "a lot of them have money, but no class."

The Jewish position in Kansas City was probably best summed up by a young Jewish lawyer who remarked, "The status of the Jews here is what you might call 'separate, but equal'—or, at least, not particularly unequal." What he meant was that most of the distinction between Gentiles and Jews in Kansas City was vertical social separation, and very little was horizontal. The Jewish population was quite well established at the upper income levels, and the Gentile community allowed individual Jews most of the symbols of success, prominence, and equality except admission into private clubs. Even when denying the latter, there was more a flavor of excluding people because they were "different'" rather than of excluding people on grounds of unworthiness.

The Protestant World: The Protestants of Kansas City, as

in other American cities, were divided into many denominations, some rated higher in popular esteem than others. Episcopalians had the reputation of having "more blue bloods than any of the rest." Presbyterians were seen as a very solid and prosperous group, right below Episcopalians in prestige. Methodists were called "a good, average, all-American group—the most powerful here, with the power that numbers give; but by the same token, they are not exclusive." Baptists were typified as "mostly working class—there are more of them in the north end of town than the south." A prominent clubwoman facetiously described the social differences between four of the major denominations with this statement: "A Methodist is a Baptist who finished high school, a Presbyterian is a Methodist who went on to college, and an Episcopalian is a Presbyterian who made money."

Episcopalians themselves felt they belonged to the highest ranking denomination, that they had a "more refined outlook on religion" than did members of other denominations. Being an Episcopalian, it was implied, elevated one socially above a non-Episcopalian unless the latter had a great deal more money and a much better house and job; the degree of elevation felt, however, depended on the other person's denomination. For example, a poor Episcopalian would not feel socially superior to a prosperous Presbyterian, but he was likely to feel superior to a prosperous Baptist because being a Baptist was in an Episcopalian's eyes "just very *common.*" Baptists, in turn, acknowledged that the Episcopalians thought they were better and seemed to realize that the larger community judged Episcopalians more favorably than it did Baptists.

In like manner, the adherents of each denomination in Kansas City had a notion of how they compared as a group with other denominations. Analysis of the comments made by Protestants about each other suggested this ranking: Episcopalians on top, followed in descending order by Presbyterians, Christian Scientists and Congregationalists, Unitarians and Quakers, Disciples of Christ (called simply the "Christian" church in Kansas City), Northern Baptists, Methodists, Lutherans, Latter-Day Saints, Evangelical and Reformed members, Southern Baptists, United Brethren, Nazarenes and members of the Church of Christ, members of the Assembly of

God and Seventh Day Adventists, and, at the bottom, members of
the "Holy Roller" sects.

In addition to ranking denominations in this fashion, Kansas
Citians also rated many of the individual Protestant churches. Of
more than four hundred churches serving the white population of
the city and suburbs in the early 1950s, five were singled out as
Society churches. Their memberships were said to be made up of
"the upper crust" or "people trying to be upper crust"; and attending these churches was felt to be a "fashionable thing to do."

The following quotations illustrate how two of these Society
churches were regarded by Kansas Citians:

> The Ward Parkway Christian Church was founded by twelve
> millionaires, and they have more millionaires in that congrega-
> tion than in any other in Kansas City. It's right in the heart of
> the wealthy neighborhood, and when anybody moves into town
> who is high up in the executive ladder he joins that church—that
> is, if he isn't strongly committed to some other denomination.
> That's the church to be with for business advantage.

> A lot of people don't know it, but the Episcopalian cathedral
> downtown is IT socially. It is supported by the real aristocracy.
> Its list of contributors reads like a Who's Who of Old Guard
> Kansas City. That's where the bishop is, and they automatically
> give him and the rector there a membership in the First Jackson
> Country Club.

The five Society Protestant churches were Christ Episcopal
(the downtown cathedral), St. James Episcopal, St. Bartholomew
Episcopal, the Third Presbyterian, and the Ward Parkway Christian. Three were located in the Country Club District, one in the
central business district, and one in the Armour area, the old Gold
Coast of Kansas City from 1900 to 1920. The reform temple, B'nai
Emunah, was considered to serve the same social function for the
Jewish community. These six churches were not the only ones attended by persons of high status, but they were the only ones which
people in Kansas City identified as dominantly Society in tone.

Ranked just below these six were four well-known churches,
centrally located on major traffic arteries, with large memberships
known to be drawn from many areas of the city. They were sometimes called "the metropolitan prestige churches." Their ministers
were considered prominent citizens and generally were offered

memberships in at least one of the leading town or country clubs. The elders in these churches were drawn almost exclusively from Ward Parkway and the Country Club District. The members were described as "people who like a big church and want to feel themselves part of the city's most important institutions."

Equal in status to these metropolitan prestige churches were several smaller churches located in the Country Club District and in the Johnson County suburbs of Fairway, Prairie Village, and Leawood. These were of many different denominations—Baptist, Congregational, Lutheran, and Methodist, as well as Presbyterian and Christian. They were highly rated because they drew their members almost exclusively from the Country Club District. Thus, their geographic location was more significant than their position on the denominational status scale. Four Catholic churches serving the southwest part of Kansas City and the high status suburbs of Johnson County also ranked at this level.

Below these top two levels, the ranks given to other Protestant congregations were based upon both denomination and geographic location. Lumped at the bottom of the status scale were all the revivalist and Pentecostal churches, irrespective of their geographic location. Some of these churches bore names like Sunnyside Gospel Tabernacle, Church of Amazing Grace, The Fountain of Life, Pilgrim Holiness, The Friendly Church, and Foursquare Gospel Tent. These and others in the Pentecostal group—the Assembly of God, the Church of God, and the Church of the Living Christ— were commonly derogated as "off-brand churches" or as being "the Holy Roller type." The people who attended them were looked down upon by most Kansas Citians. Almost the only persons held in lower esteem than the members of these churches were those who were "very poor and don't bother with church at all."

Educational Background

Kansas City residents regarded a person's educational background as a status asset or handicap but not as an absolute prerequisite for occupying any particular social position. The average Kansas Citian believed, accurately enough, that better educational backgrounds were of considerable benefit in the achievement of higher occupational and social levels; at the same time they were quite aware that advanced formal education did not guarantee success as an adult. Many took pleasure in citing examples of self-educated men and women who had achieved prominence in Kansas City. Similarly, they seemed to find it amusing, as well as pathetic, that "you can find a college graduate every now and then who's gone hobo and is down on skid row."

Thus, Kansas Citians did not think of differences in educational background as dividing their city into social class groupings. Education was simply something desirable, which people of superior status tended to have more of than did people at lower-status levels. Only two types of educational backgrounds were considered nearly infallible indices to a person's position in the social hierarchy: Illiteracy was believed inevitably to produce lowest status ("the illiterates are all at the bottom of the heap"), while an Ivy League education was thought to be "a sure ticket for admission into the top set." It was evident to Kansas Citians, however, that people with other educational backgrounds were also to be found at both status extremes, so that neither illiteracy nor an Ivy League degree was regarded as the exclusive indicator of status at these respective levels.

Outside these two specific views, Kansas Citians spoke in generalities about the educational levels of other status groups. They felt that "there are all kinds of educations" represented in every neighborhood and at every income level, so that it was meaningless to be specific in talking about most groups. Furthermore, they recognized that older people in any given neighborhood or status group usually had less education than did younger people and were inclined to think that "a high school diploma used to mean more than a college degree does today."

At the same time, it was readily agreed that people in the better neighborhoods were better educated on the whole than people in the poorer neighborhoods. "Most of your college people live in the Country Club District." "Probably the majority of people who live out south are high school graduates." "A lot of the people who live here on the North Side didn't have the opportunity to finish high school, or else they would have better jobs and live in a better neighborhood."

How much, then, were differences in educational background felt to affect the social status of people who had achieved equal economic status as adults? At least some status difference existed in most such instances. Over and over Kansas Citians revealed their feelings on this point in various anecdotes and in the way they talked about work mates, neighbors, and acquaintances. From these anecdotes and comments it was clear that differences in educational background served as one of the more common grounds for minor status differentiations within social class groups. In this respect, education acted as a status asset or handicap in Kansas City apart from its function in occupational preparation.

Finally, in spite of all the reservations Kansas Citians had about the importance of education as a determinant of social and economic status among middle-aged adults, they still viewed it as the most important route children could use to gain higher status than their parents. Everyone hoped his children would move as far up the education ladder as possible.

Chapter 4

Delineating
the Status Structure

*W*e turned next to examining the social behavior and social characteristics of a large sample of Kansas Citians and to the question of how such data would relate to the perceptions and evaluations of the status structure obtained in the first phases of the study. We had learned that residents of Kansas City were conscious of a prestige hierarchy which was not merely economic in character, although it had its base in economic differences. Kansas Citians were relating to one another as inferiors or superiors, using criteria such as church affiliation, club membership, neighborhood, and educational background in addition to economic standard of living. They rated people with whom they were personally acquainted, and they rated hundreds of others whom they did not know. In other words, Kansas Citians did not require face to face contact to judge social status; and basically they agreed on the bases for status assignments.

54

The investigator must, of course, go beyond this. Although a description of the status structure should incorporate the perceptions and belief systems of the people themselves, it must also rest upon data gathered by other methods available to the social scientist.

First Approximation

Before moving to the collection of new data, we drew up a first approximation of the Kansas City status structure. Our impression was one of a seven-layered hierarchy, an impression heavily influenced by the imagery about neighborhoods and by the fact that the most status conscious Kansas Citians described seven neighborhood ranks whose residents, in turn, they could differentiate along several other dimensions of status.

We recognized that within some of these seven status levels there were substrata—such as the differentiation among the residents of the Ward Parkway Gold Coast between those who were members of the First Jackson Country Club and hence regarded as belonging to Capital S Society and those who were members of Missoukana or Silver Hills country clubs and hence "part of the Society crowd, but not real high Society." Nevertheless, in this first approximation, we placed both the Capital S and non-Capital S layers into the top level, thinking that their similarities in neighborhood, in housing, in perceived wealth and community importance outweighed their differences.

As a second level, we recognized the "Country Club crowd," the families with memberships in one or more of the men's service clubs, country clubs, private downtown clubs, or women's social clubs. These were the people Kansas Citians themselves associated with the phrase *the upper-middle class.*

Below this second level there seemed to exist a world of people who were seen by their fellow Kansas Citians as "above the ordinary South Sider." These people were differentiated in status from "the average South Sider" because they owned better homes, lived in more desirable neighborhoods, belonged to churches or clubs of fairly high but less than upper-middle-class reputations, and pursued more esteemed occupations. It was unclear, at this point, whether these people should be considered a single social class, a middle-middle class as it were, or whether they constituted two status levels, one composed of people who primarily related upward to the Country Club world and the other composed of people who related primarily downward to the ordinary South Siders.

A large number of Kansas Citians were thought by their fellow citizens to fit the description of "average South Sider" by virtue of the housing they occupied, the neighborhoods they lived in, the jobs they held, their cultural and educational background, and their churches and club affiliations. These Kansas Citians formed a status level often referred to as "lower-middle class."

Another sizable group fitted the description of "average North Sider." They were mainly blue-collar workers whose cultural and educational levels, church and club memberships, and ways of spending their money and spare time placed them at the level often called "average working class."

Down a step, as a sixth level, was an important fraction of North Siders and blue-collar workers whose living standards as reflected in their housing or choice of neighborhood were below that of the "average working class." These people were often spoken of as "below average North Siders but not at the bottom," and seemed to include two subgroups: one, a group whom "average working class" people judged as "poor but decent" and accepted almost as social equals; the other, a group whom "average working class" people regarded as "just a cut above the 'slumdwellers'" and as people to be avoided.

The "slumdwellers"—that is, everyone living in severely deteriorated housing—were seen to be at the bottom of the social hierarchy irrespective of any other social characteristic. Persons who were observably undesirable in behavior (such as skid row winos) were also placed at this level. Whether there were further distinctions within this lowest level could not be ascertained from our interviews.

A separate status system existed for Kansas City Negroes, having apparently five levels which in some ways resembled the levels observable within the white society. The issue of which Negroes in Kansas City were socially equal to which whites could not be ascertained either by referring to social interaction, because there was so little interaction between Negroes and whites, or by reference to social perceptions, because there was no consensus beyond the general view that Negroes were "totally segregated, almost totally unequal."

Sampling and Stratifying

At this point in our research we turned to examining the social characteristics of a large sample of Kansas Citians, to see how such data would relate to the status images that prevailed. The basic sample consisted of 462 family units drawn by a random-stratified technique from a cross section of households in metropolitan Kansas City. (See Appendix B for an explanation of the sampling procedures.) Of the 462 units, 374 were married couples, twenty-four were unmarried men, and sixty-four were unmarried women (single, divorced, or widowed). In all units either the man or woman (usually both) was in the age range forty to sixty-nine at the time of contact in 1954–55. In one-third of the cases, both husband and wife were interviewed; in the other two-thirds, only one was interviewed. In these interviews, information on social participation was obtained, as well as data on occupation, income, religious affiliation, educational backgrounds, and other pertinent aspects of the life history and current life style.

For estimating the social boundaries at the higher levels of the status hierarchy, systematic data were gathered also on a special population composed of the top 3 per cent of the Kansas City, Missouri, social structure—over six thousand family units of all ages. For most of these families, relatively detailed information was obtained regarding genealogies, formal club memberships, civic participation, occupational role, schooling, and other factors. (For further information on this population, see Appendix B.) Thirty of these families were among the 462 family units comprising the cross-sectional sample of middle-aged. In addition, another sixty persons from these top levels were interviewed extensively for their observations regarding status demarcations and social interaction among the people in the top range of Kansas City life.

A series of indices for measurement of status were constructed around the dimensions which Kansas Citians most commonly employed when rating one another: residential neighborhood, occupational status, income level, quality of housing, years and type of schooling, club and association memberships, ethnic background, and church affiliation. Seven-point scales were formulated for each dimension, based upon the evaluations made by Kansas Citians. These scales came to be referred to as the Index of Kansas City Status (IKCS). (The component scales of the IKCS are shown at successive points in Table 2 and are discussed in Chapter Five.)

Data cards were filled out for all 462 family units in the cross-sectional sample, and ratings were applied for each of the dimensions of status in the IKCS. The profile of scores generated by this procedure was then used in making a tentative placement of each family into one or another of the hypothesized seven layers of the white status hierarchy or into one of the five of the Negro hierarchy.

In attempting to make placements in the way Kansas Citians would make them, we gave great importance to club memberships at the three highest levels of the white hierarchy. In the middle ranges, the patterning of several status characteristics—neighborhood, quality of housing, community participation, and occupational status—was important in determining at what level a family should be placed. At the bottom two levels, whether or not the family lived in a slum dwelling or a slum neighborhood became the critical distinction. In placing Negroes, occupation, education, and overall standard of living were utilized.

Thirteen Strata

This first classification of the sample of white Kansas Citians left certain questions unresolved. For example, meaningful distinctions could possibly be made within the first, the third, and the sixth levels. There was also the question of whether the social order was best described as a continuum of gentle gradations or as a sharply demarcated class system. To get at such questions, we carefully restudied the data on the actual characteristics of families in relation to the dimensions of status described earlier to see which groups were most distinct from adjacent groups and where the clearest continuities and discontinuities were. This analysis led to a new formulation in which five dominant classes and thirteen substrata were identified, as illustrated in Table 1.

Upper Class: There were many subtle differentiations of status among Kansas Citians at the highest level. Ultimately, however, it became clear that the demarcation of greatest importance

Table 1. KANSAS CITY STATUS STRUCTURE
(Persons Aged 40 to 69)[a]

	Total Per Cent	Whites Per Cent	Negroes Per Cent
Upper Class:			
Capital S Society	0.4	0.5	0.0
Non-Capital S upper class	1.4	1.6	0.1
Upper-Middle Class:			
Upper-middle-elite	1.3	1.5	0.2
Upper-middle-core	5.3	6.0	0.8
Upper-middle-marginals	5.0	5.6	1.2
Lower-Middle Class:			
Lower-middle-elite	5.8	6.4	1.3
Lower-middle-core	17.2	19.0	4.1
Lower-middle-marginals	10.3	11.2	3.8
Working Class:			
Working-class-elite	5.0	5.2	2.7
Working-class-core	25.5	26.2	20.0
Working-class-marginals	9.7	8.6	18.1
Lower Class:			
Lower class but not quite the lowest	6.4	4.1	22.3
"Slumdwellers" and other "disreputables"	6.7	4.1	25.4

[a] Estimated percentages have been projected to the 2,300-household master sample described in Appendix B and from that sample to the total metropolitan population in the age group.

was that between families earlier described as Capital S Society and those not Capital S. This boundary line was marked by the fact that virtually all the daughters of families in the higher group were named as debutantes in the Jewel Ball, a presentation held annually to raise money for many principal cultural institutions. Only rarely was a daughter of a non-Capital S family introduced at this event.

Upper-class status and subgroup placement within it appeared to be determined entirely by personal reputation and social acceptance, as represented both in formal club memberships and in informal clique participation. Other factors—such as the size of the family home, residential address, occupational status, or reputed family income—contributed to a family's position but were not definitive.

Almost a third of Kansas City families who lived in mansions were not accepted as part of the upper class. These people and others also reputed to be rich can be thought of as constituting a special category, "the Non-U Rich." Some of the Non-U Rich occupied positions of leadership within upper-middle-class social clubs and thus were integral members of the upper-middle-elite. Others, however, were not much better accepted by the upper-middle class than by the upper class, their wealth notwithstanding; their position could be described as "rich social outcast."

Upper-Middle-Class: Within the upper-middle world, a number of families clearly were thought of by upper-class people, by themselves, and by others in the upper-middle class as an elite group within the class. Analysis of their participation patterns and the data on their reputational status indicated that this upper-middle-elite position was distinctive. These families were regarded in comparison to other upper-middle families as richer, more socially successful, culturally and educationally superior, or as having unusually interesting or important positions in civic and cultural life.

Forming the core of the upper-middle class, and distinguishable from the upper-middle-elite, were a large number of families—approximately one-twentieth of all middle-age family units—who met almost all the expectations for people at this level. They belonged to one or more of the semielite clubs—memberships which were widely regarded as the criteria of being accepted at the upper-middle level; and they had the occupations and the standard of living perceived by Kansas Citians as being "Country Club class." The majority of these families lived in the Country Club District. They clearly formed a nucleus around which other families were clustered in both informal and formal social activities. This group we shall refer to as the upper-middle-core.

The third level of the upper-middle-class is the upper-middle-marginal. Detailed analysis of the social participation and the status characteristics of the people first identified as "above average South Siders" showed a relatively clear split into two groups. One was made up of families whose social relationships were almost exclusively with each other or with families of the upper-middle-core; the other was made up of families whose social relationships were predominantly with lower-middle families. Thus, the "above average South Siders," instead of constituting a middle-middle class as had been hypothesized at earlier stages in the research, were divided into two social strata—an upper-middle-marginal and a lower-middle-elite.

The upper-middle-marginals—almost as numerous as the upper-middle-core—were most sharply distinguished from the latter by their lack of membership in any of the semielite clubs and by being less well housed and having considerably less income. In other ways the marginals proved to be more like upper-middle-core families than like lower-middle-elites. They usually attended one of the Country Club District churches; many belonged to college alumni organizations and to cross-class clubs dominated by upper-middle people. Furthermore, if they did not live inside the Country Club District, they tended to live in those parts of the South Side of Kansas City most immediately adjacent and managed to send their children to the schools in that district. (A few had their homes in one of the still fashionable neighborhoods of old aristocracy or the newly fashionable Johnson County suburbs.) They closely resembled upper-middle-core also in that the husband or wife (or both) had almost always attended college. (In contrast, less than half of the lower-middle-elites had had any college education.)

Thus we recognized three status levels within the upper-middle class. It seemed appropriate to group them as one large social class, despite the disparities, because people of both the elite and the marginal levels related socially in formal clubs and in informal interaction almost as much with people of the upper-middle-core as with people of their own stratum. The upper-middle class was bound together by this interaction and comprised groups of people who shared many status characteristics even though they were markedly different in income and in living standards.

Lower-Middle Class: Close analysis of the social interaction and the status characteristics of persons who appeared to their fellow citizens to be lower-middle also revealed three sublevels. The group of "above average South Siders" who had very little or no contact with upper-middle-core people formed the lower-middle-elite.

The differentiation between lower-middle-core and lower-middle-marginals, however, had not been anticipated. A very large number of families could be identified who were "average South Side" in certain respects but not in others. A reexamination of the interview data revealed many references by lower-middles to neighbors and associates who were looked down upon slightly—not to the extent of being identified with the working class but enough to be considered socially below lower-middle-core.

The delineation of the lower-middle-marginal level thus reflected a set of attitudes more than a special pattern of social interaction. People of the lower-middle-core regarded themselves as being a cut above lower-middle-marginals when evaluating superficial status characteristics. Only when they became friends—as often occurred—did lower-middle-core people cease thinking in these terms. Thus, while a social distance existed between the two groups, it was bridgeable. And there was a great deal of interaction between them, although there was very little or no interaction between lower-middle-core and working class people.

Thus the lower-middle class included three social levels. At the top were the leaders in the churches, PTAs and fraternal organizations of the class, people who were also markedly better off financially or who were schoolteachers, social workers, and ministers. While the latter were only average in living standard, they were looked up to by other lower-middle people because of their professional occupations, their participation in the professional community at large, and their leadership in South Side churches and neighborhood associations.

Forming the core were approximately half of all lower-middle families, white-collar workers who lived in pleasant houses along the nicer streets of the Southeast quadrant and constituted the great bulk of membership in the Southeast Side churches and other formal associations. In almost every respect, they lived up to the Kansas City image of a Southeast Sider.

Lower-middle-marginals included those families who associated with other South Siders in clubs, churches, and informal cliques but were below average for the class in one or two major status characteristics—educational background or occupation. What distinguished lower-middle-marginals from the working class below them was that they were active in the South Side social system.

Working Class: A category not anticipated from the public imagery was the working-class-elite, although one out of every twenty middle-aged families in Kansas City seemed to belong in such a category. These families were basically identified with North Side working class but, by virtue of their participation and leadership in North Side clubs and churches or because they had a higher standard of living than many of their North Side neighbors, were looked upon by average blue-collar workers as being above themselves in status. Families of the working-class-elite, still living in the North Side and still interacting exclusively inside its social network, were not accepted by lower-middle South Siders as part of their world. They were not sufficiently educated or refined in behavior to satisfy lower-middle standards. Furthermore, many were involved in the Democratic machine, as precinct captains and officers in ward organizations. Or they were leaders in the ethnic neighborhoods, such as Balkan Hill or the Italian North End. Or they were the lesser officials in labor unions. On any one of these grounds they were inadmissible to the South Side middle class.

The great bulk of blue-collar workers and North Side residents, about one-fourth of the white middle-aged men and women, composed the working-class-core. They owned their small homes but lived in neighborhoods that were less pleasant than those occupied by lower-middles. The husbands usually were craftsmen or factory workers; neither husband nor wife had finished high school; their most likely memberships were in labor unions and churches; and they had no social contact with South Side middle class people.

The major distinction between working-class-marginals and working-class-core families lay in the manifest standard of living— the kind of housing and its location. Marginals generally appeared to be below the working class average in financial well-being. Their homes were not furnished in the same ways, and there was more evidence of want, even deprivation, in their lives. We had originally assigned these families to the sixth layer—the category of "below average North Siders but not at the bottom." However, placement of this group as marginals within the working class was regarded, in the final analysis, to be the most appropriate reflection of Kansas City thinking. Despite their poor economic situation, the marginals in overall behavior and in personal appearance came close to the standards and ethos of mainstream working class America. Interviewers described their homes as "neat and clean, if somewhat spare in furnishing"; their living habits reflected a "basic orderliness." Our best judgment from conversation with working-class-core people was that they regarded the working-class-marginals as only slightly below themselves in status and differentiated them from the group of people we have labeled "lower class but not quite the bottom," a group who were barely acceptable as neighbors and clearly unacceptable as friends.

Lower Class: The most readily identifiable members of the lower class were "slumdwellers." We initially placed these people in the seventh level, at the very bottom of the status hierarchy. Our cross-sectional sample of Kansas City families revealed, however, still another group of people who, although their housing was somewhat above the slum level, nevertheless appeared to be below the minimal standards required for acceptance into the urban working class, even at its lower margins. Some of these families were poor Mexicans, and many were "hillbillies." Others seemed unable to maintain orderliness in their lives—alcoholism, physical handicaps, or marital instability appeared to defeat them. Finally, there was a sprinkling of immigrants from such places as the Philippines, Syria, the Ukraine, and Belgium who had not managed to rise above the handicaps of language and foreign-rural origins. These people seemed to fit into a stratum of "lower class but not quite the lowest."

These two layers of the lower class were not bound together by social interaction such as characterized the other classes; one was not core and the other marginal. The only cohesion within the lower class was that, by living in or near the slums, these families constituted a social-psychological polar extreme for the entire Kansas City social structure. The two layers of the lower class were bound together by the contempt of the classes above them, despite the desire of many individuals within the class to shun one another and to escape the status assigned to them by the wider society.

Negro Status Structure

When Kansas City Negroes spoke of the status order within their own community, they almost invariably described a five-class hierarchy. Status positions were based on a combination of criteria, including standard of living, occupation, educational background, and personal connections.

The highest status group was described as "newspaper people, the successful professional families—doctors, dentists and lawyers—and men who have done well in real estate and insurance." This group was separated from the next in several ways: its members belonged to the Boulevardiers (a men's social club) or the Wednesday Discussion Club (a women's service group); they formed the leadership in the NAACP and Urban League; they were "the molders of thought among Negroes—the few who have everything and do everything." They also were the leaders in the alumni chapters of two prominent Negro college fraternities and the sister sororities and were often described as "the fraternity and sorority crowd."

The next highest group was composed of "the school-teachers, many of the clergy, social workers, chiropodists, and some of the less successful professional people who haven't yet arrived financially." These people were said to mingle with the top group at larger Negro affairs, but they were not members of the two high-status clubs and they were not leaders of the NAACP and Urban League. Although they were differentiated from the top group because they had less money, the difference was also described as the lack of "the proper educational background" or of "the social graces expected in the top group."

The third group, usually called "a lower-middle class," was described as "railroad employees like Pullman porters and dining car waiters, civil servants, and contractors in the plumbing or painting trades." Economic security, a steady job, and a fairly high income were prime criteria for acceptance at this level. Often spoken of as "good livers," members of this stratum usually owned their homes and displayed a sense of community responsibility by taking part in YMCA work, in neighborhood boys' clubs, in fund drives for the NAACP, and in food drives for poorer Negroes at Christmas time.

A fourth group was identified socially as "between the good livers and those Negroes who are the real lower class." Their incomes were low, but they were "respectable," lived in a manner that reflected personal pride, interest in "the way their children [were] raised," and "concern with appearances."

Negroes of the lowest-status group were identified and criticized by other Negroes in the same way the lower class of whites was singled out and condemned by other whites. Higher-status Negroes referred to lowest-status Negroes as having a very low living standard, "living in those slums along Troost or near the railroad tracks," unwilling to work "if you handed them a job on a silver platter," and given to brawling, fighting, and drunkenness.

White Kansas Citians in the mid-1950s were only dimly aware of these differences in status within the Negro community and certainly had no idea how to equate the various levels of the Negro status structure with their own. As far as most white informants were concerned, Negroes were either all in the bottom class, totally unequal, completely separate, or totally outside the rating system. Negroes spoke more hopefully of their position as "definitely segregated but not too unequal," meaning that Negroes of any given occupational or socioeconomic level were not too far below whites of the same level.

The relationship between Negroes and whites in Kansas City in the mid-1950s was essentially one based upon caste; Negroes were separated socially and residentially. Across the color-caste line there was no socially meaningful equality since no group of whites truly accepted any group of Negroes as worthy of the same intimate interaction or the same respect accorded a white member of the same social class. Thus, any perception of equivalence of social classes across the caste line was not a demonstrable reality.[1]

This fact notwithstanding, it is often desirable in research on social stratification to compare Negro and white status groups. This comparison was accomplished here according to a "separate but equal" principle—that is, Negro groups were considered equals of those whites to whom they were comparable in housing, educational background, income, and occupational status. While this procedure for equating Negro and white social classes has its limitations, it probably produces less distortion of social reality than the practice followed by those investigators who have referred to Negroes of the highest status as upper class and those of the second highest status as upper-middle class, even though Negroes of these

---

[1] The relationship between whites and Negroes was described as a caste system in Davis, Gardner, and Gardner (1941), and in Dollard (1949). The Negro social structure of Chicago was described in Drake and Cayton (1945). More recent descriptions of the Negro social structure are to be found in Frazier (1962) and in Billingsley (1968).

two levels were below whites of the same classes in living standard, occupation, and education, and were far below them in status reputation.

Six middle-aged families in the Negro community were considered equivalent to upper class whites in housing, income, and prominence—a Negro newspaper publisher, the minister of the most prestigious Negro church, two doctors, and two lawyers. These men and their wives were named by whites to membership on civic leadership committees. All other Negroes in the Boulevardiers and Wednesday Discussion Club were like upper-middle whites in their general living standards, their occupational status, and their educational background. Some were similar to upper-middle-elites; most were comparable to core-level upper-middles. Approximately 150 middle-aged families, 1 per cent of the Negro community, were placed at those two levels.

The second-ranked large category—the schoolteachers, social workers, and less successful professionals—included one group who associated upward with the "sorority and fraternity crowd" and another group who associated mainly with the railroad workers, postal employees, and contractors of the lower-middle class. The first group was considered equal in status to the upper-middle-marginal whites. The second group was more like the "poor but honorable professionals" of the white lower-middle-elite. The third-ranked major group of Negroes were observed to be almost identical in housing, income, and social participation to white lower-middles, either of the core group or at the marginal level. The fourth class seemed similar in all important respects to working-class whites. The lowest class of Negroes were identical to the lower-class whites in all significant status characteristics. The percentages of middle-aged Negroes in each of the social class levels were estimated as 2 per cent in the upper-middle, 9 per cent lower-middle; and 41 per cent and 48 per cent in the two remaining classes.[2]

[2] This distribution is similar to that observed in Atlanta by Hill and McCall (1950). Their placements of Atlanta Negroes were 2 per cent, 6 per cent, 28 per cent, and 54 per cent, respectively. Drake and Cayton (1945), using a different method of classification, estimated some 5 per cent of the Negroes in Chicago in the 1940s as upper and upper-middle, the rest of the middle class as another 30 per cent, and the lower class as 65 per cent. Billingsley (1968) estimated that 10 per cent of Negroes belong to an upper class group of old families with long histories of prestige and achievement

Negroes and whites in the same class groupings were most similar in income and in housing and least similar in their social participation patterns. Negro men of each class were in different work from that of their white counterparts, although the jobs were approximately equal in status. In the upper-middle class virtually all Negroes were professional men or business owners; a large proportion of upper-middle whites were managers or corporation executives. At the lower-middle level, the typical Negro male was a gray-collar worker in one of the civil services, worked for the railroads as a Pullman porter or dining car waiter, or owned a small business. The typical lower-middle white was a clerical worker, salesman, or trained technician with a white-collar job. In the working class, the typical white male was a skilled craftsman or assembly-line operative; the typical working-class Negro was in a service occupation, a janitor, chauffeur, driver, waiter, chef, barber or deliveryman, and only a minority worked in factories or in the construction trades. At the lowest level, the same distinction prevailed: the white man was more often a laborer of some sort, and the Negro more often a service worker.

In educational background, white and Negro men of the same class were virtually equal except at the upper-middle level; relatively more upper-middle Negroes held advanced professional degrees. Negro upper-middle women were like white women in that the majority had attended college but had not graduated. Lower-middle and working-class Negro women were somewhat better educated, however, than white women at these levels; for example, the median level of schooling for working-class Negro women was 10.2 as compared with 8.8 years for working-class white women. These differences reflect a widely documented fact, that Negro women tend to go farther in school than Negro men, and they also suggest that Negro women are likely to have more years of schooling than white women at the same socioeconomic level.

Patterns of club memberships, community activity, and religious participation differed considerably between Negroes and whites

---

and newer, high status families whose male heads made it to the top in their own generation; that 40 per cent belong to a middle class of professionals, clerical workers, and skilled blue-collar people; and that 50 per cent of urban Negroes are lower class, including semiskilled working nonpoor, the unskilled working poor, and the nonworking poor.

at each class level. Negroes were a great deal more active, both in churches and in formal social organizations, than whites of comparable status. Negro upper-middles, like whites, were active—but even more so—in private social clubs, college alumni organizations, professional associations, and church groups, as well as in the NAACP and the Urban League. Lower-middle Negroes reported almost twice as many club memberships as white lower-middles. Almost all were active in churches and affiliated men's and women's groups; they were also active in fraternal orders, in organizations such as Boy Scouts and PTA, and in the "race" organizations, in which they worked at fund raising.

Working-class Negroes claimed three or four times more club and church memberships than did whites of the same level.[3] Most Negro men were in one or more drinking and card-playing clubs; quite frequently they were also members of a brotherhood lodge. Many were active in the Democratic club of their neighborhood and a veterans' club and also served in their churches as deacons or ushers. Almost all working-class Negro women were active in a club or two and in their church; they were in Eastern Star or one of the other auxiliaries of a male fraternal order, in a Baptist missionary society or a comparable guild at a Methodist church; they belonged to clubs which met in members' homes for sociability and for mutual instruction in some homemaking art or to raise money for a charitable cause.

Among lower-class Negroes, half claimed membership in a club, and over 80 per cent reported an active church affiliation. Their churches were seldom affiliated with the mainstream Baptist and Methodist denominations but were more often independent offshoots such as the Bethel Pentecostal, Cross of Christ Spiritualist, Strangers Rest, The True Vine, The New Hope, and Moorish Science.

[3] This above-average club and church membership is parallel to the findings in the Deep South in the mid-1930s. However, it is not borne out in a study conducted by the senior author in which two thousand Negroes of all ages living in ten different urban areas were interviewed. That study reported a much lower volume of social activity at the working class level than did the Kansas City study. It may well be that in the 1960s urban Negroes were much less involved in the whole circle of church and social organizations than were previous generations.

Five-Class System

The preceding pages have described how the perceptions of Kansas Citians regarding the status system were combined with data regarding the social characteristics and participation patterns of a large sample of middle-aged residents. This procedure resulted in a picture of a status hierarchy composed of five major social classes elaborated into thirteen strata. The strata within each class do not represent important distinctions as seen by the wider society, nor are they social entities in the same degree as the larger class groupings. Rather, the thirteen strata represent distinctions which are significant mainly to the members of the class involved.

The five dominant social classes stand out clearly. They represent the patterns of characteristics which underlie the residents' images and belief systems regarding status differences. They also represent groups of people who characterize the community, providing prototypes for superior and inferior social ranks. They provide forces of psychosocial attraction, and they pull people in toward them, in respect to both value patterns and social participation. In so doing, they create in the status hierarchy definable boundary lines which are meaningful to the social scientist who attempts to find order in the complexity of social interaction that constitutes the social life of a city. Without this magnetizing or crystalizing effect, the status order would be more properly described as a continuum of gentle gradations; with this effect, it is best characterized as a class system.

There were, inevitably, borderline people whose identitification in the public mind with one class or the other was a matter of disagreement. These people, however, were a small minority. The great majority were easily identified as belonging to one class and only that class. Much status marginality is a reflection of the mobility processes perpetually at work within a democracy. The social classes are open to entry from below, as well as from above, as individuals rise and fall in status. Many people who appeared marginal were in the process of moving across class lines; they had not yet firmly consolidated their position at the new class level and some of the characteristics of their class of origin lingered on in their behavior, attitudes, or patterns of participation.

Influence of Wives

Often wives played an important role in influencing social class placements. Especially significant was the wife's educational background and her pattern of social participation. In cases where the husband's occupational status was higher or lower than the family's class position, analysis of the interview material usually showed that the wife's educational level, her ethnic identity, or her religious preference was the strategic influence.

The educational levels of the middle-aged women studied here, for example, proved to be more highly correlated with family income than were the educational levels of their husbands and also more highly correlated with social class position. The wife's education was almost as highly correlated with her husband's occupational status as was his own educational level. Presumably these facts reflect the influence of a wife's social aspirations on her husband's occupational choices. Those aspirations also influence the family's choice of neighborhood, style of house, and church membership. The wife's club memberships and friendships also affect her family's social status.

At all class levels wives acted as brakes or prods upon the social mobility of their families. Wives without college educations sometimes held back wealthy husbands from movement into the upper class. And the wives, in some instances, strained to keep the family in a higher social position than the husbands' occupational and economic achievements would ordinarily merit. At a different level in the social hierarchy, it was sometimes the wife whose influence determined whether the husband remained a blue-collar worker or tried to achieve white-collar, middle-class status. And, similarly, it was sometimes an uneducated, nonaspiring lower-class wife who deterred her family's upward mobility to blue-collar status.

Social Characteristics

The social characteristics of each of the thirteen social status groups are shown in Table 2. The dimensions of status that were combined to form an Index of Kansas City Status (IKCS) are indicated in the table. These dimensions were also used to form the Index of Urban Status (IUS) as described in Chapter Five.

Table 2. SOCIAL CHARACTERISTICS OF KANSAS CITY'S THIRTEEN STRATA, 1955 (Persons Aged Forty to Sixty-Nine)[a]

	Upper-Class			Upper-Middle				Lower-Middle				Working-Class				Lower-Class		
	Capital S	Non-Capital S	Total	Elite	Core	Marginal	Total	Elite	Core	Marginal	Total	Elite	Core	Marginal	Total	Not quite the lowest	"Slumdweller"	Total
	Per Cent			Per Cent				Per Cent				Per Cent				Per Cent		
A. ECONOMIC AND OCCUPATIONAL STATUS																		
Men's Occupations (by U.S. Census categories):																		
Professional, technical, kindred	25	22	23	24	30	39	33	19	15	8	13	—	2	—	1	—	3	1
Proprietors, managers, officials	72	72	72	74	63	35	52	62	31	14	31	50	10	5	14	—	—	—
Clerical and kindred	3	6	5	—	17	—	—	15	25	17	21	—	8	3	6	—	—	—
Sales and kindred	—	—	—	2	—	26	15	4	15	8	10	—	2	8	3	—	—	—
Craftsmen, foremen, skilled	—	—	—	—	—	—	—	—	12	43	19	33	40	13	32	10	12	11
Operatives, semiskilled	—	—	—	—	—	—	—	—	—	5	2	17	22	33	24	30	22	26
Service workers, public and private	—	—	—	—	—	—	—	—	2	5	4	—	14	23	15	23	19	21
Laborers, unskilled workers	—	—	—	—	—	—	—	—	—	—	—	—	2	15	5	37	44	41
Men who were:																		
Self-employed	73	74	74	62	45	16	34	35	15	6	16	24	8	6	10	82	76	79
Employees	23	24	24	36	50	79	61	60	81	88	79	70	85	85	83	14	12	13
Retired	4	2	2	2	5	5	5	5	4	6	5	6	6	6	6	**4**	12	**8**
Unemployed	—	—	—	—	—	—	—	—	—	—	—	—	1	3	1	—	—	—
Women's Occupations:																		
Homemaker or retired	93	96	96	93	83	72	79	73	74	64	71	80	69	64	69	71	**54**	62
Professional, technical, kindred	3	2	2	4	4	12	7	15	2	3	5	13	3	—	2	—	—	—
Proprietors, managers, officials	2	1	1	2	4	4	4	8	2	3	3	—	1	—	2	—	—	—
Clerical and sales	2	1	1	1	9	12	10	4	20	24	18	—	13	9	10	—	—	—
Factory operatives, inspectors	—	—	—	—	—	—	—	—	—	—	—	7	4	9	6	11	8	10
Service workers or unskilled	—	—	—	—	—	—	—	—	—	6	3	—	6	9	6	11	19	15
Private domestic service	—	—	—	—	—	—	—	—	—	—	—	—	4	9	5	7	19	13
Rating of Men's Occupations (IKCS)[b]																		
(1) Top-flight professionals, executives, proprietors	80	75	76	37	—	—	4	—	—	—	—	—	—	—	—	—	—	—

Table (rotated on page). Columns are the Kansas City social strata, identified by their 1954 median household income. Rows (2)–(7) give the distribution of men's occupations[b]; rows (1)–(7) give the distribution of household income[c].

	$41,000	$32,000	$34,000	$23,100	$14,700	$11,900	$9,300	$8,200	$6,100	$6,300	$5,400	$7,400	$4,200	$3,600	$4,300	$3,000	$2,200	$2,600
(2) Typical managers, medium-status professionals, etc.	20	25	24	63	96	13	57	8	—	—	—	1	—	—	—	—	—	—
(3) Semiprofessionals, better-paid white-collar workers	—	—	—	—	4	87	39	13	17	—	—	—	—	—	—	—	—	—
(4) Average white-collar workers, highest-paid blue-collar and gray-collar workers	—	—	—	—	—	—	—	19	77	70	54	22	21	—	8	3	—	—
(5) Average blue-collar workers, lowest-level white-collars	—	—	—	—	—	—	—	—	10	17	43	70	35	4	17	33	6	17
(6) Below-average income semi-skilled and service workers	—	—	—	—	—	—	—	—	—	13	3	—	32	54	51	53	28	53
(7) Unskilled laborers and the chronically unemployed	—	—	—	—	—	—	—	—	—	—	—	—	11	3	13	28	66	30
Household Income (1954 Dollars) (IKCS)[c]																		
(1) $25,000 and Above	85	76	78	41	—	5	—	—	—	—	—	—	—	—	—	—	—	—
(2) $12,000 to $24,999	13	22	20	54	62	44	22	17	2	4	—	6	1	—	1	—	—	—
(3) $7,500 to $11,999	2	2	2	5	32	38	52	40	23	23	15	39	21	5	5	3	2	2
(4) $5,400 to $7,499	—	—	—	—	3	9	19	23	41	37	37	44	35	21	20	14	7	11
(5) $3,900 to $5,399	—	—	—	—	3	4	7	17	25	26	33	11	32	35	32	49	36	42
(6) $2,500 to $3,899	—	—	—	—	—	—	—	3	7	7	10	—	11	32	30	34	55	45
(7) Under $2,500	—	—	—	—	—	—	—	—	2	3	5	—	—	11	12	—	—	—
Median Income: 1954	$41,000	$32,000	$34,000	$23,100	$14,700	$11,900	$9,300	$8,200	$6,100	$6,300	$5,400	$7,400	$4,200	$3,600	$4,300	$3,000	$2,200	$2,600

[a] The table is based on data obtained from interviews with one or more members in each of 462 households in the metropolitan area and—for the top three strata—on additional data gathered on several thousand families (see Appendix B). The total number of families studied at each stratum is as follows: Capital S society, 508; non-Capital S, 1,761; upper-middle-elite, 1,555; upper-middle-core, 29; upper-middle-marginal, 27; lower-middle-elite, 30; lower-middle-core, 56; lower-middle-marginal, 40; working-class-core, 102; working-class-marginal, 50; lower-class but-not-the-lowest, 35; "slumdwellers," 45.

[b] Rating of men's occupations was one of the eight dimensions included in the Index of Kansas City Status. The other dimensions (household income, quality of housing, reputation of neighborhood, community associations, church attended, men's education, and women's education) occur in successive sections of this table. Each dimension was converted into a seven-point scale, as shown. As explained in Chapter Five, the IKCS was later converted into the Index of Urban Status for use in other American cities.

[c] Given the range in income produced by the variety of family situations (multiincome to retired), this scale proved a poor index of status and was later dropped (see Chapter Five).

Table 2. Social Characteristics of Kansas City's Thirteen Strata, 1955 (Persons Aged Forty to Sixty-Nine) (cont.)

	Upper-Class			Upper-Middle				Lower-Middle				Working-Class				Lower-Class		
	Capital S	Non-Capital S	Total	Elite	Core	Marginal	Total	Elite	Core	Marginal	Total	Elite	Core	Marginal	Total	Not quite the lowest	"Slumdweller"	Total
	Per Cent			Per Cent				Per Cent				Per Cent				Per Cent		
B. HOUSING AND NEIGHBORHOOD																		
Quality of Housing (IKCS)																		
(1) Mansions and ultraluxury apartments	55	36	41	16	—	—	2	—	—	—	—	—	—	—	—	—	—	—
(2) Very good homes (typical of Country Club District)	43	58	54	81	76	33	57	17	6	3	7	—	—	—	—	—	—	—
(3) Above average homes (typical of better South Side)	2	6	5	3	24	56	36	50	39	20	35	28	—	—	3	—	—	—
(4) Average, pleasant homes (typical of average South Side neighborhoods)	—	—	—	—	—	11	5	33	51	55	49	50	29	—	24	—	—	—
(5) Ordinary, decent homes (typical of average North Side neighborhoods)	—	—	—	—	—	—	—	—	4	22	9	22	62	32	48	—	—	—
(6) Substandard housing, but above the slum level	—	—	—	—	—	—	—	—	—	—	—	—	9	68	25	100	—	49
(7) Slums: semirural shacks or dilapidated apartments	—	—	—	—	—	—	—	—	—	—	—	—	—	—	—	—	100	51
Reputation of Neighborhood (IKCS)																		
(1) Gold Coast of Ward Parkway and Mission Hills	62	41	46	22	—	—	2	—	—	—	—	—	—	—	—	—	—	—
(2) Country Club District and equivalent elsewhere	35	54	49	64	62	33	50	7	4	—	3	—	—	—	—	—	—	—
(3) Above average South Side and equivalent elsewhere	3	5	5	12	34	59	43	47	35	18	33	—	2	—	1	—	—	—
(4) Average South Side and equivalent elsewhere	—	—	—	2	4	8	5	33	46	55	46	16	15	4	12	—	—	—

(5) Average North Side and equivalent elsewhere	—	—	—	—	—	—	—	—	—	—	—	—	—	—	—	9	2	17
(6) Below average North Side and equivalent elsewhere	—	—	—	—	—	—	—	—	—	—	—	—	—	—	—	52	45	60
(7) Slum areas, including North End, River Bottoms, etc.	—	—	—	—	—	—	—	—	—	—	—	—	—	—	—	39	53	23

C. SOCIAL AND RELIGIOUS AFFILIATIONS (WHITES ONLY)

Average number of club memberships and community activities (excludes labor unions and informal clubs)

Men	7.5	6.6	6.8	5.1	3.7	2.2	3.2	2.3	1.5	1.0	1.3	0.8	0.5	0.0	0.4	0.0	0.0	0.0
Women	5.7	4.4	4.7	3.9	3.2	2.3	2.9	1.4	0.9	1.0	1.0	0.9	0.4	0.1	0.3	0.1	0.0	0.0

Men active in:

Business and professional associations	100	100	100	98	93	63	81	58	40	17	36	—	2	—	1	—	—	—
Private town or country clubs	86	78	80	57	37	24	23	—	11	11	—	—	5	—	4	—	—	—
Volunteer community service	69	52	56	45	37	5	32	19	11	—	12	13	5	—	4	—	—	—
Luncheon service clubs	63	54	56	39	27	38	18	8	2	14	2	19	5	5	5	—	—	—
Church men's groups	36	22	25	27	33	5	34	31	17	6	18	13	7	6	6	—	—	—
Sports and athletic associations	29	20	22	16	11	10	10	12	9	8	9	13	11	9	9	—	—	—
Veterans' associations	18	15	16	14	11	33	11	23	19	8	22	7	10	—	8	—	—	—
Fraternal orders	3	20	16	51	48	5	42	27	22	8	22	19	12	—	10	—	—	—
Brotherhood lodges	—	—	—	2	7	5	5	8	6	8	7	56	76	85	77	62	56	59
Labor unions	—	—	—	—	—	—	—	—	14	50	23	56	—	—	—	—	—	—

Women active in:

Women's exclusive social clubs	100	81	85	53	34	21	—	—	—	—	—	—	—	—	—	—	—	—
Volunteer community service (including PTA, scouting)	94	76	80	65	55	44	51	17	15	17	16	19	3	—	5	—	—	—
Church guilds, related groups	74	59	62	65	76	72	73	50	38	36	40	63	23	12	26	6	—	3
College alumnae clubs	55	37	41	30	24	24	25	3	—	—	1	—	—	—	—	—	—	—
Women's culture and lecture clubs	29	43	40	45	31	20	28	11	4	—	4	—	6	—	—	—	—	—
Gardening, homemaking clubs	15	8	10	9	7	8	8	7	6	5	6	6	—	—	4	—	—	—
Auxiliaries to men's fraternal, brotherhood, veterans' groups	—	—	—	17	31	20	25	30	15	14	18	13	4	—	4	—	—	—
Informal bridge, card-playing clubs	95	84	86	80	76	56	68	30	12	3	13	—	2	—	1	—	—	—

Table 2. Social Characteristics of Kansas City's Thirteen Strata, 1955 (Persons Aged Forty to Sixty-Nine) (cont.)

	Upper-Class			Upper-Middle				Lower-Middle				Working-Class				Lower-Class		
	Per Cent			Per Cent				Per Cent				Per Cent				Per Cent		
	Capital S	Non-Capital S	Total	Elite	Core	Marginal	Total	Elite	Core	Marginal	Total	Elite	Core	Marginal	Total	Not quite the lowest	"Slumdweller"	Total
Community Associations (IKCS)																		
(1) Identified with upperclass clubs or cliques	100	100	100	—	—	—	—	—	—	—	—	—	—	—	—	—	—	—
(2) Member of one or more clubs of semielite level	—	100	—	100	100	—	57	—	—	—	—	—	—	—	—	—	—	—
(3) Primarily associated with clubs and/or cliques of above-average status	—	—	—	—	—	100	43	40	—	—	7	—	—	—	—	—	—	—
(4) Associated with average South Side clubs, cliques	—	—	—	—	—	—	—	60	100	100	93	100	100	52	88	—	—	—
(5) Associated with average North Side clubs, cliques	—	—	—	—	—	—	—	—	—	—	—	—	—	48	12	—	—	—
(6) Nonmembers, but not defined "disreputable" by community	—	—	—	—	—	—	—	—	—	—	—	—	—	—	—	49	—	24
(7) "Hillbilly," "poor" Italian, Mexican—or apparently of "disreputable" character	—	—	—	—	—	—	—	—	—	—	—	—	—	—	—	51	100	76
Religious Identification, Active Membership or Preference																		
Protestant	84	71	74	64	69	77	72	73	78	82	78	53	32	79	77	64	61	62
Catholic	7	15	13	17	16	14	15	21	18	16	18	47	17	21	22	36	39	38
Jewish	9	14	13	19	15	9	13	6	4	2	4	—	1	—	1	—	—	—

Church Affiliation (IKCS)

Rated for attendance or membership in

(1) Society church	70	44	50	26	18	9	15	—	—	—	—	—	—	—	—	—	3	1
(2) Metropolitan prestige or Country Club parish church	18	38	33	48	45	47	46	7	4	—	3	—	—	—	—	—	—	—
(3) Other South Side churches of above-average reputation	3	7	6	11	14	22	17	25	9	4	10	—	1	—	1	—	—	—
(4) South Side churches in average neighborhoods and of well-known denominations	—	*	*	5	7	7	7	37	42	41	41	9	8	5	7	—	3	1
(5) North Side churches, well-known and/or "tolerated" denominations	—	—	—	—	—	—	—	4	6	12	7	50	32	32	34	3	9	6
(6) Churches in poorer neighborhoods or of so-called off-brand denominations	—	—	—	*	—	—	*	—	2	2	2	25	8	8	10	29	15	22
(7) Slum churches, store fronts, or most extreme revivalist sects	—	—	—	—	—	—	—	—	—	—	—	—	—	—	—	16	38	28
Does attend church or claim a membership	9	11	11	10	16	15	15	27	37	41	37	16	51	55	48	52	32	42

D. EDUCATION BACKGROUND

Median Years of Schooling:

Men	16.5	16.3	16.4	14.9	14.7	13.5	14.5	12.8	12.6	11.7	12.4	9.0	8.8	8.2	8.7	7.4	7.4	7.4
Women	14.5	14.3	14.4	14.1	13.9	13.7	13.8	12.7	12.4	12.2	12.4	8.8	9.2	8.7	8.9	7.8	6.5	7.2

Men born 1885–1914 who achieved

Graduate degree (M.A., LL.B., etc.)	27	21	22	17	22	15	18	4	2	—	2	—	—	—	—	—	—	—
Undergraduate degree (B.A., B.S.)	47	43	44	30	22	20	23	12	4	—	4	—	—	—	—	—	—	—
Some college attendance	18	9	11	19	19	20	19	28	27	19	25	6	4	3	4	—	3	2
High school graduation	7	20	17	20	19	30	24	36	38	27	34	22	16	13	16	17	23	20
Some high school attendance	1	6	5	9	15	10	12	8	15	30	18	22	24	15	22	26	17	21
Eighth grade completion	—	*	*	5	3	5	4	8	10	21	13	22	32	25	29	28	27	27
Fifth to seventh grade	—	*	*	*	—	—	*	4	4	3	4	17	20	22	20	26	19	23
First to fourth grade	—	—	—	—	—	—	—	—	—	—	—	11	4	22	9	3	11	7
No formal schooling	—	—	—	—	—	—	—	—	—	—	—	—	—	—	—	—	—	—

Table 2. Social Characteristics of Kansas City's Thirteen Strata, 1955 (Persons Aged Forty to Sixty-Nine) (cont.)

| | Upper-Class | | | Upper-Middle | | | | Working-Class | | | | Lower-Middle | | | | Lower-Class | | |
| | Per Cent | | | Per Cent | | | | Per Cent | | | | Per Cent | | | | Per Cent | | |
	Capital S	Non-Capital S	Total	Elite	Core	Marginal	Total	Elite	Core	Marginal	Total	Elite	Core	Marginal	Total	Not quite the lowest	"Slumdweller"	Total
Women born 1885–1914 who achieved																		
College degree (B.A. or higher)	38	36	37	31	26	24	26	14	4	—	4	—	—	—	—	—	—	—
Some college attendance	56	35	40	32	34	34	34	24	16	24	20	4	4	2	3	—	—	—
High school graduation	6	25	20	29	29	34	31	42	50	33	44	27	22	10	20	4	6	5
Some high school attendance	—	4	3	7	7	8	7	17	21	27	22	17	26	28	25	19	9	14
Eighth grade completion	—	—	—	1	4	—	2	3	9	13	9	33	34	36	34	24	23	23
Fifth to seventh grade	—	—	—	—	—	—	—	—	—	3	1	17	14	12	14	24	20	25
First to fourth grade	—	—	—	—	—	—	—	—	—	—	—	6	—	12	4	24	28	26
No formal schooling	—	—	—	—	—	—	—	—	—	—	—	—	—	—	—	—	14	7
Education of children in families studied																		
Attended one year or more of college	97	94	95	91	89	86	88	71	63	57	62	29	16	12	17	4	—	2
Graduated from high school	99	99	99	98	98	97	98	96	94	93	94	71	67	57	65	25	14	19
IKCS Rating for Men on Educational Background																		
(1) Prestige education: Ivy League undergraduate and/or top-ranked professional schools	44	8	17	3	—	—	*	—	—	—	—	—	—	—	—	—	—	—
(2) Advanced degrees or undergrad years in good colleges, fraternities	44	60	56	40	41	30	36	11	4	—	4	—	—	—	—	—	—	—
(3) Above average for men of era: degrees from lesser colleges or some post-high school training	7	11	10	27	26	26	26	28	23	14	21	—	—	3	1	—	—	—

	C1	C2	C3	C4	C5	C6	C7	C8	C9	C10	C11	C12	C13	C14	C15	C16	C17	C18
(4) Average preparation for white-collar jobs: ten, eleven, or twelve grades	5	17	14	21	22	35	29	46	46	52	48	39	30	18	28	—	6	3
(5) Average for "blue-collar" workers: eighth or ninth grade	—	4	3	9	11	9	9	11	23	29	23	33	48	28	41	40	38	39
(6) Below blue-collar average for boys of their era	—	—	—	*	—	—	*	4	4	5	4	17	20	28	22	27	25	26
(7) Lowest 12-13 per cent in years of schooling for boys of their era	—	—	—	—	—	—	—	—	—	—	—	11	2	23	8	33	31	32

IKCS Rating for Women on Educational Background

	C1	C2	C3	C4	C5	C6	C7	C8	C9	C10	C11	C12	C13	C14	C15	C16	C17	C18
(1) Fashionably educated: at finishing schools or top-ranked women's colleges	60	15	25	3	—	—	*	—	—	—	—	—	—	—	—	—	—	—
(2) Attendance at better colleges and/or membership in good sorority	31	43	40	35	34	32	33	7	—	—	1	—	—	—	—	—	—	—
(3) Degrees from lesser colleges or other post-high school training	5	18	15	26	28	28	28	24	15	18	18	28	3	2	2	—	—	—
(4) Average for girls from white-collar families: eleven or twelve grades	4	20	17	32	34	36	35	53	57	51	54	28	35	20	30	3	10	7
(5) Average for girls from blue-collar families: eight, nine, or ten grades	—	4	3	4	4	4	4	13	24	26	23	44	47	51	48	34	23	28
(6) Next-to-lowest 20-25 per cent in years of schooling for girls of era	—	—	—	—	—	—	—	3	4	5	4	22	15	18	17	45	26	35
(7) Lowest 12-13 per cent in years of schooling for girls of era	—	—	—	—	—	—	—	—	—	—	—	6	—	9	3	18	41	30

Chapter 5

The Index of Urban Status

*M*any aspects of the status system found to operate in a metropolitan center are not properly reflected by scales developed previously for measuring social status. Some scales are based upon an inadequate number of variables; some employ scoring principles that do not accord with the relationships observed in many communities (Knupfer, 1946; Kahl and Davis, 1955). The Index of Status Characteristics, for example, included scales for only four variables—reputation of neighborhood, quality of housing, type of occupation, and source of income (Warner, Meeker, and Eells, 1949). Source of income was observed to be almost irrelevant in the Kansas City setting; and the occupation scale did not reflect the fact that Kansas Citians attached more significance to degree of success at occupation, as measured by apparent income, than to type of occupation. Furthermore, in Kansas City, ethnic identity, church affiliation, club memberships, and certain other forms of community participation had important status significance.

The Index of Kansas City Status was developed to take into account all the variables just mentioned and, in doing so, to imitate the practices followed by Kansas Citians themselves in judging status. Everything learned in this regard from the Kansas City newspapers and from interview materials was used in devising the Index.

The Index of Kansas City Status (IKCS) measured eight dimensions, each in terms of the *evaluations* made by Kansas Citians: occupation of male head of household, total family income, neighborhood of residence, quality of housing, education of male head, education of female head or wife, church affiliation, and community associations (including the factor of ethnic identity). For each of these eight dimensions, a seven-step scale was devised, with each step on the scale roughly equated with one or another of the social status levels perceived by Kansas Citians. The distributions of ratings on these dimensions within each of the five social classes and for strata-within-class are shown as parts of Table 2 in Chapter Four. As already pointed out in Chapter Four, the IKCS yielded a profile of status ratings for each family; that eight-dimension profile (rather than a summed total score) was used in arraying the 462 families in the sample, in delineating social class boundaries, and then in making social class placements for each family. Analysis of these profiles proved most useful in arriving at the thirteen-stratum status hierarchy.

In the years since the Kansas City study was completed, revisions and modifications of the IKCS have been made in studying other urban communities.[1] The result is the Index of Urban Status (IUS) described in this chapter. In the Index of Urban Status, seven of the dimensions used in the original IKCS have been retained. The one that was dropped—total family income—was replaced by a scale for rating occupation of female head of household or employed wife. Each of the scales has been generalized from the original Kansas City scoring to apply to a wide range of American cities. Procedures to be followed for continual revision and updating of the scales are indicated in the discussion to follow. (A more detailed version of the Index as a manual of instructions for classifying a sample is available from the senior author.)

[1] The Index of Urban Status was refined through twelve years of research in consumer behavior at Social Research, Inc., of Chicago. It has been used in three major studies (as well as in smaller studies) for (1) classification of a national sample of 2,500 families used as a continuing panel, (2) classification of a national panel of 1,300 families for a television rating service, and (3) classification of 2,100 Chicago men participating in a study at the University of Illinois Medical School on the correlates of heart disease.

A principal advantage of the Index of Urban Status is that, unlike other status measures, score values are the same for all dimensions. Thus, on any dimension, a score of:

1 is predictive of upper-class status;
2 is predictive of upper-middle-core (or upper-middle-elite);
3 is almost equally predictive of either upper-middle-marginal or lower-middle-elite;
4 is predictive of lower-middle-core or possible lower-middle-marginal;
5 is almost equally predictive of working-class status, at the core level or possibly elite;
6 is almost equally predictive of working-class status at the lower margin or lower-class status; and
7 is predictive of lower-class status at its bottom level.

In the paragraphs that follow scale points are described, for purposes of convenience, in terms of their social class equivalence in Kansas City. In subsequent sections of this chapter, however, scale points are described in terms of actual social and economic characteristics. Thus the IUS can be utilized whether or not the investigator chooses to use the social class nomenclature used here.

The establishment of comparable score values for all variables yields a status profile wherein a family's status assets and liabilities are quickly revealed. For example, if the male head of a family receives an occupation score of 2 but the family's address and community associations are both rated 4, it is immediately suggested that the family is higher in economic-occupational status than in social aspiration and participation and that the family is at the lower-middle-elite level. If the husband and wife are both rated 5 in educational background, it is likely that they have moved up from working class origins, which might explain why the husband's occupational success has not led to higher social status. Thus the IUS makes explicit for a given family the components of its status position. The profile also reveals the extent to which a family is in a position of high status crystallization, when all characteristics are rated nearly the same, or of low status crystallization, when the various status characteristics are rated quite differently (Lenski, 1954).

Ideally, judgments of status should be made subjectively according to the patterning of scores, instead of from a total score which can often be misleading. In certain instances, a score on a single variable is by itself definitive of status. Thus, whenever a family has a 7—or slum—rating on housing quality, the family is regarded as lower class regardless of its scores on other variables. Similarly, if a family has a 1 rating on community participation, it is automatically placed as upper class. This subjective use of the Index can be considered a parallel to the evaluated participation technique recommended by Warner and his associates for research in small towns (Warner, Meeker, and Eells, 1949).

The IUS can also be used more objectively by averaging the several part-scores to obtain a total score. When it is used this way, it is not necessary to use all eight dimensions, although to do so is always the optimum course. Whether two or three or all eight dimensions are used, average scores which are closer to 1 than to 2 indicate upper-class status, averages which are closer to 2 than to 4 indicate upper-middle-class status, and so on.

If an investigator wishes to develop an additional scale, or substitute different dimensions, he may do so as long as equivalent score values are used. Thus, another advantage of the equal score values is that interpretation does not depend on the use of any particular scale or combination of scales.

Finally, it should be repeated that the IUS mirrors the methods and the status imagery of city dwellers themselves. In a metropolis, social class is evaluated in terms of the observable social characteristics of hypothetical equals, rather than by reference to specific individuals. As a consequence, status in a city can be assessed in almost exactly the same way that residents themselves assess it.

Occupation Status Scale

The IUS occupation status scale reflects several assumptions about the relationship between occupation and social status which are not always incorporated into other occupational scales.[2]

[2] The original scale developed for rating Kansas Citians was drawn from the occupational characterizations applied to each of the seven strata of neighborhoods. This provided a rudimentary base. As a second step, the data from the sample of middle-aged families were used to clarify income boundary lines for the various levels of occupational success and to determine the range in occupations which were likely to be found at each level. Other occupational scales were examined, as well as opinion surveys regarding the

Occupational Success: For middle class (or white-collar) occupations—business, managerial, executive, clerical, sales, and professional jobs—the degree of success a man has achieved at his occupation is critical to his family's social status. This is true particularly for men over forty years of age. It is almost as true in the blue-collar world, except that income level does not vary as much for blue-collar workers as for white-collar workers.

In any particular white-collar occupation, the range of success as measured by income is so broad that the occupation quite commonly spreads over three or four class levels. In the Kansas City sample, for instance, there were dentists with annual incomes ranging from eight thousand dollars a year (1955 dollars) to fifty thousand dollars or more. This was also the case with sales managers and company presidents. In the imagery of the community, the occupational ratings of these men ranged from "side-street dentists," "small-time sales manager," and "president of an unimportant little company" up to "society dentists," "phenomenally successful salesman," and "a big wheel among executives." In social position they ranged from the lower-middle-core up to Capital S society. The adjectives used to describe degree of occupational success are more important in defining the layman's view of an individual's status than the occupational title. The occupation scale reflects this fact by offering a range of ratings for almost every occupation. The suggested income ranges shown in Table 3 are the quantitative equivalents for the degree-of-success-at-occupation adjectives used by the American public.

Occupational Field: The status significance suggested by a given income can vary sharply from one occupational field to another. Schoolteachers, social workers, ministers, and bank clerks, for example, have more social and occupational status per dollar of income than plumbing contractors, tavern owners, or truckers. The occupational status scale is designed to reflect such differences.

---

prestige ranking of various occupations and data from the 1960 census on the relationship between income and occupation. The most fruitful sources were: Hatt and North (1953); Reiss (1957); Reiss, Duncan, Hatt, and North (1961); and Hodge, Siegel, and Rossi (1964). Especially helpful was the detailed analysis of occupation and income trends reported in Bogue (1959). Edwards (1943) was also consulted. Recent findings on occupational status are given in Blau and Duncan (1967).

To illustrate, a 3 rating is given as the lowest rating for all college faculty members or male schoolteachers, no matter how low their income. This is because 3 is the status level generally attributed to men in the educational field, regardless of their income or apparent success. At the other extreme there are many occupations, such as lithographer or milk delivery driver, where a 3 rating is impossible no matter how high the income, because these occupations virtually close out a family from the lower-middle-elite level or higher. In between these extremes, our research has shown that the government employees with incomes which are as low as $10,600 a year (1970 dollars) qualify for a 3 rating, white-collar workers in private industry need to earn a bit more ($11,800), and men in other fields even more—a building superintendent, $14,700, a plumbing contractor, $16,300, and a union official, at least $19,700. (The relationships between income and occupational field change with time; the occupational status scale shown in Table 3 refers to 1970 dollar values in urban America.)

Such relationships between occupational field and range of income apply in all occupational categories. The concept of field is relevant to entrepreneurs in a special way. A division of these men into (1) owners of luxury goods stores and banking-financial enterprises, (2) proprietors of construction, trucking, and other low-status enterprises, and (3) all other owners makes it possible to measure the occupational status of entrepreneurs in hundreds of different fields with only a few income breakdowns. (Income ranges are irrelevant in judging the status of owners of illegitimate and/or disreputable businesses. Their occupational rating is 0, meaning that they cannot be classified.)

Occupational Title: The IUS occupational status scale places virtually all white-collar employees who are not professionals or proprietors into one category: executives, managers, clerical, and sales. All executives, managers, and clerical workers are then subdivided according to whether they work for private corporations or government, and then further subdivided by whether they work in certain prestige fields and by whether they work for the federal government. (All sales workers are singled out for separate grouping.) This procedure avoids the problem of separately rating the myriad of occupational titles like president, vice-president, secretary, treasurer, manager, assistant manager, section head, division chief,

Rating Assigned Occupation	PROFESSIONALS AND TECHNICIANS (Male)	EXECUTIVES, MANAGERS CLERICALS AND SALES (Male)	PROPRIETORS, INCLUDING CONTRACTORS, ALL SELF-EMPLOYED BUSINESSMEN (Male)
ONE	Physicians, lawyers, architects, other fee professionals: $42,000 or more. Prominent clergymen, educators: from $36,000 (inc. house)	Corporation executives: above $42,000. Federal, state, local officials: over $37,200	Owners, partners in manufacturing, retailing, wholesaling: above $50,000. Contractors, truckers, laundry owners: $58,000 up
TWO	Professionals (fee or salaried—CPAs, scientists, doctors, lawyers: $19,100–$41,999. College faculty, other educators, social workers, clergy: $15,900–$35,999	Corporation managers, officials: $19,100–$41,999. Government officials, department chiefs: $16,900–$37,199	Proprietors in manufacturing, retailing, wholesaling: $23,000–$49,999. Brokers, luxury goods retailers: $20,700–$44,999
THREE	Accountants, engineers, miscellaneous salaried and fee professionals: $11,800–$19,099. Teachers, social workers, clergy: most all with B.A.s	Higher-level corporate office workers, junior executives, top clerical: $11,800–$19,099. Government bureaucrats: $10,600–$16,899. Salesmen: $13,000–$22,299	Proprietors of small businesses—primarily retailing, wholesaling: $14,200–$22,999. Contractors, truckers: $16,300–$26,299
FOUR	Draftsmen, surveyors, x-ray technicians, radio operators, photographers, miscellaneous technicians: $8,150 up	White-collar business employees, auditors, payroll clerks: $7,250–$11,799; government employees: $6,700–$10,599	Small business owners—grocery stores, service stations, barber shops: $8,700–$14,199. Contractors, truckers: $10,000–$16,299
FIVE	Technicians, as above: $5,650–$8,149. Ministers of storefront churches, low-status evangelist sects	Office workers: $5,100–$7,249; government clericals: $4,800–$6,699. Salesmen: $5,400–$7,849. Shipping clerks: $5,850–$8,399	Miscellaneous proprietors, contractors, no employees or 2 or 3 (corner grocers, cafe owners, filling station lessees): $6,100–$8,699
SIX		Shipping clerks, baggagemen, messengers: $3,350–$5,849. Salesmen: at least $3,000, but less than $5,400	Fruitstand owners, other hole-in-wall business enterprisers, newsstand operators: $2,650–$6,099. Self-employed truckers: $3,900–$6,949
SEVEN		Shipping clerks, salesmen: below minimums above; other census-classified clerical workers: below $3,000	Trashhaulers, peddlers, hucksters who are self-employed: less than $4,700

Rating Assigned Occupation	FOREMEN, CRAFTSMEN, OPERATIVES, SERVICE WORKERS, AND LABORERS (Male)	MILITARY PERSONNEL AND PUBLIC SERVICE EMPLOYEES	WOMEN: PRINCIPAL OCCUPATIONS AT EACH RATING
ONE		Generals, admirals, and commodores	Well-known entertainers, writers, classical artists, dress designers, locally prominent decorators, professionals, executives, business owners who qualify at this level by men's scale criteria
TWO	Labor union officials: $36,000 or more	Colonels, lieutenant colonels (Army, Air Force, Marines), and captains, commanders in Navy Police, fire commissioners in larger cities: $22,500 or more	Educators, social workers, other professional women: $15,900–$35,999 Salaried businesswomen: $16,700–$41,999 Moderately prosperous specialty shop owners
THREE	Labor union officers: $19,700–$35,999	Majors and captains (Army, Air Force, Marines), lieutenant commanders and 1st lieutenants (Navy) Police, fire, law enforcement officials, top level assistants: $15,000–$22,499	Schoolteachers, social workers, librarians, other professional women past apprentice level Saleswomen, private secretaries, administrative aides: $8,900–$16,699
FOUR	Union personnel, foremen: $10,650–$19,699 High-skill craftsmen—engravers, jewelers, opticians—and inspectors: above $9,500 RR engineers, bus drivers, butchers, telephone men: above $10,650	1st and 2nd lieutenants (Army, Air Force, Marines), Jr. lieutenants, ensigns (Navy), warrant officers Fire, police, law enforcement officers: $10,000–$14,999 Mailmen: 21 years service	Secretaries, other women in office jobs: $4,850–$8,899 Salesclerks in middle class shops, department stores Registered nurses, dental hygienists, medical technicians, $5,700 up
FIVE	Foremen, medium-skill craftsmen—carpenters, machinists, painters, plumbers—and assembly line operatives: $6,950–$10,649 Inspectors, barbers, milk route delivery drivers, other gray-collar types: $6,400–$9,499 Dirty-blue-collars: above $7,650	Career sergeants, career petty officers Policemen, firemen, highway patrolmen without supervisory title: $6,550–$9,999 Most postal carriers	Typists, other office workers: $3,300–$4,849 Salesclerks in lower status stores; cashiers in grocery, drug stores, etc. Beauty operators, higher level waitresses, practical nurses Factory workers: above $4,850
SIX	Assembly line operatives and lesser skill or lower-pay service workers, craftsmen: $3,920–$6,949 Dirty-blue-collar types—longshoremen, truck drivers, janitors, construction workers: $4,300–$7,649	Career enlisted men—corporals, privates, airmen, seamen, petty officers 3rd class (Navy) Prison guards, fire, police workers: $3,700–$6,549	Assembly line workers, packers, graders: $2,800–$4,849 Hotel maids, nurses' aides, fountain girls, hash-house waitresses, dimestore clerks, hospital attendants: $2,550–$4,450 Domestics in personal service
SEVEN	Dishwashers, ditch diggers, street-sweepers, garbage collectors, hod carriers, menial laborers: less than $4,300 Blue-collar or service workers: less than $3,900 Chronic unemployed and odd-jobbers		Assembly line workers, laundry employees: below $2,800 Scrubwomen, janitresses: less than $3,100; day workers irregularly employed A.D.C. mothers

and so on; it also accounts for discrepancies in status of titles from one enterprise to another.

In the final analysis, salary, not title, provides the primary measuring stick Americans use in evaluating the status of any particular bureaucratic-managerial position. Rating white-collar business employees according to their salary level, not their titles, reflects the social realities of the situation. The same practice has been followed with blue-collar occupations, where status is scored mainly on annual wages and minimal attention is paid to differences in level or type of skill. There is considerable overlap in income ranges between skill levels, and thus in the America of the 1950s and 1960s blue-collar income had more influence on family status than the skill-level of the job at which it was earned.

The occupation status scale is presented in summary form in Table 3 below. The income figures cited are appropriate only to those American communities where income levels are average relative to urban areas across the nation.[3]

Women's Occupations: It should be noted that income levels are often omitted for women's occupations. This is done because the status of the clientele served, not the income derived, is often the major consideration in the status accorded. Women's occupation ratings are most useful when subjective analysis is made of a family's status profile. For example, all the occupations in the women's part of the scale rated at the 4 level or higher are eminently acceptable employment for middle class women but, by and large, those rated 5 or below are not. Women's occupational ratings are also useful in suggesting whether the wife, by working, has raised her family's social status, as is likely when the wife has a job with higher occupational status than her husband's.

Correlation with Social Class: In the Kansas City sample of middle-aged adults, the correlation between male head of household's occupation rating and identification with one or another of the thirteen substrata was 0.89. The correlation between occupation rating for women and class position was 0.65. It cannot be expected

[3] With respect to the occupation status scale, the IUS manual of instructions referred to above provides: (1) a more detailed listing of occupations than shown in Table 3, (2) recommendations for adjusting income ranges to take account of regional variations in salary and wage levels, and (3) procedures for updating income ranges in line with the changing value of the dollar. Detailed instructions on ratings of retirees, unemployed, and deceased spouses are also offered.

that a sample including all age groups would yield such high correlations. For example, for men under thirty-five in managerial and professional occupations, ratings on the occupation scale can be expected to underestimate their status. For such men, it is occupational potential—as judged by initial achievements, educational credentials, family background, and peer groups relationships—which is crucial in estimating their social position, not their occupational level of the moment.

Neighborhood Status Scale

Kansas Citians regarded address as a key fact in making status evaluations. Neighborhood distinctions played a vital role, also, in determining the social participation ratings of most middle-status families, because these families usually attended nearby churches and associated almost exclusively with people who lived in the same part of the city. The impact of neighborhood was particularly important in child raising. Children attended schools in their own neighborhoods, and their parents worked together in parent-teacher associations and youth-serving organizations. Many of the larger fraternal orders and brotherhood lodges, with their women's auxiliaries, were subdivided into neighborhood chapter units. All these informal and formal relationships oriented around neighborhood contributed heavily to a family's place within the status system.

All this meant that Kansas Citians looked upon address not only as evidence of financial status but also as an important sign of a family's status goals. Most Kansas City neighborhoods offered a range in prices for housing, and, recognizing this, Kansas Citians felt that neighborhood choice indicated whether a family cared enough about status to spend more money to buy a house in a desirable neighborhood than would be required to purchase an equivalent house in a less desirable neighborhood.

Almost everywhere that social class has been studied, a great deal of class consciousness has revolved around neighborhood differentiation. Lynd described Muncie, Indiana, as roughly split into North Side Business Class and South Side Working Class worlds, with children's attitudes toward their acceptance in the peer world of the Muncie Central High School strongly influenced by this division (Lynd and Lynd, 1929). The numerous geographic labels used by the people of Yankee City, Deep South, and Jonesville as stratification terms prompted Warner and his associates (Warner and Lunt, 1941; Warner et al., 1949; and Warner, Meeker, and Eells, 1949) to choose dwelling area as one of the four main status characteristics to be rated in their index of status characteristics. Similarly, Hollingshead (Hollingshead and Redlich, 1958), in developing a three-variable index of social position, included a residential scale for evaluating addresses.

In Kansas City: Three types of data were employed in developing the neighborhood scale in Kansas City: general reputation of the city's neighborhoods and adjacent suburban areas obtained from interviews; consultations with real estate experts to determine where there were specific streets or blocks with reputations different from the surrounding areas; and examination of block-by-block census statistics on housing values to determine relationships between community reputation, expert opinion, and these officially published valuations.

The widespread community agreement on ranking of seven major areas of Kansas City, Missouri, and its suburbs, as described in Chapter Three provided the guidelines—that is, each of the seven ranks of neighborhood was equated with one of the seven points on the IKCS. The Ward Parkway Gold Coast area served as the reference for a 1 rating, the Country Club District for a 2, and so on. Pockets of more or less desirable housing within these larger areas were given separate ratings. Neighborhoods in Independence, Missouri, and Kansas City, Kansas, were equated to one or another of these seven levels. The neighborhood map which resulted represented a compromise between a scale based on general neighborhood reputation and one based on individual block evaluation, as determined from census statistics and appraisal by real estate experts. Benton Boulevard, for example, though superior in appearance to the rest of the South East Side, was regarded as a place where people lived who were identified as leaders in the lower-middle class rather than part of the Country Club social world. Accordingly, Benton Boulevard was given a score no higher than that of the blocks surrounding it. On the other hand, Armour Boulevard, in the South Central area, and Gladstone Boulevard, in the Northeast, were awarded higher ratings than the areas surrounding them, because it was considered quite acceptable for people of high status to live on these streets despite the lower rating of surrounding neighborhoods.

Correlation with Social Class: The correlation between neighborhood rating and social class position in the Kansas City sample of middle-aged families was 0.85. The correlation would undoubtedly have been lower had the sample included the entire age range of household heads. Before age forty, many middle class families cannot afford as good a house or neighborhood as is expected of middle-aged persons of the same status; after age fifty-five, many families at various class levels stay on in declining neighborhoods.

A neighborhood scale is unlikely to be equally status-predictive in all cities, or in smaller communities where neighborhoods tend to be less homogeneous in housing. The particular pattern of social geography of Kansas City in 1955 very likely placed it among the most neighborhood-conscious communities of the United States. There are few cities in the United States where a gradient of residential desirability prevails that is as neat as Kansas City's north-south rule. Even in Kansas City this rule has broken down considerably in recent years, as desirable new areas have been built north of the river, to the southeast, and also to the southwest. In communities where the status geography is not as easily perceived by the residents and where neighborhoods are less homogeneous, a lower correlation between status and neighborhood rating should be expected; also, the construction of a status map will require greater reliance on census data and real estate judgments.

Constructing Scales for Other Communities: A neighborhood status scale is easy to construct for communities where neighborhoods are relatively homogeneous. In communities where there is variation within blocks or from block to block, such a scale is not only more difficult to construct but also less meaningful as a measure of status. In either case, a single scale point should represent a balance between the reputation of small areas and the reputation of larger subdivisions of the city.

In isolating seven ranks of neighborhoods, the following criteria can be followed:

> 1 indicates neighborhoods, special blocks, or apartment complexes reputed to be where the city's social, professional, and executive elite live, and where a majority or at least 40 per cent of the houses or apartments are of the mansion or top luxury class as rated by the IUS Housing Quality scale.

2 indicates neighborhoods, special blocks, or apartment buildings which, in public opinion, are appropriate residential
locations for prosperous managerial and professional families. The public impression should be that a majority of
the residents are firmly established at a fairly high occupational and social status level.

3 indicates neighborhoods, special areas, or apartment buildings which are considered above average in desirability
either because they are: favored by aspiring young college-
educated professional and managerial families, not so
highly regarded as in former years but still occupied by
many older high status families, or aspired to by the most
socially sensitive white-collar and semiprofessional families.

4 indicates neighborhoods which are basically white-collar
and/or middle class in the public eye, but do not merit a
higher rank than this within the middle class world. Some
of these neighborhoods may contain more blue-collar than
white-collar workers, but if so, these will be blue-collar
families who are thought to be aspiring to higher status,
as distinguished from those who accept a definition of
themselves as prosperous but not socially minded working
class people.

5 indicates neighborhoods which are blue-collar or ordinary
working class in the public eye but not substandard or
markedly below average in desirability or appearance. The
quality of housing may appear to be almost as good as in
some neighborhoods given a 4 rating, but they will be given
this lower rating because, in the opinion of the city's
white-collar residents, these neighborhoods are on the
wrong side of town, or in an undesirable school district.

6 indicates areas which are widely considered substandard
in housing, or undesirable by virtue of proximity to industry, commerce, railroad tracks, or slums, or where more
than half of the housing rates no better than a 6 on the
IUS Housing Quality scale.

7 indicates neighborhoods viewed as "the worst in the city"
in appearance and reputation, where the majority of housing units are rated as slums or which public opinion has
condemned as inhabited by bad people, reliefers, or the
poor of a widely disapproved ethnic group.

Quality of Housing Scale

Americans tend to regard housing as the foremost visible
indicator of a family's level of economic well-being. Actually, it is
not as good an index as is commonly supposed, for families vary

greatly in the proportion of income they spend on housing. Nevertheless, in most status-measuring instruments, including the earliest scales for measuring socioeconomic status, the quality and appearance of a family's housing have been included as one of the indices (for example, Chapin, 1933). Thus, the precedent is strong for including such a scale in any multidimensional status measure.

In Kansas City: The scale for scoring Kansas City housing was relatively easy to construct. The imagery on the seven levels of neighborhoods and the descriptions of realtors about the market values of homes in these neighborhoods were used as starting points. Typical blocks were then surveyed to determine what types of houses were characteristic, and market values and rentals were determined for typical houses in each area. The approximate market value or rental of a respondent's home was sometimes elicited in an interview. In all instances, however, the housing unit was rated by two members of the research team, using guidelines acquired from realtors for estimating value or rents. Table 4 illustrates the relationship between these market and rental values and the seven scale points.

Correlation with Social Class: For the middle-aged families in the Kansas City sample, the correlation between housing quality scores and social class was .85, about the same as between neighborhood ratings and social class. As with the neighborhood, this correlation is almost certainly greatest for middle-aged couples, who are housed more in line with social class expectations than are single people of the same age, or older or younger couples.

There is reason to believe that in the future, as more Americans of working-class level share in the general prosperity and occupy houses of the same quality as those occupied by lower-middle-class people, the correlation between social class and housing will be reduced. Similarly, further increases in federally subsidized housing may reduce the significance of housing in differentiating social levels among the lower income levels. Real estate newspaper columns in the late 1960s warned that housing costs, in rents or mortgage payments, are advancing more rapidly than the average rate of inflation. These changing relationships between housing costs and income may decrease further the correlations between housing and social class identification.

Table 4. QUALITY OF HOUSING SCALE FOR KANSAS CITY, 1955

Scale Value	Type of House	Market Value[a]	Monthly Rental
1	Mansions, nine rooms or more, built in 1920s or later; luxurious ranch or modern homes of postwar period; spacious luxury apartments	Over $36,000	Over $270
2	Seven or eight rooms of good architecture built in 1920s or later; six- and seven-room ranch homes of postwar period; larger, older homes in good condition	$18,000 to $35,000	$135 to $269
3	Brick bungalows, six rooms, built in 1920s or later; houses of seven or eight rooms, in good condition dating from World War I period, luxury four-room apartments in higher status areas	$12,200 to $17,900	$92 to $134
4	Five-room frame or brick bungalows, built in the 1920s or later; six- and seven-room older houses in good repair; well-maintained five-room duplexes, four-room apartments in good areas	$9,000 to $12,200	$67.50 to $91
5	Four-room houses, dating to 1900, if well maintained; older five- and six-room houses in fair condition; four-room apartments in satisfactory condition, North Side location.	$6,300 to $8,900	$49.50 to $67.00

[a] These market values—given in 1955 dollars—applied to houses fifteen years old or more; for newer houses a gradient was used, ranging up to 25 per cent above the suggested range if the house were new, needed no reconditioning upon purchase, and could be financed with minimum down payment.

Table 4. QUALITY OF HOUSING SCALE FOR KANSAS CITY, 1955 (cont.)

Scale Value	Type of House	Market Value	Monthly[b] Rental
6	Well-maintained three-room cottages; larger houses, run-down but not dilapidated; small apartments in only slight disrepair; veterans' housing projects; decent trailer camps.	$3,600 to $6,200	$35.00[c] to $49.00
7	Housing units that are dilapidated or in considerable disrepair; makeshift dwellings built by the occupants; shacks on edge of city, at backs of lots; badly crowded and deteriorating apartment buildings and old houses.	Less than $3,600	Less[c] than $35

[b] In Kansas City as of 1955 Negroes paid slightly more than whites for apartments or homes of equal size, appearance, condition. The rental ranges used in scoring Negroes were thus $5 higher than the ranges shown here.

[c] Because slum and substandard rents are often exorbitant, the real rent reported by respondents should on occasion be disregarded in favor of interviewer verdicts.

Developing Scales for Other Communities: To adapt the housing quality scale to other communities, citizens and realtors should be interviewed about what kind of housing they consider typical of the main occupational levels. These judgments can be scored as follows:

1 indicates housing associated with corporation presidents and other rich people—typically only 1 per cent of a city's housing.

2 indicates housing associated with the full-fledged manager level of businessman—typically 5 per cent to 7 per cent of a city's housing.

3 indicates housing associated with better paid white-collar workers—typically 12 per cent to 15 per cent of a city's housing.

4 indicates housing associated with average white-collar workers and better paid blue-collar workers—typically 24 per cent to 27 per cent of a city's housing.

5 indicates housing associated with average blue-collar workers, but somewhat below average in desirability for modern, prosperous American families—about 28 per cent to 30 per cent of a city's housing in the 1950s and early 1960s.

6 indicates substandard housing associated with families who are struggling to make ends meet—18 per cent or 20 per cent of a city's housing.

7 indicates housing derogated as slums and shacks, barely fit for human habitation, plus public housing projects for low-income people—7 per cent to 10 per cent of a city's housing.

The market prices and rental ranges should be determined for each scale point. Market value and rentals paid are used as the key considerations in rating dwelling units in the IUS not only because they are easily scaled—but in addition, because they are more closely correlated to the status symbolism of a house or apartment than any other factors, such as size or condition or number of rooms or grounds, taken singly or in combination. Market value or rentals, indeed, should be thought of as the best summation of what these other factors taken together contribute to the status of a dwelling unit in the eyes of the public. Using this concept, it is not necessary to rate a house for details of size, condition, architectural style, and yard. When used in the past, such scales have proved cumbersome and often inaccurate in reflecting the overall social value of a home or its economic value. The housing scale proposed here disregards people-per-room, but our empirical work has shown this variable to be of little importance except at the lower end of the scale, where it affects less than 15 per cent of the cases. Nevertheless, in more recent applications of the IUS to large samples, a modification for crowdedness has been worked out.

Educational Status Scales

In the course of the Kansas City research, it became apparent that the influence of educational background on social class position is complex and that previous scales for rating education as a status factor had been inadequate. In the first place, they did not take into account the dramatic changes in educational standards and expectations of the American people. Only one scale was used for all age levels, with, for example, all persons who had completed ten years of school rated as equal, despite the fact that the social meaning of such an educational background has changed drastically through the years. In the second place, the education scales often omitted altogether a rating for the wife's education or applied the same scaling to men and women, thus overlooking differences between the sexes in expectations and educational goals. Finally, the scales did not take into account the social reality that at the college level the prestige of the college attended often takes precedence as a status factor over how many years were spent in college and how many academic degrees were earned.

The IUS educational status scales for men and women have been designed to take these factors into account, and thus they differ considerably from the education scales developed by Warner, Hollingshead and others (Warner, Meeker, and Eells, 1949; Hollingshead and Redlich, 1958).

Educational background influences adult life status somewhat differently from other variables measured in the IUS. Its role can be described as that of a status *platform* from which an individual is launched into adulthood. After leaving school, a man or woman remains at the status provided by this platform, moves up socially by being successful at his occupation, or drops down because of personal or economic failure. The status of a young adult is heavily influenced by this education platform, but as a person moves through adulthood his educational background becomes increasingly less relevant in judging his status. These changes notwithstanding, it is clear that education should be measured in any index of status. It usually remains as an ingredient of current status, and it adds a dimension to the status profile which is helpful in understanding the movement of a person toward his present social class position.

Patterns of education changed in the thirty years (1900–1930) during which Kansas City respondents were passing through their teen-age years, with the result that at each social class level the men and women who were in their forties in 1955 averaged two years more schooling than those in their sixties. Since the 1930s changes have proceeded even more rapidly, with college attendance doubling and high school graduation becoming the rule, not the exception. This means that for a proper measure of education as a status platform, these differing patterns of school attendance must be taken into account.

To this end, census information was consulted for years of schooling completed by persons born in each five-year period from 1865 through 1949. The percentage of people achieving a given level of education was used as the best evidence of the kind of schooling which served at each point in time as one or another of the seven status platforms. For example, we assumed that the 14 per cent of persons who were least well educated among those born between 1865 and 1876—those who had not gone beyond the second grade—constituted the group in that generation whose educational level was a lower class platform. In like fashion, the educational levels indicative of the other six status platforms were worked out for that age group and for each of the others. Estimates of class distributions in previous eras were used to determine the percentage of people to be assigned to each platform. Since lower status groups have always had more children per family, the percentage quotas were modified accordingly. On the average, 12 per cent of each age group was assigned a 7 rating, the next 20 per cent a 6, the next 30 per cent a 5, the next 25 per cent a 4, and the top 13 per cent a 3, 2, or 1.

At the upper-class level generally, the particular college attended is often more important than how many years of college were completed. In Kansas City, for example, one year of undergraduate study at Harvard constituted a better credential for upper-class status than a Ph.D. from the University of Missouri. Similarly, among middle-aged men and women, more people who had attended a college of high or middle level prestige for two years were in the upper-middle class than people who had received a B.A. from a low prestige institution. Furthermore, a history of fraternity and sorority membership took social precedence over how many years were spent in college (and to a certain extent took precedence over the particular college attended). This was particularly true for women—that is, those who had attended a state university or a good private college and had joined one of the better sororities were almost invariably upper-middle-core or above, even if they had attended college for as little as one year, whereas women who grad-

uated from a lower ranked private college or teacher training institution and who were without a sorority membership were more
commonly upper-middle-marginal or lower-middle-elite.

Wife's Education: The Kansas City findings highlighted
the importance of including a wife's educational background when
assessing the social status of a family. The social status of families
in the middle-aged sample correlated slightly more with the wife's
educational background (0.68) than with the husband's (0.65);
also, the correlation between wife's education and family income,
as scored in the IKCS, exceeded that between husband's education
and income. Plainly, a wife plays an important role in establishing
a family's reputation (high or low) for breeding and culture, or
respectability. It is she who aspires for status in its more purely
social aspects or declines to make the effort and hence holds a family
at a lower social level than her husband's occupational status might
permit. The wife's status aspirations are often closely associated with
her educational experience. While the wife's education is not an
infallible index to her social aspirations and to her contribution to
family status, it is the most easily determined index of what her
contribution is likely to be, and thus it should be used whenever
possible in measuring family status.

Abbreviated Scales: To take into account the various
factors mentioned above, an educational platform scale was developed utilizing status rankings of 1,400 colleges and universities
plus rankings of the various social fraternities and sororities. These
rankings were in turn weighted according to historical era. (For the
IKCS, the ranking of colleges and the ranking of fraternities and
sororities were based on interviews with Kansas Citians of upper
status levels. Later, for the IUS, additional insight was gained from
consultation with college administrators and journalists specializing
in the field of education and from examination of a variety of source
books on American college life.) The details are beyond the scope
of the present volume—and, indeed, are not relevant to the needs
of most researchers in classifying a large sample of survey respondents. (In most such surveys, the only information obtained on
college attendance is number of years completed and degrees received.)

An abbreviated version of the educational platform scale to
be used when the only data available are date of birth and the

number of years of schooling completed is shown in Table 5. This scale incorporates historical era in its scoring, but not place of college, and is thus of much less value for status prediction at the upper social levels.

The relevance of place of college, as it modifies the ratings on the abbreviated education scale, can be briefly illustrated in the following summary of the differences in status rating produced by four different college backgrounds. (The detailed versions of the educational platform scale for men and women are presented in the manual of instructions referred to earlier.)

1 indicates an *upper class platform rating,* given to *men* with a socially prestigious college background—Harvard, Yale, Princeton, Williams or similar colleges of extremely high social status in previous eras; men who may not have attended so highly honored an undergraduate school but who earned law degrees at schools such as Harvard or Columbia or medical degrees at Pennsylvania and Johns Hopkins; and men who attended a semiprestigious private college and while there joined one of the nationally elite fraternities such as Beta Theta Pi or Phi Gamma Delta. This same rating is given to *women* who were educated at a four-year woman's college such as Vassar, Smith, or Bryn Mawr, or at an exclusive finishing school (Briarcliff Junior College, for example); also women who attended one of the semiprestigious private schools such as Northwestern or Duke and while there became affiliated with one of the nationally elite sororities such as Kappa Alpha Theta, Kappa Kappa Gamma, or Pi Beta Phi.

2 indicates an *upper-middle platform rating,* given to all *men* with professional degrees in law, medicine, dentistry, or architecture, which require typically more than four years of college attendance, or to men with master's degrees in an academic discipline; also all graduates of colleges in the same level of prestige as Beloit, Colgate, De-Pauw, Holy Cross, Massachusetts Institute of Technology, Notre Dame, Reed, Tulane, Vanderbilt, or Wooster—irrespective of era; men born before 1919 but who graduated from state universities on the prestige level of University of Arkansas or Pennsylvania State University or Purdue or private colleges of approximately similar social rank (Baylor, University of Cincinnati, Texas Christian). This same rating is given to *women* graduates of the same schools, with the same degrees, and at the same era; it is also

given to those who attended college without graduating but who joined one or another of the more socially prominent sororities (Delta Delta Delta, Delta Gamma, and Gamma Phi Beta are examples).

3 indicates a *middle-middle platform,* given to graduates of all the lesser private colleges, municipal universities, and teachers' colleges, irrespective of era; among older men and women it is given to those who attended colleges of medium status but did not graduate; among the youngest people it is given to those who graduated from the typical state university or one of the medium-status private colleges without membership in a socially significant fraternity or sorority. For men born before 1890 this rating can be applied even to graduates of business colleges or special technical schools, and for both men and women it is often granted in recognition of attendance at a recognized music school or art institute.

4 indicates an *average lower-middle platform,* given to men born after 1920 if they attended a municipal-type college, a teachers' college (or college formerly of this type transformed into a state university after World War II in the education boom of the 1950s), or lowly regarded private college without graduating—even up to three years of attendance; just one or two years of college at such schools also grants a 4 rating for men born between 1900 and 1919; and more recently, for men and women born in 1940 or after, this is the rating even for those who attended the recognized state universities and high-average private schools without graduating or without affiliating with one of the more prestigious of fraternities or sororities.

Religious Affiliation Scale

Religious affiliation can best be viewed as a status asset or handicap, not as a basic component of class position. Nevertheless, at almost all social levels, religion is sometimes significant in judgments people make of one another's status and in revealing a person's own social aspiration level. Many Kansas Citians were found in a lower social stratum than they otherwise might have been because their religious attitudes and church membership reduced their social acceptability in the eyes of persons of equal economic status or educational background.

Each church in a community has a reputation regarding the social desirability or undesirability of belonging to it. For example,

Table 5. IUS Education Scales (Abbreviated Version)

Birth Years	MEN ONLY Collegiate Years Completed						WOMEN ONLY Collegiate Years Completed					
	All Advanced Degrees	B.A. or B.S.	Three Years	Two Years	One Year	Post H.S. Commercial or Technical Institute	All Advanced Degrees	B.A. or B.S.	Three Years	Two Years	One Year	Post H.S. Secretarial, Nursing
1945–49	2	3	4	4	4	5	2	3	3	4	4	5
1940–44	2	3	4	4	4	4	2	3	3	4	4	4
1935–39	2	3	4	4	4	4	2	3	3	3	4	4
1930–34	2	3	4	4	4	4	2	3	3	3	4	4
1925–29	2	3	3	4	4	4	2	3	3	3	3	4
1920–24	2	3	3	4	4	4	2	3	3	3	3	4
1915–19	2	2	3	3	3	4	2	2	3	3	3	4
1910–14	2	2	3	3	3	4	2	2	3	3	3	4
1905–09	2	2	3	3	3	4	2	2	3	3	3	4
1900–04	2	2	3	3	3	4	2	2	3	3	3	4
1895–99	2	2	3	3	3	4	2	2	3	3	3	4
1890–94	2	2	3	3	3	4	2	2	2	3	3	4
1885–89	2	2	3	3	3	4	2	2	2	3	3	4
1880–84	2	2	3	3	3	3	2	2	2	3	3	4
1875–79	2	2	3	3	3	3	2	2	2	3	3	4
Pre 1875	2	2	3	3	3	3	2	2	2	3	3	4

Table 5. IUS Education Scales (Abbreviated Version) (cont.)

MEN AND WOMEN

Birth Years	Secondary Years Completed				Grades of Elementary Schooling Completed								
	12th Grade	11th Grade	10th Grade	9th Grade	8th Grade	7th Grade	6th Grade	5th Grade	4th Grade	3rd Grade	2nd Grade	1st Grade	No Schooling
1945–49	5	6	6	6	7	7	7	7	7	7	7	7	7
1940–44	5	6	6	6	7	7	7	7	7	7	7	7	7
1935–39	5	5	6	6	7	7	7	7	7	7	7	7	7
1930–34	5	5	6	6	6	7	7	7	7	7	7	7	7
1925–29	5	5	5	6	6	7	7	7	7	7	7	7	7
1920–24	5	5	5	6	6	6	7	7	7	7	7	7	7
1915–19	4	5	5	5	6	6	7	7	7	7	7	7	7
1910–14	4	5	5	5	6	6	6	7	7	7	7	7	7
1905–09	4	5	5	5	5	6	6	7	7	7	7	7	7
1900–04	4	4	5	5	5	6	6	6	7	7	7	7	7
1895–99	4	4	4	5	5	6	6	6	7	7	7	7	7
1890–94	4	4	4	4	5	5	6	6	6	7	7	7	7
1885–89	4	4	4	4	5	5	6	6	6	7	7	7	7
1880–84	4	4	4	4	5	5	6	6	6	7	7	7	7
1875–79	4	4	4	4	5	5	6	6	6	7	7	7	7
Pre 1875	4	4	4	4	5	5	6	6	6	6	7	7	7

a church will be rated as a Society church if many members are reputed to be of the Society stratum, and if it is reported that others have joined in order to be associated with a Society institution. Off-brand or undesirable churches are those at which membership constitutes a social handicap to acceptance within the middle class or at which attendance signifies indifference to middle class proscriptions against such affiliation.

Including the religious affiliation scale in the IUS gives an additional weight to community participation and formal affiliations. This is appropriate, since a great many people, from the middle levels of the status system on down, consider their church activities and religious beliefs a vitally significant aspect of their lives and of their relationship to the community. For many, the church is the only organized form of social life.

Previously developed scales of religious affiliation have used only denominational ratings and have not given attention to specific congregational membership. In Kansas City, however, the attitude prevailed that "it's not your denomination, but your congregation that counts socially." Indeed, had this attitude been ignored and only denominational preference used in the IKCS, religious affiliation would have correlated with social class less than any other dimension. Instead, by scoring for congregational membership, the correlation was considerably above either the education factor or the income factor. The correlation was 0.78 for the middle-aged sample.

This attitude that the congregation exceeds the denomination in status significance is likely to be typical of most cities, although perhaps in ways different from Kansas City where much of the status of any particular church is derived from its neighborhood location. When neighborhood patterning is not as clearly defined as in Kansas City, and when relatively more of the churches are located in the downtown district, the status of a congregation may be more dependent on denomination and less dependent on location. In smaller communities where most denominations are represented only by one congregation, this attitude is presumably not so prominent.

The religious affiliation scale requires information about community imagery of the rank of specific churches and about the degree to which certain denominational affiliations are a local status asset or handicap. Society churches are to be identified, as are metropolitan prestige churches. The status of neighborhood churches is investigated, although generally such churches are rated according to their neighborhood locations more than their denominations.

Churches are ranked as follows:

1 indicates churches which in public reputation are Society-oriented in membership and appeal.

2 indicates churches of the metropolitan prestige type, which are reputed to draw their leadership mainly from the managerial, executive, and professional strata, and thus are considered very desirable churches to attend. Also included are smaller churches of reputable denominations which serve a primarily upper-management or country-club neighborhood.

3 indicates churches reputed to draw their membership from the middle echelons of the white-collar and semiprofessional world, that are of reputable denomination and generally regarded as above average in social status but not particularly prestigeful.

4 indicates churches reputed to draw their congregants mainly from white-collar neighborhoods and to be affiliated with one of the accepted mainstream denominations.

5 indicates churches reputed to draw their congregants mainly from average working class neighborhoods and thought to be composed dominantly of blue-collar people. Also included are churches of off-brand denominations located in middle class sections of the city and assumed to attract some white-collar people.

6 indicates churches of mainstream denomination which draw heavily from lower-level neighborhoods or churches of off-brand denominations which by virtue of their location and/or their reputation are assumed to draw their membership mainly from average working class neighborhoods but not from substandard areas.

7 indicates churches in slum neighborhoods or of the "store front" and revivalist type which are the targets of scorn from solidly-established working class people as well as from those higher up.

The following guidelines are employed in determining at which level any given church should be placed.

For a church to be rated 1, it need not be dominantly upper class in membership, although upper class people should constitute an important fraction of the members. In some cities there will be no church rated 1—instead there will be several metropolitan prestige churches—rated 2—serving people both of upper class and higher middle class status.

Metropolitan prestige churches rated 2 are usually the city's Protestant churches and Jewish synagogues or temples with the largest memberships; the ministers or rabbis at these institutions are considered prominent citizens; the lay leadership is drawn from persons who occupy other positions of leadership in the community; and it is generally presumed that persons of lesser status who attend do so to "feel part of one of their city's most important institutions."

Churches of the following denominations are, by middle-class standards, somewhat off-brand, not in the mainstream: Church of Christ, Evangelical Brethren, United Brethren, Church of Nazarene, and Church of the Brethren; they cannot be rated even 5 unless located in a white-collar neighborhood and drawing many members from this occupational level; usually they are rated 6. Eastern Orthodox churches and Orthodox Jewish synagogues are never rated above 5 because they represent old country approaches to religion (although individual members of these denominations may have middle class status); if in very low-status neighborhoods, they will be rated 6.

A church is usually rated 6 or 7 if it is affiliated with the Assembly of God, Seventh Day Adventist, Jehovah's Witnesses, or other revivalistic, fundamentalist sects, for these sects are usually disparaged even by average working class people.

The main distinction between churches at the 6 level and those at 7 is that the former are not store fronts, nor revivalist tents, and they are not located in slum neighborhoods. Only rarely is a mainstream denomination of Protestantism or a Catholic church given a 7 rating, and then only when the neighborhood served is Mexican-Catholic or Puerto Rican-Catholic or because the church is not truly affiliated with the denomination whose name it carries (as is the case with many churches in poor neighborhoods bearing the word Methodist or Baptist as part of their title).

Associations Scale

Developing a scale for community associations in a metropolitan area requires a systematic survey of community attitudes about every club and association of any prominence, and also about the reputation of various ethnic groups. Questions to be asked about clubs and associations include the following: Is membership in this club thought to be limited exclusively to persons from one status level, so that the club acts to define its members' status level? (If so, of course, what is the level?) If members come from more than one level, what is the typical status level? What are the membership floor and ceiling—that is, what are the lowest and highest statuses found among members of the organization? Does membership in the club automatically hold an individual down to a given level?

In scoring for the IKCS, as much information as possible was obtained from each person regarding his formal and informal associations. Information was obtained regarding:

First, the husband's formal memberships in clubs, associations, organizations, business and professional groups;

Second, the wife's formal memberships in clubs, associations, organizations, business and professional groups;

Third, the husband and wife's ethnicity, and current formal and informal participation in an ethnic group;

Fourth, the husband's friends, their occupations, where they live, and what associations and activities he shares with them;

Fifth, the wife's friends, where they live, and activities she shares with these women.

The methods used to arrive at an overall rating for individual families are too detailed to be presented here, except to note that the status value of each club membership, and also the value for ethnicity where appropriate was entered in the status protocol; the estimated status position of friends and clique groups was also indicated. The rater then evaluated the various scores, keeping in mind the following points:

First, most clubs and formal organizations which are not class-limited have status defining properties insofar as they provide a floor for class membership or a ceiling. In almost all cases, an individual's associations scale score falls between the ceiling and the floor level of those organizations in which he holds memberships.

Second, when an individual is a member of two or more organizations, the most appropriate rating is likely to be one which represents the central tendency or average value of the various organizations.

Third, when an individual is not a member of any formal organizations, he is assigned a status rating that represents the social level of his clique participation. In cases of doubt, the lower of two possible ratings is usually given, since the lack of associational membership is something of a status liability in the United States.

It must not be expected in an urban setting that the associations scale will yield a crucial rating in any more than a minority of cases. It is useful mainly in determining upper-class status and in distinguishing those who are solidly established within the upper-middle class from those who are marginal. The associations scale is also helpful in determining who among those of middle occupational-economic status are upward-oriented and who are downward-oriented in their social participations. It is also of central importance in separating working-class-elite people from lower-middle-marginals. At the lower status levels, its ratings of ethnicity are helpful in determining whether families are identified in the public eye mainly with the working class at its lower margins or with the lower class.

In only 9 per cent of the cases in the Kansas City sample was the information on formal affiliations regarded as *conclusive* of status position in terms of one of the thirteen levels. Another 12 per cent of the sample were placed conclusively within one of the five social classes, but the evidence was not precise enough to determine placement at the specific level. Most of these 21 per cent of cases where placement could be made from the record of community participation alone were at Kansas City's upper- and upper-middle class levels. In the other 79 per cent of cases, the associations data provided only a best estimate of status position. In all but 11 per cent of cases, however, this best estimate on the associations scale agreed with the status placements ultimately made from evaluation of the entire status profile.

Scoring and Interpreting the IUS

The protocol of the David Austin family which follows (see Table 6) illustrates how ratings from the eight IKCS scales were compiled to achieve a status profile and arrive at a social class placement; it indicates how, with appropriate revisions, the IUS can be used in future studies. A protocol such as the one illustrated may be used to produce an objective (that is, a numerical score) estimate of a family's class position by averaging the several scores, or to obtain a more subjective evaluation of status.

When the IUS is used subjectively, the patterning of a family's ratings on its several scales is interpreted in light of what such a pattern represents in the particular community being studied, and a status placement is made in direct imitation of how community residents would place the family. In the illustration, the rater has used the circled score on associations to arrive at a subjective placement of the family in the upper-middle-core. (Had the objective method been used, the placement would have been the same in this case, because the average of the ratings is the same as this associations scale rating.)

In general, the subjective method of evaluation requires knowledge of the particular status symbols of the community being examined. It should be kept in mind, also, that the educational ratings and data on family background are especially meaningful in evaluating younger couples, but less so in evaluating families who have reached middle age.

When the IUS is employed objectively, a family's status is determined by averaging the scores in its status profile and determining in which social class range this average score places the family. Status predicted by averaged IUS score is as follows:

Averaged IUS Score	Estimated Social Class
1.00–1.50	Upper class
1.51–3.00	Upper-middle class
3.01–4.49	Lower-middle class
4.50–5.99	Working class
6.00–7.00	Lower class

Average scores do not predict position—elite, core, or marginal—within class with sufficient accuracy to make it worth specifying score ranges associated with these strata. Position within class depends heavily on the patterning of scores, especially the relationship between economic status, educational background, and associational pattern.

The scoring interpretation shown above calls attention to one of the essential characteristics of the IUS. The significance of the averaged score is an inherent property of the instrument, because the scores on the several scales carry equivalent status significance.

Table 6. RECOMMENDED IUS PROTOCOL CARD[a]

CASE **David T. Austin**
(Martha Ruth)

SOCIAL CLASS **Upper**
PLACEMENT **Middle (Core)**

H's Year Birth: **1904**

W's Year Birth: **1906**

AVERAGE OF
SCORES **2.1**

INDICES OF URBAN STATUS

Neighborhood
Reputation   **2**

Address: **114 West 65th Terrace**
(note: this is in heart of Kansas City's Country Club District)

Housing
Quality   **2**

Interviewer's Description and Evaluation:
Seven-room Dutch Colonial, brick and wood siding; estimated market value $24,000–$25,000 (1954–55)

Husband's
Occupation   **2**
(weighted double if no wife's occupation)

Personnel Director for Mid-American Life Insurance Company at salary of $15,000 a year (1954–55)

Wife's
Occupation   —

Housewife, not employed

Total Family Income: **$15,000+[b]**

IKCS Rating (Income) **2**

Income
Evaluations: "Overprivileged"

Average for Class

"Underprivileged"

---

[a] Also recommended for IUS Protocol Card is space for recording the following information (which is helpful in understanding social mobility):
  (1) history of marital status, including number of marriages and age at which contracted
  (2) facts about children, number, age, and educational status
  (3) career history of husband
  (4) facts about husband's parents—father's occupational status and education, mother's education, and ancestry on both sides
  (5) facts about wife's parents (same as about husband's)

[b] On this form, space is provided for recording total family income, then for rating the family as "overprivileged," "average income for class," or "underprivileged." Many studies have shown that income status within class is important in explaining a family's consumption patterns and recreational choices. See Coleman (1960).

Table 6. RECOMMENDED IUS PROTOCOL CARD (cont.)

Husband's Education	2	University of Iowa, B.A., (1926) in business administration; Drake University night classes in personnel management, no degree; local fraternity at Iowa
Wife's Education	3	Simpson College (1 year), Curtis Institute of Music (2 years)
Religious Affiliation	2	Wornall Road Congregational; both husband and wife attend fairly regularly; husband, former deacon and wife in women's circle group
Associations	2	Husband's Membership:

Husband's Membership:
Nodaway Yacht Club   2[e]
Optimists Club (downtown chapter) (2–3)
Personnel Club, former officer   (2–3)
K. C. chapter of American
   Management Association,
   president 1954–55   (2–3)

Wife's Membership:
Kansas City Musical Club   (1–2–3)
Horizon Club Committee (Camp
   Fire Senior High Mother's)   (2–3–4)
Phi Delta Theta Mother's Club (1–2–4)
Midday Woman's Club   (1–2)

Informal Cliques: **Dance and Bridge Club,
   twelve couples**   2 (estimate)

Best Friends
   **Bensons: lawyer, also Country Club
     district, in church, neighborhood,
     cliques, and children same age**   2
   **Knowles: employment agency proprietor,
     also Country Club district, through
     business and Dance and Bridge Club 2**
   **Coates: K. C. editor of Farm Belt
     Daily, in clique, also in K. C. Musical
     Club, neighbor**   2

Ethnicity of Husband: **several generations
   in U.S.A., Scotch-English-Dutch**

Wife: **several generations in U.S.A.,
   English-German**

---

[e] The numbers written to right of associations data are the rater's estimates of the range in status level of the association's membership. When a particular rating is circled, that rating is considered conclusive in placing the family at the indicated social level.

The final score thus automatically signifies a social class position, regardless of how many scales are included. (In other status indices, interpretation of the final score depends upon the weighting assigned to each subscore.)

IUS Efficiency as Status Predictor

The IKCS, when applied to the Kansas City sample as an objective measure of status, produced a correlation above the 0.90 level between the averaged scores and the subjective estimates of social class placement. This correlation is unusually high and implies greater predictive efficiency of the IUS technique than it is likely to show if samples include all age groups, if fewer than all eight dimensions are used, or if less care is employed in determining the individual scale intervals.

When all eight factors were used, as in Kansas City, the Index proved extremely accurate in predicting class membership at the three middle levels—there was agreement, for example, for 94 per cent of working class families in the sample (all, of course, middle-aged) between the objective and subjective placements; for 92 per cent of the lower-middle families; and for 89 per cent of the upper-middles. The Index was slightly less efficient at the lower class level, where there was agreement for 86 per cent of the cases, with disagreements coming about largely because so many lower class families claimed an educational background much higher than is theoretically associated with this status level.

At the upper class level, however, the eight-factor IKCS did a rather poor job of predicting subjective judgment; only 47 per cent of upper class Kansas City families had eight-factor averages predicting this status, while 53 per cent scored as upper-middle class. This happened because so many upper class families did not live in the mansions expected of them, some did not live in the Gold Coast area, barely half attended Society churches, and only a small percentage had been educated in a manner that could be described as an upper class educational platform. The majority of Kansas City's upper class families had moved up from the lower levels and had not, indeed could not, always shed some of the symbols of their past. For most upward-mobile upper class families it would have been better to calculate a median of their ratings rather than the average or, better still, to have relied only on their associations rating in combination with their occupational status rating.

All told, and even including the upper class discrepancies, objective placements from the eight-factor IKCS yielded a 91 per cent agreement with subjective evaluations. In this it compares favorably with the four-factor Warner I.S.C., which was tested in Kansas City but yielded correct prediction of social class affiliation in less than three out of four cases, and with the three-factor Hollingshead I.S.P., which predicted class membership in less than two out of three cases.

In the manual of instructions for use of the IUS, alternative versions of an abbreviated IUS are offered, to be used when only three, four, or five dimensions are available for scoring. These versions, with special weightings determined by regression analysis, yield correlations with social class at or above the 0.84 level.

Part Two

Social
Classes

Chapter 6

People
at the Top

*K*ansas Citians at middle and high status levels liked to believe that a spirit of social democracy prevailed in their city and that all people of merit had a chance to rise to the top. More realistically, those at or near the top of the social ladder stated it as a rule that "the better a family's total qualifications and connections, the higher it ranks." By qualifications they meant intelligence, charm, cultural level, civic contribution, and breeding as well as occupational success. By connections they meant occupational associations or ties of kinship or friendship which produced social advantage.

Two beliefs pervaded the discussion of status at the upper levels. One belief was that membership in one of the country club crowds constituted the final criterion of status; the other was that position at the top levels was determined through a social-free-for-all wherein no single factor such as wealth or lineage could be definitive. ("Social-free-for-all" was the title of a pictorial essay on the social life of Kansas City which appeared in *Life* magazine in March, 1954; the phrase became immediately popular in Kansas City.)

Kansas Citians were convinced that the distinction between old families and new was less important at the top levels of

their community than in older cities of the South and East. As one
prominent citizen put it:

> In the last forty years there has been very little snobbery here
> concerning the nouveau riche versus the blueblood. I think
> Kansas City has reflected the spirit of democracy far more than
> other cities. Of course, you'll hear people make fun of some
> newly wealthy family's overly obvious efforts to climb the social
> ladder, but I think you will find that our very highest levels
> represent a wedding between the old families and what some
> people call "the aristocracy of the greenbacks." The First Jack-
> son Country Club is that way: it has almost all the old guard
> bluebloods, and then it has the most popular and well-respected
> families who have earned their wealth in the present generation
> —the "greenbacks," so to speak.

Kansas Citians did not automatically credit old families with
social superiority, perhaps because such families were of several types.
One, often referred to as prairie aristocrats, consisted of "rather
plain people who got here first and have always had a lot of money,
but have never been too socially conscious and hence have not been
accepted into the highest social circles." A second type, said to be
concentrated at the First Jackson Country Club, were families described as having "charm and culture—they have always had a flair
for Society with a capital S." The latter families were considered
old guard Kansas City, whether or not they had been wealthy or
prominent as long as the prairie aristocrats.

Furthermore it was said, "In Kansas City an old family
name is absolutely meaningless unless attached to a sizable amount
of money." Frequently the men and women of Kansas City's higher
echelons proudly stated that their city was not like others in the
United States where "you can be poor as church mice and still rate
high socially, as long as you had the right grandparents." It was
generally understood that many old families were no longer well-off
and that such families, if without enough money to operate successfully, had not remained in the forefront of the Society scene.
Operating successfully meant maintaining a country club membership, or at least a downtown club membership, entertaining enough
to meet social obligations, sending children to private schools and
Eastern colleges, and giving time, if not money, to civic causes.

At the same time, a charitable attitude was maintained

toward new wealth. A common phrase was: "Nobody holds it against a man that he's just recently made his money, as long as he's a good Joe." Very few of Kansas City's leading families could trace their wealth back as far as the Civil War—a short time compared to the East and South. Kansas Citians applied the phrase *old families* to any who had acquired their wealth before the stock market crash and even to the offspring of men who had established their prominence more recently. Finally, the exodus of many leading families of earlier eras—a phenomenon commonly lamented among Kansas City's old guard—helped diminish the distinction between old and new families.

Upper Class Strata

Intensive study of attitudes and interaction patterns among the upper strata revealed four major levels, two within the Capital S Society bracket and two in the non-Capital S bracket. In turn, within each of the two major levels subsumed under capital s society were two layers of cliques. At the top of this finely graded system were about twenty families of greatest prominence and social power in the city—pinnacle people, as it were.

Of Kansas City's 360,000 adults, forty-five men and women were seen as "reigning over High Society." Several of the city's greatest fortunes which had passed into the second or third generation were represented among these men and women. Their names were the ones most impressive to the average Kansas Citian—they represented the city's great banks, the leading department stores, the real estate fortunes memorialized in street names, and the largest manufacturing firms. The most prominent among this group were the Galbraiths, nine men and women plus their spouses.

The Galbraith fortune had originally been made in lumber, but more recently the family business had branched out to include banks, downtown real estate, and manufacturing enterprises. The Galbraith family first became identified with Capital S Society in the 1920s. During the Depression, when other fortunes crumbled theirs grew, and they gained admission into the First Jackson Country Club. During World War II they moved up to the top level, and as the third generation entered adulthood, the family came to dominate the pinnacle position. One reason often cited for their leadership was that they were thought to display a minimum of snobbishness. As one pinnacle woman put it, "The Galbraiths are always fair, socially speaking."

The men of the pinnacle group, who ranged in age from the early twenties up to the eighties, were represented on the board of directors of Kansas City's six most important banks—usually two or three per bank—and also in the directorships of all the city's utility companies and of every leading manufacturing, insurance, or transportation firm. There were at least five men and women from this pinnacle group serving as trustees of each major cultural institution: the university, the art gallery, the art institute, and the symphony. And as many were counted in the leadership of the Chamber of Commerce, American Royal, Starlight Theater, and other organizations devoted to civic promotion. A majority of the men were listed in *Who's Who in America* of 1955.

The women of this group were similarly prominent. One, the widow of Kansas City's wealthiest grain broker, was renowned throughout the Midwest as an art collector and donor to galleries; another, a daughter of the founder of Kansas City's finest department store, was a nationally known horsewoman whose stables had produced Kentucky Derby winners; a third was the daughter of a former United States cabinet member and had herself been a Democratic Party committeewoman from Missouri, a regent of the University of Missouri, and national president of the Junior League.

The pinnacle people were not necessarily the most personally popular members of the First Jackson Country Club. But the combination of their wealth, reputation, and personal achievement placed them in a special category, and an extra measure of deference was shown them. For the most part these people worked hard at serving the community. There was, however, one small clique among them who were more social than serious.

Level I Society: In addition to the pinnacle people, about five hundred other men and women ranked in the top level of Capital S Society in Kansas City in 1954–55. Many of these people were related to each other, and there were several families who were represented by three generations. Thus, fewer than one hundred different family names were represented in this group.

An example was the Sheldon family, who traced their prominence in Kansas City back to pre-Civil War days. In 1866 Alexander Price Sheldon, who had been a captain in the Confederate army, came to Kansas City to start a hardware wholesaling business. Shortly after he arrived, he married Eliza Holmes, daughter of a pioneer landholder for whom one of Kansas City's downtown streets was named. With Eliza's inheritance as one of his assets, Alexander Sheldon built his company into a position of considerable importance. Alexander and Eliza Sheldon had two children. Their son Prescott went to the University of Virginia, where the captain had been enrolled. Upon graduation he married Caroline Richey, a Kansas City society belle of the early 1890s. When the First Jackson Country Club was founded, Prescott and his wife became charter members. Alexander and Eliza's daughter Cynthia was sent to Baltimore for her finishing education at a fashionable seminary for young ladies. She married Arthur Shartel Wood, whose family had founded one of Kansas City's great banks.

In 1954, each of the families named above—Holmes, Richey, Wood, and Sheldon—was represented in the top level status group at the First Jackson Country Club. The Sheldon name was represented by two of Prescott's sons, William and Price, who were president and secretary-treasurer of Sheldon Hardware. The Sheldon Hardware company had not grown much through the years, and the Sheldon brothers were not especially wealthy men. The older brother's annual income was assumed by people who knew him to be somewhere between fifty and sixty thousand dollars, and the younger brother's, in the vicinity of forty thousand dollars. Such incomes, while not great, were adequate for maintaining status in Kansas City Society's top tier, although in a slightly circumscribed manner.

The Sheldon brothers and their wives were, in different ways, typical of many top level First Jackson families. William Sheldon had once served as president of the club and was on the board of directors for the Kansas City Art Institute and the Young Men's Christian Association. He was thought of as a civic leader. Price Sheldon spent much time playing golf or tennis at the Club. He was not involved in any major civic activity, although he was usually on the men's board at St. Bartholomew Episcopal church. Both men were members of the Quadrangle Club downtown, for both, following family tradition, had attended The University of Virginia.

Both the Sheldon wives were sustaining members of the

Kansas City Junior League. Mrs. Price Sheldon was considered one of the real workers among Kansas City's civic committee-women, but Mrs. William Sheldon was a more retiring type whose favorite activities were gardening and attending meetings of the Art Gallery Garden Club, a group composed of thirty women from the top level.

The Sheldons were often named by Kansas Citians as "good examples of what's left of old guard Kansas City." In their long history of affiliation with the First Jackson Country Club, they were the exception, not the rule; indeed, of the 120 middle-aged couples holding Level I status in 1954, only twenty could trace family membership back to the founding of the Club in the 1890s. The Sheldons were also exceptional in that all of them, wives and husbands, had grown up in Kansas City.

In certain respects, Andrew and Helen Bradshaw were more typical of top-level First Jackson people than the Sheldons. Helen was a third-generation Kansas Citian, but her husband grew up in Columbia, Missouri, where his father was president of the University of Missouri.

Bradshaw came to Kansas City in 1923 to join one of Kansas City"s "fine old law firms." Two years later he married Helen Holton, whose family had been respected as prairie aristocrats in Kansas City ever since 1855, when her grandfather founded a bank. By 1954, Bradshaw had become one of Kansas City's most highly respected lawyers. The income from his law practice and his wife's inheritance provided the Bradshaws with "close to one hundred thousand dollars a year," an income that was well above average for top level families.

Members of the First Jackson spoke of Bradshaw as "one of the best-loved men in Kansas City Society." He had been on the First Jackson's board of directors for ten years. He was a trustee of Mercy Hospital, director of the Red Cross, president of the City Housing Authority, trustee of the University of Kansas City, and governor of the Kansas City Historical Museum. Mrs. Bradshaw was very popular with other women of the top level, but not at all active in civic or church groups.

Located four blocks from Ward Parkway in a neighborhood considered the "real center of old aristocracy," the Bradshaws' home was an ample ten room Tudor style dwelling, easily classified as a mansion in Kansas City terms. It was not, however, one of the city's true showpieces.

The education of the Bradshaws' children was halfway typical for top-level young people. Their son attended the University of Missouri, in deference to his father's conviction that "a young man is better off going to college in the area where he's going to earn his living." Their daughter had gone to Vassar, married a Yale man, and resided in Manhattan.

Many Level I families, like the Bradshaws, had achieved either social or geographic ascent into this status in their own lifetime. Several, like Helen Bradshaw, had made the transition from being prairie aristocrats into old guard. Another large number of husbands and wives, like Andrew Bradshaw, were descended from families who had been part of the pioneer elite of smaller Kansas or Missouri cities (cities which a hundred years earlier had been as important as Kansas City but had long since ceased to grow). The top level also included families who had transferred their high status to Kansas City from other parts of the United States.

(Not all families who came to Kansas City with *Social Register* listings in other cities were accepted into the First Jackson Country Club, or even into the third or fourth levels of Kansas City's' upper class. The position of such families was determined by their popularity, the husband's business or professional achievement, and other credentials.)

Every middle-aged Level I family in Kansas City in 1955 could claim social prominence through husband or wife for at least one preceding generation, either in Kansas City or elsewhere. Inasmuch as less than half were born into the very top level, however, it can be said that even at this level a social-free-for-all operated, with important limitations. In the final analysis, a family history of high status, while essential for top-level acceptance, was not sufficient. Ongoing achievement or personal attractiveness was necessary in addition to proper family background.

Level I families were distinguishable on the basis of other factors in addition to lineage. They were also (on the average) wealthier, more often civic leaders, more often educated at prestigious institutions, and more socially proper in their church memberships than families at other levels. It is probably also true that they were perceived as physically more attractive—the men more handsome, the women more beautiful than the people lower down the social ladder. The top-level families exercised leadership primarily by virtue of social rank and function. They were noted for being "the crowd that runs the social life of this city—things like the Jewel Ball and the Junior League"; they were less important in the political and governmental arena than was the leadership clique at the Tavern and Trail Club or the Missouri Establishment group of Level II.

Level II: There were 490 married couples and 210 single men and women who were identified in 1954 with the lower tier of Capital S Society, as evidenced by their clique participation and by rankings made by upper-status informants. These Level II Kansas Citians were identified in four ways. Some were members of the First Jackson Country Club; others were families in which the wife was a member of the Junior League and who, through that membership, associated extensively with First Jackson women; another group were the higher-status families in the Missoukana Country Club; and some were members of the Bluff Club. (The Bluff Club, founded as part of downtown renewal efforts in the old Quality Hill section, was a recent arrival on the Kansas City club scene. It became established immediately as an ultra-exclusive downtown club noted for posh entertainment. Its membership represented a union of the wealthiest of old families with the most socially successful newly rich.)

Second-level families formed two categories, with those identified through membership or clique participation as part of the First Jackson social whirl being afforded greater prestige than those associated with Missoukana Country Club. Some second-level Kansas Citians who were members of the First Jackson Country Club had fallen from top-level status. Prescott Sheldon, Jr., for example, had been married three times, and his latest wife was twenty years younger than he and had been a beauty-contest winner. It was said of Prescott that he might get back into the top level if he divorced his present wife and married a woman of "his own class."

The Gerlachs, in contrast, were a family on their way up and likely to be accepted into the top level in a few more years. Frederick Gerlach had grown up in Kansas City's upper class, but in the non-Capital S level as son of the founder of Gerlach Paint

Company, one of the city's biggest manufacturing firms. By 1954, his father was dead and he himself was president of the company, with an annual income estimated at two hundred to four hundred thousand dollars. His wife, a former movie starlet, lived in the city thirteen years before being invited to join the Junior League; seven years later the Gerlachs were asked into the First Jackson.

One-fourth of the Level II families had their country club memberships at the Missoukana. These were the most socially prominent of the prairie aristocrats, the old guard of Missoukana, and the most intensely civic and welfare minded families in the top levels of society. They frequently served on official governing groups such as the City Park Board, the Election Commission, and the School Board. They were often Honorary Fire Marshals and Police Commissioners and were pillars of the most prestigious Baptist, Methodist, or Presbyterian churches.

Many of the prairie aristocrat men were lawyers or third-generation family physicians; several were vice-presidents of downtown banks; numerous others were in real estate and insurance businesses. Very few had gone to colleges outside the Midwest; the men were graduates of the University of Missouri or the University of Kansas or Westminster College (a semi-fashionable men's institution in Fulton, Missouri). Most of the women had attended either these same state universities or women's junior colleges in the region. These families had been prominent in Kansas City for such a long time that they earned Capital S status without being really social figures.

The prairie aristocrat families had many contacts in the smaller towns of Missouri and Kansas. Many of the men had business and political ties in the courthouse towns throughout northern and western Missouri; and both the men and the women were often related to the principal families in these communities. The prairie aristocrats of Kansas City, along with their best friends in Independence, constituted the Jackson County branch of what was sometimes referred to as the Missouri Establishment. They exercised the silent political power which often determined who was nominated for governor and senator and who sat on the state supreme court bench. Their role in Missouri life was one of knitting together the big city's elite with the statewide small town aristocracy.

Another type of old family commonly found in the second

level were offspring of higher-status famiiles who were finding it
financially difficult to maintain their inherited social position. These
families held no country club memberships; their continued acceptance in the Society world was dependent on their personal
popularity and on their ability to remain active in some civic and
social affairs. The Edgerton family was an example. Keith Edgerton's father had been a prominent Kansas City lawyer, and because
he had been counsellor to so many First Jackson Country Club
families, he had been taken into the club. Keith did not repeat his
father's success, but ended up as a salesman for the city's most
prestigious realty firm where his connections with the city's wealthy
families were useful.

Mrs. Edgerton came from a family of pinched gentility, from
whom she inherited a Junior League membership. The early 1950s
found her teaching art at one of Kansas City's private schools in
order to supplement her husband's earnings. A great deal of the
Edgertons' income—which was somewhat less than the twenty-five
thousand dollars a year generally considered necessary for maintaining Society-class living—was used for the education of their
children. Edgerton held a membership only at the Quadrangle
Club, one of the smaller downtown men's clubs; long ago the
Edgertons had dropped the membership at the First Jackson Country Club which they had held during the first years of their marriage.

Also in Level II of Capital S Society but at the opposite end
of the financial scale from the Edgertons were families known as
Bluff Clubbers. Among Bluff Club members were the city's most
legendary successes, men who had founded large manufacturing
firms or commercial organizations and thereby made the jump from
average circles into the social elite (although not into the First
Jackson Country Club). A. Walter Hallstrom was such a man.
Walter Hallstrom's father came from Sweden as a young man in the
late 1880s and soon established a small brick-contracting business.
Walter worked his way through Kansas City Business College.
During World War I, he became fascinated with early developments in radio and navigation equipment, and he started a manufacturing company in this field.

Thirty-three years later, Hallstrom, Inc., was known
throughout the Midwest for its high quality radios. Hallstrom also
made electronic equipment, and the company expanded greatly

during World War II. When it added television sets to its list of products, it became the second-largest Kansas City-owned industrial firm. The result was that A. Walter Hallstrom became one of Kansas City's wealthiest men. Three qualifications other than wealth, however, brought the Hallstroms into the Society world. First, everybody in Kansas City's top circles "liked Walter and Edith." They had not been invited into the First Jackson Country Club, but Walter was second in line for presidency of the Bluff Club; Mrs. Hallstrom had served for many years as an officer in the Midday Woman's Club. Second, their children were immensely popular. Their two daughters had made "brilliant" marriages; their son was attending Yale and had been elected to one of the top senior societies there. Finally, the Hallstroms had given millions of dollars to Kansas City's cultural institutions. Walter Hallstrom had for ten years been on the board of trustees at the University of Kansas City, and in the early 1950s he served as chairman of the board.

Most business leaders who had reached the social summit, like Walter Hallstrom, were known for the munificence of their gifts to the symphony, the university, the art institute, and so on— and also for their service as governors and trustees of such institutions. They had proved themselves more than just successful businessmen; they had become philanthropists.

The second level of Capital S Society contained people who were widely divergent. Some of them hardly knew each other, for they traveled in different cliques and sets. The Hallstroms circulated mainly with the civic minded "big rich," while the Edgertons generally participated in the circle of "slightly fallen old guard." The Gerlachs were in a third set of the socially flamboyant, using their wealth for travel and entertainment, not community service. Still another group was composed of "fascinating new people" who had moved to Kansas City from other places, and might move on again, depending on where their professional or business connections took them.

Level III: The third level of Kansas City's upper class— that is, the upper layer of its non-Capital S branch—was organized around those members of the Missoukana Country Club who were not Capital S. The role of the Missoukana Country Club in Kansas City life is explained in the following pair of comments: "Missoukana costs a lot of money, so it naturally has a lot of big wheels and top flight businessmen. It's the prestige country club for the self-made man." "Missoukana doesn't have quite the aristocracy that you'd find among the First Jackson members. . . . Money talks louder there than at First Jackson, and the other qualifications aren't quite as important. But, don't get me wrong, Missoukana doesn't let just anybody with big money in. They've got a nice bunch of people there. It's a fine membership."

Approximately 730 Kansas City families—including the married sons and daughters of Missoukana members, elderly couples who had retired from active participation, and the close friends who, though not actually members of the club, had earned designation as "members of the Missoukana crowd"—were identified with the third level. Another 270 men and women—widowed, divorced, or single—were also ranked here. Within the group there were gradations in status. The dominant figures were men like Tex Grasselli, president of the Missouri and Gulf Coast Railroad; Bert Williamson, multimillionaire Chevrolet dealer with the biggest auto agency in Kansas City; Frank Bell, founder of Bell Plate Glass, one of the city's twenty largest manufacturing firms; and Frank Yarnall, a Missouri farm boy who came to Kansas City to study law in night school, made his fame as the prosecuting attorney who sent Pendergast to prison, and shortly thereafter became reform mayor of the city.

The names of these men were regularly in the newspapers. They stood, in the public eye, at or near the summit of financial status, executive prominence, and political power. Each had served a term as president of the Tavern and Trail Club, and all were members of Missoukana Country Club. Two were members of the Bluff Club, which provided them occasional connections with the upper two levels of society. The less prominent Warren Knights were more typical of the people at this stratum. Warren Knight was vice-president and partner of the Valley Steel company, with an income around forty-five thousand dollars a year. Born in Junction City, Kansas, where his father was division foreman for the Rock Island Railroad, Warren worked summers so he could go to Kansas State College at nearby Manhattan; but in 1917 he quit school because he "wanted in on the action" of World War I. In the service, Warren Knight began a friendship with Tom McIntosh from Kansas City, whose father had established the small but thriving McIntosh Fence and Iron Works. When the war was over, Tom persuaded Warren to join his father's firm.

Thus Warren Knight came to Kansas City with a social as well as a financial sponsor, for Tom McIntosh's family was by then in Kansas City's upper class. The McIntoshes started Warren off by getting him a junior membership in the newly-founded Silver Hills Country Club. Three years later Warren established his second important connection by marrying Genny Wallace, a roommate of Tom McIntosh's younger sister at Kansas University, an attractive and popular girl who was friendly with socially prominent girls in Kansas City. Soon after their marriage, Warren and Genny became what *The Chatterbox,* Kansas City's weekly magazine of social news, described as "one of our town's most popular young couples." During the Depression, the McIntosh Fence and Iron Works remained solvent, then grew into the Valley Steel Company. Tom became president; Warren, vice-president. The Depression had taken its toll of Missoukana members and when the chance arose in 1938, the Knights took the membership offered them and became fully accepted members of Kansas City's upper class at the third level.

The families of many of the city's topflight professional men —the leading physicians, dentists, architects, engineers, and lawyers —constituted an important source for membership in the third level. Whether these families were accepted as part of the Missoukana world or were at Level IV was due as much to the ambition and charm of the wives as to the professional stature of the husbands. Another large number of Level III people were second- or third-generation inheritors of this status, of which the Sartains were an example.

The Sartains were a very active family, with memberships in Missoukana Country Club, Cibola Lake Yacht Club, Westport Tennis Club, and the Kan-Citian. Beth Sartain, however, had been passed over by the Junior League, even though her father, Russell Janeway, was the multimillionaire owner of Janeway Cereals. (She had gone to the public high school instead of one of the two fashionable private schools, so she had not become an intimate of the prospective Junior League group in her younger years.) She was a member of the Service Club and the Historiennes Club, a group of younger women whose activities helped support the Kansas City

Historical Museum. There were no signs that the Sartains aspired to move higher on the social ladder. They had no friends of higher status, and they seemed satisfied to remain leaders in the lower echelons of the Society world.

Level IV: The fourth level of Kansas City's upper class included approximately 1,250 families, plus 470 widows, widowers, and single or divorced persons. The most important segment of this group came from "the higher half of the Silver Hills Country Club crowd." Generally speaking, upper status Kansas City people defined Silver Hills members as "well-to-do, but not really rich" or "almost big wheels, but not quite." The position of Silver Hills as third among the city's country clubs was unchallenged, but the degree to which the club and its members were part of the upper class was a subject of debate. Clique analysis, however, revealed two basic levels of Silver Hills members. In one, the men were top-flight in business and professional status; in the other, most of the men were at semi-executive levels of large businesses; frequently their memberships in Silver Hills were paid for by their firms. The daughters of the first group were usually named Belles of the American Royal; the daughters of the second group never were.

Other groups at the fourth level were the Irish elite of Emerald Hills Country Club and those members of the Tavern and Trail Club who were not members of Missoukana. The Tavern and Trail ranked higher in the social scale than the Silver Hills Country Club; many of its members were in Missoukana and some were even drawn from the uppermost circle of Society.

"The quiet professional elite at the Quadrangle Club" made up the last main group of fourth-level families; these were editors, ministers, architects, jurists, college deans, as well as physicians and lawyers. Their lineage was usually distinguished to some extent (for example, a college president father or an ancestor who had been a Randolph of Virginia) and each in his own right was of some note on the local scene. Almost anyone in the Quadrangle Club was assumed to be of at least Level IV upper class status.

Old families in the third and fourth levels were distinguished from those in Capital S Society by their failure to maintain the social pace set by the higher-status group. They were different, in turn, from those who had fallen out of the upper class, because they still maintained extensive formal and informal ties with other upper-class families.

The Jewish Upper Class

In 1955, 350 Jewish families plus another 135 single Jewish men and women ranked as members of Kansas City's upper class. These people were divided by informal clique participation and personal reputation into four status levels which were roughly equivalent to the four levels of the non-Jewish upper class, with certain tenuous interconnections existing between the separate worlds of Gentile and Jew at each level.

Most upper-class Jews were members of the Standard Country Club, a club which had been in existence for over forty years. At its founding, all members were affiliated with reform Judaism and were of German ancestry. During the 1940s the Standard began to admit Jews affiliated with conservative Judaism. It remained, however, the center of much of the social activity of Kansas City's higher-status Jewish families. The other Jewish country club, Idlewild, was formed in the early 1950s. Its members were almost entirely conservative Jews of Russian and Polish background. This club included many wealthy families who were not acceptable to the Standard Club group, plus many of upper-middle status.

The top rung of the Jewish social ladder was composed of an exclusive circle of twenty-five families. Their importance to the wider world of Kansas City's Level I Society, as well as to the Jewish community at large, was reflected in the comment made by a member of the Jewel Ball planning committee: "Whenever we're drawing up the list of debutantes we always consult the Kiels and Rosenthals and Brenners for their choices on which girls to include from the Jewish circles."

Just below this group in status were another fifty-five families. Their daughters were always invited to be debutantes in the Jewel Ball, and they frequently socialized with the top twenty-five families, especially at larger parties. A leader in the Jewish community remarked, in clarifying the status of these second-level families: "If you want to know who count as the good old families in the Jewish community, you'd have to get a list of the people Florence Kiel invites to her Christmas party or Kitty Brenner to her

New Year's Eve party every year—that would cover everyone who rates in the top group." The second-level families were included at these parties.

As in the non-Jewish world, a meaningful division between upper class and upper-middle status was whether a daughter was invited to serve as a Belle of the American Royal. Another criterion was whether or not the family participated across the religious barrier with non-Jews of high status. Whenever top status Jews mingled with non-Jews at private parties, the latter were almost always of the capital s society world. And whenever Jews in the lower levels of the upper class socialized across the barrier, it was usually with those who were similarly from the third or fourth levels.[1]

The Non-U Rich

Certain families were not accepted by upper class Kansas Citians despite sufficient wealth. In some, the men were reputed to be racketeers; in others, the families were rejected as uncouth. Many were considered socially uninteresting, "just plain people who made money." We have borrowed the phrase of the British social observer, Nancy Mitford, to denote this group as the "Non-U Rich," —non-upper class, though rich (Mitford, 1956).

These Non-U Rich families were not accepted wholeheartedly by the upper-middle class elite any more than by the upper class. They constituted a separate social category, in some ways isolated from the Kansas City social structure. The Non-U Rich differed in several ways from the adjacent groups: they were less active in civic affairs that the upper-middle-elite, and held no more

[1] The authors estimated the Jewish status distribution to be 8 per cent upper class, 45 per cent upper-middle, 42 per cent lower-middle, and 5 per cent upper-lower. This is similar to the Jewish community of Peoria, Illinois, described by Peter E. Siegle (1958) as 9 per cent upper class, 38 per cent upper-middle, 49 per cent lower-middle, and 5 per cent upper-lower. (In Peoria, as in Kansas City, the Jewish population constituted 3 to 4 per cent of the total.) The pattern in these two midwestern cities was different from that reported for two East coast cities. In Yankee City in the early 1930s, the distribution was reported by Warner and Lunt (1941) as 3 per cent upper-middle, 42 per cent lower-middle, 48 per cent upper-lower, and 8 per cent lower-lower. The evidence on ethnic groups given by Hollingshead and Redlich (1958) suggests the following for New Haven, where the Jewish population was about one-tenth of the total in the early 1950s: 3.5 per cent upper class, 25 per cent upper-middle, 31 per cent lower-middle, 34 per cent upper-lower, and 6.5 per cent lower-lower.

memberships in social clubs. They were no better, or less well, educated than lower-middle class people: only 7 per cent of the wives had gone to college, approximately the same percentage as among working class women. There was an overrepresentation of Catholics, and ten times as many Jews as in the city as a whole. Few were of upper-middle origin, and more than a third were of working or lower class origin.

The occupations of the Non-U Rich often explained the great discrepancy between their income level and social status. Seventeen per cent operated retail stores or service stores which catered mainly to working or lower class Kansas Citians. They had entered these businesses at the bottom and risen to top financial levels without forming social relationships to high-status people. Some were in the restaurant and entertainment business. The legitimate operators owned cafeterias and restaurants, bowling alleys, neighborhood movie houses and drive-in theaters. The illegitimate operated taverns and night clubs thought to be in syndicate control; some ran pinball machine and jukebox concessions or were wholesale liquor dealers. Contractors in the building trades who could achieve great financial success with little social polish, Jewish clothing manufacturers who spoke with accents, and lawyers who were known to "defend the criminal element" also were among the group. Several Non-U Rich men in Kansas City had achieved their wealth through inventions, and some of these inventors were considered "strange," or were unacceptable because they were "too plain" or "too roughhewn" in appearance. Several Non-U Rich men had achieved wealth in livestock and produce trading or farm real estate; they were rejected as "too rural" in manner.

The Upper Class of the Satellite Cities

The upper strata of Kansas City, Kansas, and Independence, Missouri, could be analyzed in much the same way as Kansas City, Missouri. There was little interaction among the upper-class men and women of the three communities; each upper class was a self-centered group. What little interaction occurred across the city lines followed the same pattern observed between Kansas City, Missouri's Jews and non-Jews—that is, Independence and Kansas City, Kansas, people socialized with persons in Kansas City, Missouri, who were of the same status as themselves. On this basis the levels of upper-class people of Independence and Kansas City, Kansas, could be equated with those of the central city.

Following such a rule, only ten or twelve families in Kansas City, Kansas, qualified as Capital S Society in metropolitan terms, and none could be equated with the number one level in Kansas City, Missouri. These leading Kansas families socialized almost entirely with second-level Capital S Missouri families; the memberships they held were at the Missoukana and the Tavern and Trail clubs, or in the Bluff Club and the Kan-Citian. A similarly small number of families in Independence qualified as Capital S Society. They were more integrated, however, with their counterparts in Kansas City, Missouri, because in most cases they were related to Kansas Citians. Daughters of these families were usually elected to membership in the Junior League of Kansas City, Missouri, and through the years there had almost always been one or two families from Independence among the membership at the First Jackson Country Club. (Indeed, many of the top-level families in Kansas City traced their origins back to Independence.) More typically, however, the leading families in Independence, like those in Kansas City, Kansas, were affiliated with the Missoukana Country Club. There they were friends of the "top circle of prairie aristocrats," part of the group referred to earlier as the Missouri Establishment.

At lower levels of the upper class in Kansas City, Kansas, and Independence, there was much less intermingling with people from Kansas City, Missouri. Memberships in the central city's town and country clubs were not common; instead these people were members of the leading golf clubs serving their own communities. Men in Kansas City, Kansas, had a downtown club atop the leading Kansas-side bank. Festivities centering around the American Royal provided one of the few occasions for extensive intercity social interaction. Girls from upper class Kansas City, Kansas, and Independence families served along with those from Kansas City, Missouri, as Belles.

Entrance Requirements

The most striking difference between the Capital S Society and non-Capital S groups was in class origin (see Appendix C). The majority of middle-aged Capital S couples (54 per cent) had originated at the Capital S level—that is, the husband or wife or both had parents in that stratum—and only 5 per cent had moved up to Capital S levels from middle-class origins. This finding suggests that myth more than reality underlay the image of the upper-class world as open to all. Although club affiliations were claimed to be the final status criterion, the relation between lineage and club affiliation indicates that lineage was a potent determinant of acceptability for the highest-status clubs and was perhaps the most significant factor.

This is not to say that the image of the social free-for-all was totally without foundation. Families with newly acquired wealth were frequently admitted to non-Capital S Society, for instance. What was meant by a free-for-all was that all who were well-to-do were eligible for upper-class status but that competition then determined who was accepted into the upper class and at what stratum therein. Bloodlines began to apply once a family was in the upper class. Connections and qualifications rather than bloodlines were important in making families socially acceptable. Connections were gained through personal or corporate sponsorship; certain executive positions, for example, automatically enabled membership in certain clubs and cliques. Valued qualifications included a prestigious educational background, as well as leadership and social skills. The social abilities of a wife were as important as her husband's. Non-U Rich families were always judged to be lacking in these qualifications.

Level II contained the clearest examples of upward mobility —families who had risen from middle class status to Capital S in one generation. These cases strengthened the belief in the free-for-all, but with little warrant, since they constituted only 7 per cent of the families at their level. These mobile families were headed by spectacularly successful entrepreneurs or by eminent lawyers, doctors, or banking executives. The entrepreneurs had impressed elite Kansas Citians by their philanthropies perhaps even more than with their business success; the lawyers were partners in the city's biggest firms and counselors to old guard families; the physicians were men who had earned national reputations in their specialty. The banking and investment executives were those who controlled the most important estate and corporate funds. Only Level I appeared closed to families who had no forebears of upper-class status.

Age and Status

The mobility observed in the upper class refers mostly to older families. Of the families at Level I in which the husband was under forty years old, 84 per cent had inherited this position and 16 per cent had moved up; but in families in which the husband was over sixty-five, 43 per cent had moved up from Level II and 39 per cent from Levels III and IV. Whether this pattern of mobility at the top level would have prevailed had more high-status families of previous eras remained in Kansas City is a moot question. The majority of Level II families in which the husband was under fifty-five had inherited this status position. Where the husband was older than fifty-five, the majority were newcomers to Capital S Society, even though many had moved up from only one step below and had already been within the upper class.

Age also was associated with movement into Level III. Almost all of the younger Level III families were second- or third-generation upper class. Level IV received newcomers who were five or ten years younger than newcomers to Level III, because less occupational success was required for acceptance at this level. This factor, coupled with the dropping out of many young adults born into Level IV, meant that the majority of younger families in Level IV had not inherited upper-class status. This age-related mobility meant that the percentage of upper class families in the population increased considerably with age. The percentage of people over seventy who were upper class was twice the number in the twenty-two to thirty-nine age group. While some of this difference can perhaps be attributed to greater longevity among upper-class people than in the general population, the more important factor is undoubtedly that of mobility increasing with age.

Whether these relationships between age and mobility into the upper class apply to Kansas City in the late 1960s has not been determined. They reflect what happened to people whose adulthood was marked by a succession of dramatic events: the economic boom of the 1920s, the Great Depression of the 1930s, World War II, and the prosperity of the postwar years. Downward mobility could often be traced to financial losses suffered in the Depression, or by the inflation of the 1940s and early 1950s which devalued inheritances; in more instances, however, downward mobility was a product of personality disorders or career failure among inheritors of high status. As described in Chapter Eleven, our best estimate is that at least 30 per cent or 35 per cent of children born to upper-class status had dropped out of the class in their adulthood.

Mobility into the upper class usually occurred between the ages of forty and fifty-five. By then a man's career line was established; his attainments to date and probable future achievements could be assessed by his associates. If a man made a great deal of money after age fifty-five, it seemed to be too late to translate the wealth into increased social status. Some of the Non-U Rich were people of this type: they prospered too late in life to care about changing their patterns of living or seeking new friends. Kansas City's economic and occupational leadership, nevertheless, was concentrated in the hands of men fifty-five and over. For all but a few, their earlier adult years constituted a period of steady but not spectacular ascent; leadership came primarily in their fifties. This meant that Society was dominated by men and women who were fifty-five and over.

To give younger men and women the opportunity for appropriate social participation without having to compete financially with their elders, special organizations and special categories of junior memberships had been created in most of the high-status clubs. A junior membership with reduced annual dues and initiation fees could be maintained until age thirty-five or forty. This arrangement was explained on the grounds that "you can't tell how high a man is going until he reaches his early forties." In the high status clubs for women, junior memberships almost always lasted until age forty and sometimes until forty-five. This higher age limit, as compared to the men's clubs, was justified on the grounds that as long as women still had children at home to care for they would not be able to invest much energy in organizational activities.

"Society" Occupations

The point has already been made that for a family in Kansas City to attain upper-class status it was necessary that the husband hold a topflight executive position or a commensurate reputation as a professional. To move above Level IV usually required greater occupational success than being merely topflight. Where a husband or wife were originally of upper-class status, however, the relationship between current occupation and social position was complicated by other factors, such as the inherited social position of the couple and the social ambitions of the previous generation.

The interaction of occupational and economic factors with inherited position explains the considerable variation in economic status at each level within the upper class, even in men of the same age. Capital S and non-Capital S men also differed in the kinds of occupations they pursued and the clienteles they served. Almost twice as many Capital S men were owners or chief executives of banks, investment houses, insurance companies, and real estate firms. It was common for second-generation upper-class men to enter these fields even when they had not inherited such businesses. The concentration of Levels I and II men in these fields reflected the prestige and power attached to the control of money and land.

A number of families, although the husbands were in retailing, were accepted at a high level in the upper class because they served an upper-status clientele. Lawyers, doctors, dentists, and architects whose clients were upper class were nearly always upper class themselves, often second- or third-generation. The clientele principle also governed the service professions—the ministry, education, and government. Ministers serving upper-class congregations were always upper class. The headmasters of Kansas City's three private schools were all upper class. (Many of the teachers at these schools had inherited upper-class status.) So, too, were the deans of the Art Institute and the Conservatory of Music, the president of the local university, the director of the Philharmonic orchestra, the curator of the Art Gallery, and others whose jobs required continual solicitation of city leaders.

Elected officials, who were generally seen as serving the masses, held upper-class status only if they came from upper-class families or if, in addition to their elected office, they were moving toward high status via their private careers. Appointed federal or state judges were accepted into the upper class if the appointment was recognized as a reward for merit. Elected judges and those whose appointments were thought to accrue from patronage were generally restricted to upper-middle class participation.

Civic Leadership

The upper class supplied virtually all the leadership of the important civic institutions—cultural enterprises, welfare agencies, and city or county commissions—as well as the various voluntary organizations devoted to promoting the city's economic interests. The greatest share of this leadership was carried by Capital S men and women; and such activities were well-nigh imperative for families wishing to move upward from non-Capital S. Most families viewed civic participation more as an obligation than as fun, and they sought occasional respite from its demands on their time and energy. Thus, at any given time many persons who ordinarily were active were counted among the inactive—they were taking their sabbaticals, as it were. Only those men and women who felt "lost" without these activities or who felt themselves indispensable to Kansas City's civic leadership did not take an occasional "leave of absence." (See Appendix C for statistical detail.)

Educational Patterns

The typical upper-class man in the forty to sixty-nine age group was a college graduate; what differentiated Capital S men from the others was the particular colleges attended. Most Capital S men had attended an Eastern college or had gone to a state university and joined a top-rated fraternity, whereas most of those below Capital S levels had not. These differences simply reflected the fact that the majority of Capital S men had been born into the upper class and thus been given an education typical for their class, while the majority of the others had made their way into the upper class through adult occupational success. (See Appendix C.)

The importance of prestigious colleges as part of Capital S life is reflected in the educational experiences parents of this level provided their children. For example, slightly over half of Level I sons born between 1915 and 1934, who therefore entered college between 1933 and 1952, were sent to Harvard, Yale, or Princeton; this reflected the extent to which their parents were Eastern-oriented in their concepts of appropriate male education. Sons from other levels of the upper class more commonly attended a nearby state university or a private college in the South, Midwest, or West where they mingled socially with the more popular of upper-middle young men.

The educational backgrounds of upper-class women were even more closely linked to their position in adult life than was true of men. Capital S women differed far more from non-Capital S in the college or finishing school they had attended than in the number of years they had spent in college. Women at Levels I and II were usually educated at Eastern women's colleges or finishing schools; at Levels III and IV, usually at the midwestern state universities where they joined high-status sororities. From the early 1900s until the middle 1950s the latter was an eminently acceptable educational experience for an upper-class girl in Kansas City, especially during the Depression and in the post-World War II period.

Religious Preferences

The exalted position of Episcopalianism was reflected in the finding that 23 per cent of the upper class were affiliated with this denomination, as compared with only 2 per cent of the total Kansas City population; 53 per cent of Level I men and women belonged to one or another of the three Society Episcopalian churches. At Level II, the Presbyterians included many of the professional elite and newcomers to high status. Christians, Methodists, and Baptists at Level II were mainly prairie aristocrats and Missouri Establishment families—they had remained in the churches of their fathers, even though these denominations were less fashionable than the Episcopalian or Presbyterian.

Catholics, although they constituted 20 per cent of white Kansas City, constituted only 7 per cent of Capital S, 15 per cent of non-Capital S, but 23 per cent of the Non-U Rich. The relative exclusion of Catholics at the top status levels was associated with rejection of overly ethnic behavior (Irish, Italian, or eastern European), so that persons were more often rejected for their non-assimilation than for their Catholicism per se.

The acceptance of Jews in Kansas City's upper class appears high when it is noted that 12 per cent of the Kansas City upper class, but only 3 per cent of Kansas Citians, were Jewish. To be Jewish was nevertheless a handicap, as shown by another comparison: of Jewish middle-aged men with high-income occupations, 45 per cent were not part of the upper class; the comparable figure for non-Jews was 29 per cent. As with Catholics, rejection of Jews was usually based on their ethnic behavior—foreign origin, accent, or failure to abandon traditional religious practices. Virtually all upper-class Jews who were affiliated with a congregation were members of the most religiously liberal of the five Kansas City temples. Indeed, the reform Jewish congregation, B'nai Emunah, ranked easily as one of the top four among Kansas City's religious institutions in total number of upper-class families included in its membership.

Style of Housing

The average Kansas City resident would have been surprised at how many of the city's upper class did not live in mansions. Only 36 per cent of middle-aged families in non-Capital S and 55 per cent of Capital S occupied homes of the size and impressiveness which Kansas Citians had in mind when they spoke of Ward Parkway mansions. Partly this was because in the early 1950s a mansion was no longer the most sought after acquisition for many upper-class families. Entertainment, club dues, charitable donations, clothes, recreational equipment, educational expenses for children, and vacation homes took a large share of the upper-class dollar.

Despite these changing values, the majority of families headed by men between fifty and sixty did live in mansions. Not too many men under fifty could afford them, and those over sixty had often moved into smaller homes or apartments. Location of the home tended to take precedence over size and impressiveness. Society people lived in the right neighborhoods and avoided offbeat or nonrespected areas. The exceptions to this rule were mostly families who lived in neighborhoods of fading aristocracy.

Social Sets

It would be a mistake to conclude that upper-status Kansas Citians were preoccupied with the stratifying function of their clubs or that climbing the Society ladder was their only goal. On the contrary, most of the elite clubs were seen as bringing together Kansas Citians who, though of diverse statuses within the upper-middle and upper class, shared common interests and recreational enthusiasms. Organizations like the Cibola Lake Yacht Club, the Westport Tennis Club, the Brush Creek Hunt Club, and the Indian

Fields Polo Club were known to attract members from three or four levels of the upper strata.

Another example is provided by a comparison of the two largest high-status downtown men's clubs: the Quadrangle Club was thought to be the haven of Kansas City's "intellectual crowd" and "professional elite," while the Kan-Citian Club was described as the center of "business and executive leadership," where the social tone was dominated by expense-account entertaining. The Kan-Citian Club contained several inner clubs of less than a hundred members each; their colorful names—The Seven-Come-Eleven Club, The Saturday Afternoon Chowder and Marching Society, The Tuesday Poker and Sewing Circle—were said to reflect quite well their gregarious and masculine spirit.

Kansas City society figures referred to their vertical cliques as "sets." This term was especially widely employed in characterizing the social life of upper-status women. Widely recognized women's groups were "the issues-and-culture set," "the tea-and-crumpets set of sweet old ladies," "the Hattie Carnegie set who go to all the fashion shows," "the past worshippers who are in the 'Daughters' series of clubs," "the symphony women," and "the amateur do-gooder set."

While some of the sets that Kansas City people talked about were really only small cliques within a single status level, most of them drew their members from three or more social strata. Because of the great number of sets at the upper and upper-middle levels, and because a great proportion of social interaction occurred within sets, rather than within same-status cliques, the network of social interaction at higher levels can only partially be described in terms of social class. In Kansas City, and presumably in other cities, dimensions other than social status operated to produce social cohesion as well as divisiveness in the community—race, ethnicity, religious affiliation, and political ideology, to mention only a few. The sets described here constitute only one dimension of social participation. We shall return, at a later point in this book, to a further consideration of the utility of the concept of social class in studying urban communities. Meanwhile, it is evident that sets engage only part of an individual's social life; they do not define his status or his position on the social ladder.

Chapter 7

Upper-Middle Class

$\mathscr{I}$n every community study, sociologists have identified a group midway between the rich and aristocratic and the average white-collar worker.[1] Kansas City proved no exception, and Kansas Citians themselves spoke of such a group as "an upper-middle class," the "managerial class," or "the country club class."

Upper-Middle-Core

The aptness of these characterizations is demonstrated in the profile of the David T. Austin family, who typified the life style of that 6 per cent of white, middle-aged Kansas Citians who in 1955 formed the core level of the metropolitan upper-middle class:

> David Austin had reached his fifteen thousand dollars a year position (about twenty-five thousand dollars in 1970 dollars) as personnel director of the Mid-American Life Insurance Company by a familiar career route. Born in Iowa in 1904, the son of a self-taught bookkeeper, he attended the State University of Iowa and graduated with a B.A. in business administration. He held a variety of part-time jobs while a student and led a somewhat limited social life until his junior year at college, when he joined

[1] For a summary of research on upper-middle class life, see Kahl (1957). For comparison of New Haven to Kansas City, see Hollingshead and Redlich (1958).

a fraternity. Upon graduation he began work for the Equitable Life Insurance of Iowa in Mason City and married Ruth Taylor, the daughter of his supervisor. Ruth had spent a year at Simpson, a small Methodist college in Iowa, before transferring to a conservatory in Minneapolis for further study of piano and composition. After studying music for two years, she decided to forego a career and settle instead into a family and home life. A year after the Austins were married, David transferred to the Equitable home office in Des Moines.

The Austins were relatively unaffected by the Depression of the 1930s. David advanced slowly but surely at Equitable Life, studying personnel management at night. He had decided he would rather "work with people than with numbers" and he wanted to be in on the ground floor of a developing field. In 1940 the Mid-West Insurance Company, with home offices in Kansas City, established a Personnel Department and hired Austin as an assistant. In 1947 he was promoted to Personnel Director. Thus, by 1954, at age fifty, David Austin occupied a secure position as a fully established member of the managerial class in the Kansas City business world. He was responsible for hiring all the clerical workers (approximately three hundred), all salesmen who worked in the Kansas City territory, and the maintenance staff.

The Austins lived in a seven room Dutch colonial house in the center of the Country Club District, two blocks away from Kansas City's top-ranked public high school and one block away from their church, the Wornall Road Congregational, a typical parish church serving the Country Club District. Their son Jack had already graduated from Kansas University and was an ensign in the United States Navy. Their daughter Jean, a junior in high school, was a very good student who hoped to attend Oberlin College.

The Austins did not hold a country club membership, but they belonged to the Nodaway Lake Yacht Club (the city's second-rank yacht club) where they kept a sailboat. Austin was not a member of a private downtown men's club, but he belonged to the Optimists Club as Midwest's representative, and also to the Personnel Club, of which he had often been an officer. He was president of the Kansas City chapter of the American Management Association at the time he was interviewed. In past years he had been on the board of deacons of his church, but he had decided not to serve again, explaining: "I have enough of people and human relations problems from nine to five." In place of church work, he planned to devote his winter evenings to reading and "watching television (then new in Kansas City) until I get tired of it" and his summer evenings to sailing ("until I get too old") or to "growing something here in the yard."

Ruth Austin had maintained her interest in music, and was a member of the Kansas City Musical Club; one of her small disappointments in life was that neither of her children cared about music. At forty-eight, Ruth felt that the mothering stage of her life was almost over: "My PTA days are behind me, and my work with the Camp Fire Girls comes to an end next year. I've been on the Horizon Club committee [for senior Camp Fire Girls] in the southwest neighborhood the past two years, and probably will be again next year when Jean's a senior. When Jack was at Kansas University, I was in the Phi Delta Theta Mother's Club—but if Jean goes to Oberlin there won't be anything like that." Mrs. Austin wasn't sure what she would be doing "along the club line" in future years; one thing she wanted to avoid was becoming "the kind of woman who spends half her afternoons around the bridge table." She looked forward to going downtown more often and taking advantage of her membership at the Midday Woman's Club: "They have a committee on hearing conservation which I would like to work on. I haven't had time til now, but that is something I have thought about."

The Austins' social links to members of many of the private clubs are illustrated in Ruth Austin's description of the twelve couples in a "dance and bridge" club to which she and her husband belonged:

> The Dance and Bridge Club meets every other week during the winter. One time we play bridge, then the next time we have dinner out. We have three special parties every year. In the fall, we all go over to Lawrence for a University of Kansas football game, then come back to the Shawnee Woods Country Club, which the Gilberts belong to, to end the day with dinner and drinks—we call that our "football frolic." Then some time in the middle of the winter we have dinner at the Commercial Club, where the Eckles are members, and go on to the theater to see a play or musical which has come to town. Finally, in May, we have our last fling of the year by dancing on the roof garden of the Kan-Citian Club—that's where the Highets belong, and we call them our "fanciest members" as a result.
>
> This club has been going on a long time, and the membership keeps changing as couples leave town, and as we bring new ones in. There are twelve couples all told. We have been in it eight years now. We were brought in by one of the women I was working with in Camp Fire Girls. We have other long time friends in the club—some we met at a church, and one is my regular car pool pal at the Musical Club. One of the men has been in the Optimist Club with my husband, another helped him start the Personnel Club, and others are at Nodaway with us. Most of the couples live some place here in the Country Club District and are about our age. The men do a variety of things. One is a lawyer with the Department of Commerce in the motor carriage division, another has a display advertising company;

then we have a dentist, a research engineer at the telephone company, a CPA, a public relations man at Missouri-Kansas Natural Gas, and some district managers for big national firms like Pittsburgh Glass & Jar and Riteline Typewriter.

Most upper-middle class persons sampled in the Adult Life study belonged to one or two informal groups like the Dance and Bridge Club. Thus, while it appeared that fewer upper-middle class people held private town and country club memberships than Kansas Citians supposed, most had access to these clubs through their clique associations.

In occupation, income, and type of residence, David Austin was representative of the upper-middle pattern. Managers such as Austin—men with titles like personnel director, head of public relations, district sales managers, and assistant secretary-treasurer—constituted the largest occupational group. Together with salaried professionals like lawyers, engineers, accountants, and editors, they constituted two-thirds of upper-middle-core men.

Independent businessmen—24 per cent of the core group—constituted the third-largest occupational group. Although most of these independent businessmen had higher incomes than the managerial and salaried professionals and were more active in organizations and civic affairs, they had had less education. Few had gone to college, and many had dropped out of high school, whereas the majority of managerial men at this level were college graduates.

The organizational activities of these independent businessmen centered around business promotion organizations such as the Chamber of Commerce, the Blue Valley Businessman's League, or the Real Estate Board, or luncheon clubs such as Kiwanis, Cosmopolitan, Exchange, Cooperative, or Lions. Through these organizations, men from various enterprises got together and unofficially pledged to trade with one another. These men were also usually members of a fraternal order, although they regarded such memberships primarily as a means of promoting their businesses.

Approximately half the upper-middle independent businessmen were Jewish. Like their non-Jewish counterparts, they were active in business organizations—particularly the Merchants Association—and a few belonged to the luncheon clubs. Many were members of B'nai B'rith, a men's philanthropic and social organization; wives were active in Hadassah, a philanthropic organization for Jewish women. Most upper-middle class Jewish families were affiliated with one or another of the three Conservative synagogues.

Independent professionals were the smallest occupational group, comprising only 10 per cent of the middle-aged core men in the sample. Evidence from other sources (city directories and telephone directories) suggests that among independent professionals at this level lawyers were most numerous, followed by dentists, accountants, engineers, physicians, osteopaths, optometrists, and architects. For the most part, Kansas Citians considered these men below average in professional attainments. The lawyers, for example, were in small, two- or three-partner firms, sometimes father-and-son practices, or in offices by themselves. Doctors at this level were usually general practitioners, old-style family physicians. The dentists served southeast side or north side families, not other upper-middles. The accountants, architects, and engineers were only moderately successful in their respective professions; and the osteopaths were among the more successful in the city—but that occupation itself was looked upon as an inferior branch of the medical profession.

Just a few men of the upper-middle-core were widely known in Kansas City. These were supervisors in the school system, several ministers of medium-large but not high-status churches, and some higher level employees of the local and federal governments. Men in public positions of this type were often mentioned in the newspapers, and they were frequently speakers at public meetings; they were virtually the only upper-middle-core men who ever served on civic boards and commissions. Such men did not amount to even 1 per cent of the upper-middle-core, although as individuals they were the most visible.

Upper-Middle-Elite

Approximately 1,300 middle-aged Kansas City families could be characterized as upper-middle-elite. While these people were identified more broadly as "part of the upper-middle class," they had unusual qualifications or connections which gave them extra status in the eyes of other upper-middle people. These families were usually headed by men whom Kansas Citians called "semi-executives," meaning they were not yet at the level of executive responsibility characteristic of the upper class. Semi-executives were usually in the eighteen to twenty-four thousand dollar salary range; they were members of the Silver Hills or Emerald Hills country clubs, or sometimes of a downtown club. Durward Gregory and his wife were a typical middle-aged couple of the upper-middle-elite.

As general manager of King's (Kansas City's leading department store) branch in the Country Club shopping center, Gregory at forty-four earned over twenty thousand dollars (which is approximately thirty-four thousand in 1970 dollars). Somewhat more active in voluntary organizations than most men of his status (because he felt his position more public than that of many semi-executives), he was vice-president of the promotional organization of his shopping center, and treasurer of the Mercury Club (a men's luncheon club described as "a very smart group"). He was also on the social committee of the Military Order of World Wars (composed of ex-officers), on the membership committee of the Chamber of Commerce, on the board of directors of the Fairway Estates Association (the suburb he lived in), and past president of Kansas City's Northwestern University Alumni Association.

Mrs. Gregory was one of Silver Hills Country Club's two representatives to the Kansas City Women Golfer's Association and also the representative of her college sorority to the Kansas City Panhellenic. A mother of three, she had never taken part in parent-teacher activities or scouting. "I'd rather play golf or go to parties than tie myself down to parent organizations. When I get out of the house I want to enjoy myself." To this end, the Gregorys belonged to the Silver Dollar Club, a swankier Dance and Bridge Club.

To the man on the street and to those in the highest echelons of the upper class, families like the Gregorys—who were close to executive level—seemed only slightly different from families like the Austins. Within the upper-middle class, however, these two types were perceived as quite distinct. Upper-middle-elites were awarded greater prestige because they had closer ties to the upper class.

Those who acquired elite status in their fifties generally remained in the upper-middle class. It was mainly the younger families like the Gregorys who moved into the upper class as they entered their late forties. (A follow-up—made in 1965 on the thirteen couples who had been in the Silver Dollar Club in 1955—indicated that six of the thirteen couples had become part of Kansas City's upper class.)

Exceptionally successful businessmen in their fifties or sixties and older professional men, who had developed good practices but had not become known as topflight, made up the rest of the upper-middle-elite. These men were more frequently of lower-middle class origin, and they had prospered later in life than those who moved into the upper class. Many of the professional men had completed their training three or four years later than average and had been handicapped by the late start.

Much of the leadership in upper-middle and large cross-class organizations in Kansas City was provided by these older, higher-status upper-middle-elite men. Through the years this group contributed most of Kansas City's Shrine potentates, American Legion commanders, Knights of Columbus and B'nai B'rith officers, presidents of the lesser-ranked luncheon clubs, and elders and deacons in the metropolitan prestige churches. Their wives officiated in church guilds and organizations like the Forum Federation, the Kansas City Musical Club, Daughters of the American Revolution, the Catholic Women's Circle, or Hadassah.

Elvin Porch was a typical member of this group. His law practice had been built almost entirely on services to individual clients. His only large client was the firm of a boyhood friend whose invention of an optical device resulted in a multi-million dollar business. Without this company and its patent rights, Elvin Porch would not have been so prosperous.

Elvin grew up in Sarcoxie, Missouri, and came to Kansas City to study law in night school. His wife was a small town girl, who went to a teachers' college in Kansas for two years. The Porches lived in a large, older Country Club District house, which was probably considered a mansion back in the early 1920s when it was built.

Elvin Porch was a Shriner and an ex-president of the Kansas City Bar Association. His wife had been very active through the years in a club that sponsored a small woman's college in Missouri and provided scholarships for deserving girls. She was also a past officer of the women's guild at the Country Club Baptist church, a few blocks from the Porch home.

Elvin Porch claimed to have "no interest whatsoever in Society doings." He did, however, maintain his membership at the Downtown Athletic Club, which he had joined in his younger days when he had enjoyed handball and swimming. Now, at sixty, he went to the club only occasionally for lunch or when he and his wife wanted to entertain guests.

Most of the lawyers, doctors, dentists, and other professional men who had reached upper-middle-elite status but had not moved higher were like Elvin Porch. Their backgrounds were small town, usually lower-middle; they were night school law graduates or men who for some reason had received their professional degrees three or four years later than average; and they had generally been slow in achieving their prosperity. Their clients or patients were usually Kansas City's "little people."

Upper-Middle-Marginal

The upper-middle-marginal life style might best be illustrated by referring again to the Austins and what their life style would have been had David Austin been somewhat less successful. The family would probably have lived in a smaller house in the Country Club District; they could not have afforded many of the activities of the Dance and Bridge Club, nor could they have managed to have a boat at the Nodaway Yacht Club. Ruth Austin would still have been active in the Kansas City Musical Club, the PTA, and Camp Fire Girls. She would probably have played bridge in the afternoon with at least some of the women in the Dance and Bridge Club, plus a few others who lived on more moderate incomes like herself. The Austins would have entertained their friends at home, instead of dining out frequently. In short, they would probably have done whatever they could on a below-average upper-middle income to maintain their connections with upper-middle friends.

About 6 per cent of white middle-aged families in Kansas City were marginal in status within the upper-middle class; this represents slightly over two-fifths of the total class. The men were educationally as well prepared as those of the core group. But they had achieved less occupational status by their middle years, and their standard of living was affected accordingly. A fourth of the wives in this group worked to help the family maintain an upper-middle life style. All of the marginal women maintained informal clique ties with upper-middle-core women and participated with them in those formal organizations which were not beyond their means.

The Wellmans were one type of upper-middle-marginal. The Wellmans lived in Prairie Village, a suburb often chosen by younger upper-middle couples. Their house was one of the smallest in Prairie Village and sparsely furnished compared to their neighbors' homes. Their car was an old model. Mr. Wellman taught high school English and journalism. Mrs. Wellman worked part time for a travel agency; she also wrote for a neighborhood newspaper. A sizable part of the Wellmans' combined income of ten thousand dollars a year was spent on classical records, books, prints, and theater tickets. They enjoyed participating in amateur theatrical productions and were also active in the Johnson County Democratic Club, a very small but vocal group in an overwhelming Republican area. The Wellmans did not use the swimming, tennis, and party facilities of the semiprivate Prairie Village Club.

The Wellmans were representative of a small, somewhat deviant group of upper-middles in Kansas City—concerned with cultural affairs but economically marginal and minimally integrated into the mainstream of upper-middle social life. The majority of the academic people and most of the ministers in the upper-middle class were more conventional than the Wellmans—they were Republicans and devoted church workers. The Wellmans' political behavior illustrates a point made by Seymour Lipset and Mildred A. Schwartz (Vollmer and Mills, 1966). They comment that, although persons in professional occupations are generally conservative politically, those in the lower-paid professions—such as teaching—are often liberal. Those liberal views result from frustration and the belief that the prevailing social order does not properly reward persons of their educational achievement and occupational contribution. Many low-salaried professionals—writers, artists, musicians, as well as schoolteachers—were connected, like the Wellmans, with the upper-middle class through their participation in semiprestigious community organizations.

Another type of marginal upper-middle were impoverished gentility like Ned and Alice Clay. The Clays' parents had been respected higher-status upper-middles. In his own adulthood, however, Mr. Clay had shifted from job to job as an artist for advertising agencies and department stores. Intermittently he experienced periods of ill health. Mrs. Clay had a small inherited income, but the Clays' standard of living was not up to average for the Country Club District. Despite their relative impoverishment, Mrs. Clay maintained several ties with the friends of her childhood and participated in several organizations composed mainly of upper-middle-elite and upper-class women. Mr. Clay had dropped all organizational activities.

Women like Mrs. Clay sometimes thought of themselves as part of the upper-middle-elite, but families like the Austins were inclined to disparage people like the Clays, referring to them as "the past-worshipping set"; they looked upon them as individuals who had fallen in status over the years but maintained pretensions of grandeur.

Age and Status

Upper-middle people who fit the public image of the managerial Country Club group were usually fifty to sixty-five years old. Had the study sample included families headed by men under forty, relatively few would yet have moved into the Country Club District, and only a few would have been members of a downtown men's club or a country club. It took most men the first twenty years of their adult lives to acquire these marks of upper-middle status.

The first ten or twelve years of adulthood, from age twenty-one through thirty-two, were, in the 1950s, a period for demonstrating one's abilities. At this age, inclusion in the upper-middle class was based on the potential provided by occupation, education, and family background. Young men and women were regarded as upper-middle if they were born into the class and had fulfilled its educational expectations, or if they were from lower-status groups but had acquired the appropriate educational qualifications and were accepted by established upper-middle young people. (David Austin was an example of this type. Although he was of lower-middle origin, he was clearly moving into the upper-middle world when he completed his college education. Graduation from college was achieved by only 7 per cent of American men born, as he was, between 1900 and 1904.)

In Kansas City in 1955, the typical upper-middle young man

was a managerial trainee moving into a job euphemistically called junior executive; he and his wife were living at a standard approximately equal to that of the average lower-middle family ten years their senior. The symbols of upper-middle status for such a couple were their anticipations for the future as well as their education.

The second ten years of adulthood, from approximately thirty-two to forty-two, was a period of increasing achievement. The majority of upper-middle men in this age bracket in 1954 were nearing full managerial status, were still living in a Prairie Village home, and had not yet joined a luncheon club or exclusive private club. (Many, however, had joined the Prairie Village Club, a neighborhood country club with tennis, swimming, and a clubhouse where members could dine out and entertain.)

The years between forty-three and fifty-five served as the period when a family's status crystallized at the core, elite, or marginal upper-middle level or when the move up to upper class was made.

In the ten years between fifty-five and sixty-five, the typical upper-middle family was experiencing a period of reward when the years of hard work paid off. It was common for companies to honor their long-time managerial-level employees with more honorific titles at this point in their careers. The change in job title was more of an honorarium, however, than a sign of increased responsibilities. Sometimes the men would be given a long-sought club membership and a salary increment, but seldom was he brought into the group of company officers who made the decisions on broad corporate policy.

This was the kind of final ten-year career with Mid-American Life that David Austin could look forward to. It meant the Austins could take longer vacations, even travel abroad if they wished, and that Mrs. Austin could have a mink coat. The Austins could save enough money during these years to retire later to Florida and to pass on a modest estate to their children.

This pattern of relationships between age and status characteristics was true of the upper-middle-core group. Men who moved faster tended to end up as elite, those who fell behind, as marginal.

The Corporate Class

The upper-middle class in Kansas City was essentially a class of managers and salaried professionals—or, in the vocabulary of William H. Whyte, Jr., of "organization men"—rather than independent business and professional people (Whyte, 1956). This stands somewhat in contrast to the upper-middle groups described in earlier community studies. The difference is mostly a reflection of the difference in size between Kansas City and the communities studied previously, but it also reflects the differences in American economic and occupational life in the 1950s as compared to the 1930s and 1940s. Among the middle-aged upper-middle men in the Kansas City sample, 66 per cent were organization men. Three-fourths of these men were employed by private enterprises, the rest by government agencies or religious, educational, and other service organizations. (It was estimated that 74 per cent of upper-middle men of all ages were salaried employees.) The dominance of salaried employees reflected Kansas City's urban economy, its position as one of America's main distribution centers, and its status as a branch office town for many large corporations. The middle-aged managerial men in Kansas City had, for the most part, been born elsewhere and moved to Kansas City as adults to advance their careers. The majority had moved up to the upper-middle status from lower-middle origins.

The veneration historically given in America to self-employment had been overturned among upper-middle Kansas Citians by the mid-1950s; the salary dollar purchased greater status at this level than the profit dollar or the fee dollar. Independent professional men in the upper-middle class were considered only moderately successful. Corporation lawyers, for example, were somewhat more esteemed than lawyers in their own small firms; similarly, the accountant or engineer who worked for a large consulting firm or held a high-level position within a corporation was of higher status than his self-employed counterpart of equal income.

Participation Patterns

Upper-middles in Kansas City were not a group who occupied visible positions of leadership in civic affairs; these positions were held, instead, by upper-class men and women. Nor, as has been described of upper-middles in other communities, were they a front group for the upper class. Rather, they were the grass roots (as one Capital S man put it) who aided the upper class in a manner that was by and large unnoticed by the wider Kansas City public.

A spirit of reform dominated Kansas City government in the early 1950s (a reaction to the machine-dominated government that had controlled the city under Pendergast from the 1920s to the early 1940s). The mayor and city council members had been elected by a nonpartisan citizens' association, and appointees to municipal boards and commissions were chosen by the mayor in consultation with the leaders of this association. One influential citizen said of the political structure of the city government: "The country clubs are running Kansas City now—people from the First Jackson and Missoukana country clubs are the leaders in the Citizens' Association, and the people who live in the Country Club District give them the numerical support which insures their victory at the polls." This statement aptly described the roles of upper- and upper-middle class men and women in Kansas City government and in civic and cultural affairs. Almost all the city's leaders came from the upper class and their helper-followers from the upper-middle. Comparatively few upper-middle people—mostly from the younger upper-middle-elites who were moving toward upper-class status—served on boards and committees of citywide importance. Other upper-middle people were given leadership posts only when they possessed a special, relevant expertise.

The role of upper-middle people in city affairs was mainly to support Citizens' Association candidates, raise money during fund drives, and serve as leaders in their own neighborhoods. In a city as large as Kansas City there was not much room for people in leadership positions who were not near the social, financial, and professional summits—opportunities were occasionally given to young upper-middles showing leadership potential. (Only in small, predominantly upper-middle suburbs did upper-middles play important governmental roles—on their suburban town councils, park boards, school committees, and zoning commissions.)

As the generation of upper-middles who had come into adulthood during the 1930s was reaching middle age, Kansas Citians of this class were noticing changes in the kind of clubs and social activities that were popular. Among men, the major change perceived was a shift from the old dominance of fraternal organizations to expense-account social life in the private clubs. An older upper-middle man, a little unhappy with the change, commented: "Today all the clubs are run by businessmen whose companies pay their dues so they can entertain out there. The volume of business transacted at the clubs probably exceeds the amount done in business offices. This is a big change from the days when fraternal organizations—which now seem to be dying out—were the thing. It's all part of the expense-account revolution. None of the younger men in my organization are joining the Masons and bothering with all those rituals and degrees you have to go through in order to become a Shriner."

Much of this change was a by-product of the upper-middle class transition from being a group of independent business and professional men to being the class of organization men. Earlier much of the reason for joining fraternal orders was to meet people in other businesses who could become customers or clients. Part of the change was generational, however, almost irrespective of occupations. The older men in the study sample were much more often members of fraternal groups than the younger men. (Of those over fifty-five years of age, 67 per cent were either Masons, Knights of Columbus, or members of B'nai B'rith; of those under fifty-five, only 37 per cent were in one of these fraternal groups.)

Among women, the most noticeable change was a decline in interest in the clubs that emphasized a "ladylike interest in culture," and an increasing interest in clubs devoted to social issues, causes, and charities. Concern with self-uplift had given way to social welfare. An older woman not entirely pleased with this trend said: "All our women's groups are possessed with the idea of raising money for some cause or another. We have to spend all our time on charity projects, and we are eternally having bazaars to raise money—well, there's nothing bizarre about bazaars anymore."

In the 1920s the Forum Federation had been the dominant upper-middle women's club. (One of its presidents said, "We think of it as the married woman's college.") In the middle 1950s it had yielded its position to The Service Club, the American Association of University Women, the League of Women Voters, and The Philharmonic League. These were the clubs that younger upper-middle women hoped to have time for, along with the Kansas City Panhellenic and their sorority alumnae units. In these clubs the spirit of "being politically active," "doing for others," and "raising money" reigned. The members no longer "sat back and absorbed" culture.

Chapter 8

Lower-Middle Class

*T*hroughout the 1950s American magazines carried many articles asking: "Are blue-collar workers becoming middle class?" The assumption was that the middle class had earlier been restricted to white-collar workers, professionals, and businessmen. The view—probably inaccurate—that in previous periods there were no middle class blue-collar workers stems perhaps from the presumption of an inherent separation between management and labor. Such a view does not fit the everyday realities of social interaction observed in small towns through the past forty years nor does it fit Kansas City in the mid-1950s.[1]

[1] In Yankee City, only a small majority of lower-middle men (54 per cent) were in white-collar employment, with 46 per cent in blue-collar jobs (Warner and Lunt, 1941). Those data refer to 1934 and provide persuasive evidence that for a long time there has not been a clear line in social interaction between white-collar and blue-collar workers. Ten years later, the situation in Jonesville was much the same; 62 per cent of the lower-middle class men were classified as white-collar (Hollingshead, 1949). And the Lynds (Lynd and Lynd, 1937), viewing Middletown in 1935, said "trusted foremen, building trades craftsmen of long standing, and the pick of [its] experienced and highly-skilled machinists" were socially closer, as a group, to the "clerks, clerical workers, and civil servants" than to the "mass of wage earners . . . the numerically dominant working class." The lowest proportion of blue-collar workers in the lower-middle class is the 16 per cent re-

158

If the sample studied in Kansas City were classified according to census categories, 75 per cent of the middle-aged, lower-middle class men would be grouped as white-collar (professional, technical, proprietary, managerial, sales, and clerical) and 25 per cent as blue-collar (craftsmen, foremen, skilled or semi-skilled operatives, and service workers). If the popular meaning in Kansas City of blue-collar versus white-collar were followed, the blue-collar group would be increased by 13 per cent, to a total of 38 per cent of the lower-middle men. In either case, the Kansas City lower-middle class consisted mainly of white-collar sales, clerical, and semi-professional employees. The real factor in Kansas City was not a split between blue-collar and white-collar workers but in the life styles of families as shown in choice of neighborhood, friends, and formal associations.

When Kansas Citians talked about "a lower-middle class group," they meant people who lived in "nice, pleasant five or six room frame bungalows in the South East side along Benton Boulevard and Prospect, or in suburbs like Mission, Kansas, or Overland Park or Shawnee." They meant home- or church-centered people who voted Republican in national and state elections and for the reform Citizens' Association in city elections, and who sent their children to college. Lower-middle class was a designation most such people applied to themselves, and it was a phrase other Kansas Citians found most natural in characterizing the third of their city's population who fit these descriptions.

Lower-middle class families were linked to one another by a formal network of organizations, churches, and schools, and by an informal network of socializing in the neighborhood and/or with "friends from the job" and "just old friends." They were separated into elite, core, and marginal levels not so much by participation and interaction patterns as by the deference accorded to particular

---

ported for New Haven (Hollingshead and Redlich, 1958). In Kansas City the lower-middle class could appropriately be described as white-collar, however, with regard to its employed women. Twenty-five per cent of lower-middle women in the age range were employed, almost all as teachers, social workers, secretaries, or salesclerks. Beauty operators who owned their shops or worked part-time in a friend's shop came closest to being employed in demeaning work. For a woman to work in a factory or in certain kinds of stores or service capacities was regarded by Kansas Citians as not sufficiently proper for a middle-class person.

occupations, levels of education and income, and aspects of residence. The differences between the people of these three levels were not so sharp as to preclude interaction or make it uncomfortable. Indeed, it was through formal and informal interaction patterns that the class was unified.

Lower-Middle-Core

Seventy per cent of the middle-aged men in the lower-middle-core were white-collar clerical, sales, and technical workers; the rest of the core was split between the families of proprietors and contractors and those of respected blue-collar workers. These core-level families constituted over half of the middle-aged lower-middle population, and their way of life defined characteristic styles of the class. In keeping with the image, they were home- or church-centered people; they lived in "pleasant, average" homes, almost always on the "right side of town"; and they attended churches near their homes. Usually both husbands and wives were high school graduates and a great many of these men and women had received additional education from a business college or technical institute.

Changing Patterns: In speaking of this class, Kansas Citians overdrew the picture of the punctilious clerk, a picture that was probably more realistic in bygone years than in the 1950s. In 1954, only 11 per cent of the men in the lower-middle sample were reminiscent of that type, and they were all nearing retirement, like Wallace Parkinson. At fifty-three, Parkinson was a freight rate clerk for the Missouri and Gulf Coast Railroad. He had been with the line for thirty-four years and prided himself both on his loyalty to the company and his arrival at the office at 8:00 a.m. each day. In 1954 he received a salary of about four hundred dollars a month, which placed him near the bottom of the income scale for middle-aged lower-middle men. He and his wife lived in a six room bungalow located in a South Side neighborhood that real estate men called the center of low-paid white-collar workers in Kansas City.

The difference in the education of the Parkinsons and their children reflected the changing times. The Parkinsons were high school graduates; their children had graduated from junior colleges. The Parkinsons each belonged to only one club, but they usually attended services at the neighborhood Methodist church. When not "remaining quietly at home," they spent their leisure "visiting their few old friends, going to a movie, or taking a drive to some place of historical interest." The advent of television had meant that Parkinson devoted less time to his coin collection. His wife managed to crochet and watch TV at the same time, so that her habits were little changed by this invention. Men like Parkinson had become something of an anachronism by 1954, because most jobs like his had been taken over by women or by machines. Technicians were taking the place of the "tight white-collar" man at the lower-middle levels of Kansas City corporations. They usually worked in industrial laboratories or in the computer rooms of businesses, universities, or government offices.

In Kansas City in 1954, most men in the latter jobs were under forty. A few, however, like Perry Harnischfeger were older. Harnischfeger earned $6,300 a year as a laboratory assistant at the National Oil Refinery. The Harnischfegers occupied a moderately priced, newer home in suburban Raytown. Harnischfeger drove to work; there was no public transportation to the industrial area where he worked. The Harnischfegers seldom went into downtown Kansas City, doing all their shopping in the Raytown Village Center. The Harnischfegers were typical mid-1950s suburbanites. They exemplified the postwar trend wherein lower-middle people in city after city moved from older urban neighborhoods to newer suburban ones.

The Johansen and Scott families illustrate the change in participation patterns from the older style joiners to the new style doers that was also taking place in the lower-middle class in the 1950s. Chris Johansen was a grocer in an old, lower-middle section of the city. He was an active member of the Benton Boulevard Masons, the fraternal order of Modern Woodmen, and the 40 Et 8 Society of the American Legion. He was also on the executive committee of the Retail Grocers Association—an organization composed of most of the city's smaller neighborhood grocers—and had served it in the past as secretary, treasurer, and vice-president. Both Mr. and Mrs. Johansen were active in the Immanuel Augustana Lutheran Church a block down the street from their store; Chris had frequently been chairman of its board of deacons.

The social life of joiners like the Johansens coincides with one of the dominant images about the lower-middle class which has emerged from studies of America's small towns dating from the 1920s through the early 1940s. In Kansas City, lower-middle joiners were commonly found among men and women over fifty and among the families of independent businessmen. Most of Kansas City's lower-middle tradesmen maintained social interaction patterns like those of their social equals in the Jonesvilles and Prairie Cities of America. They were the most socially active members of the lower-middle-core in fraternal orders, brotherhood lodges, and veterans' associations. Of necessity, they belonged to a commercial association or two. It was also to their interest to join social organizations where they might develop customers. For them, these organizations served much the same function as country clubs and luncheon clubs did for upper-middle and upper class businessmen.

The community activity engaged in by the Ralph Scotts, on the other hand, was more typical of the younger, salaried families in the lower-middle-core. As a supervisor of PBX installations and repairs for Missouri Bell Telephone, Ralph Scott earned nine thousand dollars in 1954. The Scott home, a one-and-one-half story seven room brick house, was located in a neighborhood ranked just below the Country Club District in social desirability. Ralph was a scoutmaster and he was also coach to one of the neighborhood's little league baseball teams. He was serving on a committee trying to build a neighborhood youth center. Mrs. Scott was a room mother for her daughter's grade school class, and PTA membership chairman at the high school her son attended. The Scotts were not interested in the fraternal organizations and auxiliaries, for as Ralph Scott put it: "I can't see the purpose in them—you can't feel you're doing something for your children, and for the young people, in organizations like that."

There were always a certain number of lower-middle people who were active in organizations serving young people, but the postwar years in Kansas City witnessed a tremendous increase in their number. There were more children to do for in the 1950s than before, and their parents had more leisure hours in which to participate in these organizations. Moreover, this change in lower-middle participation from social to community service paralleled the changes observed at upper-middle and upper class levels.

Typical Patterns: The lower-middle-core families already described, although they symbolized the most notable changes in life styles of people at this level, were not numerically dominant types. Church-centered families and very quiet, home-centered families were more common types to be found in the lower-middle-core.

The Enoch Smiths were very devoted to their church, the Reorganized Latter Day Saints (the Missouri brand of Mormonism) and donated one-tenth of their income to it. They were among the highest income couples in the lower-middle-core because both of them were employed. Enoch Smith was the office manager of a small manufacturing concern, and Mrs. Smith was the bookkeeper and secretary for a small insurance office. Their combined income totaled slightly over ten thousand dollars in 1954, and they felt "comfortably fixed." The Smiths had an adopted son who was attending college in Idaho on a scholarship provided by the church. The Smiths described themselves as "quiet—not social at all." Their friends were "all nice church people."

The Briskobies also considered themselves "quiet-living," but they were home-centered rather than church-centered. Harry Briskobie, fifty-five, was a salesman for one of Kansas City's large wholesale grocery houses. His income of about six thousand dollars a year placed him almost in the middle of the lower-middle-core. He and his wife lived in an eighteen thousand dollar Cape Cod house considered "one of the nicest homes in Prairie Village." The Briskobies' terraced garden was the showplace of their block. Mrs. Briskobie gardened outdoors in summer and in a glassed-in porch in the winter. Mr. Briskobie also preferred to spend his spare time at home and in the garden rather than "at some lodge meeting."

The quiet lives of the Briskobies and the Smiths were characteristic of 40 per cent of middle-aged lower-middle men and women. For these families, having a "dream home" took primacy, and they usually occupied housing that was considered "above Southside average" in quality. In almost half of these families, the wife was employed—a major reason being her desire to furnish "the house of her dreams" according to her wishes.

Lower-Middle-Elite

Seventeen per cent of lower-middle families occupied a position of superior status within the class because of their jobs or their income level. The average lower-middle person deferred to schoolteachers and to ministers, for example, as men and women of superior education who performed a more valued service than he did. He also respected the moderately prospering independent enter- prisers and the higher-income, semi-managerial families who lived in the above average houses which lined the leading boulevards or occupied corner lots in his neighborhood.

The professional and higher income families were expected to provide leadership for the rest of the lower-middle class in the churches, PTAs, fraternal lodges, and American Legion posts. Whether or not they actually exercised such leadership, the men and women of elite status were regarded as the most competent people in the lower-middle class.

Kansas Citians had a name, The Benton Boulevard Crowd, for one type of lower-middle-elite who lived along the street that earlier had been a center of the upper-middle class. The Benton Boulevard people, who were looked down upon by contemporary upper-middles as "behind the times" or "just sort of corny" people, in turn made fun of "the Country Club crowd." They ridiculed its "pretensions" and took pride in their own lack of them. One of the most effective spokesmen for the Benton Boulevard ethic was a school administrator:

> We've got a stabilized middle-class group of people here who only buy what they can afford to pay for. And we don't run from the doorbell, for fear it's a bill collector on overdue pay- ments. That's what a lot of those people who live out in the Country Club District do. . . . We aren't trying to keep up with the Joneses here like they are out in Southwest and John- son County. We don't go traipsing around from one part of the city to another keeping up with the social swim. But, now, if you go to the pop concerts where the public doesn't get dressed up and act highbrow, you'll find a good many of us. We've got a genuine appreciation of good music and art and fine literature, and we don't want to be bothered with folderol and rigamarole that has nothing to do with real culture. We're not your codfish aristocracy.

Most of the families in the Benton Boulevard Crowd were prosperous self-employed business or professional men. A great many of them were raised on midwestern farms or in very small towns, an important factor in explaining their decision to move in the less sophisticated lower-middle world instead of the upper-middle.

At the opposite end of the lower-middle income scale were low salaried professionals, like Reverend Raymond Doering. At sixty, Reverend Doering was sent by the national board of his denomination to Raytown, a lower-middle class suburb, to found a new church. He had been chosen for this task because the national board considered him a successful minister and a man likely to appeal to the young families of Raytown. Reverend Doering's success as a minister, nevertheless, was not like that of the ministers of Kansas City's prestigious metropolitan or Country Club churches. He had steadily advanced through a succession of ever larger churches in ever larger centers of commerce scattered through the Midwest, but he had always served congregations of small town and farm people like the families among whom he had grown up.

As in Reverend Doering's case, the social class of ministers quite often depends on the kind of religion preached and the type of parishioners. The largest number of ministers in Kansas City were found among the lower-middle-elite; they led the smaller churches which served mainstream denominations and were located in ordinary middle-class or working-class neighborhoods. Ministers who were affiliated with the smallest churches of respected denominations or with larger fundamentalist churches were generally marginal within the lower-middle class.

The range in the status of teachers was smaller than for ministers. Most public schoolteachers were either upper-middle-marginals or lower-middle-elite, a matter usually determined by their social origins or by the subject they taught. For example, most vocational arts teachers were lower-middle-elite, whereas journalism teachers and drama teachers tended to be upper-middle-marginals.

No other group of families in Kansas City felt as underappreciated and economically underprivileged as the schoolteachers, ministers, and social workers of the lower-middle-elite and upper-middle-marginal levels. If only the husband was employed, and if he was not holding a second job, the family's income was $5,500 or $6,000 a year, slightly below average for lower-middle families. To meet the material standards of lower-middle life was difficult for these families, who often had special professional and cultural expenses. These highly educated but low-income professionals were examples of extreme disparity between educational background on the one hand and income and social position on the other.

A happier balance between education, income, and social position occurred in the higher-income white-collar families, where the men had typically graduated from high school, gone to business college, and then gotten a job in the office of a local manufacturing firm or utility company. By middle age, these men had been promoted to semi-managerial positions or were semi-successful in medium sized businesses, where they earned, in 1954, from $7,500 to $10,000. The way these higher-income families in the lower-middle-elite spent their money and the goals they pursued contrasted sharply with those of families at the same income level who were upper-middle-marginals. They felt they had already achieved the house and the neighborhood they wanted to live in; they had basement recreation rooms instead of addresses in the Country Club District. They drove Buicks, Oldsmobiles, or Chryslers, not Chevrolets, Fords or Plymouths like the upper-middle-marginals. Many of them owned motor boats. They frequently went out to dinner, and every now and then to one of Kansas City's night spots, but they had not tried to enter the more formal and organized world of the town and country clubs.

By and large it was the women of these families who did not aspire for the upper-middle-marginal associations which their husbands' occupations or incomes might permit. These wives had chosen to live in lower-middle neighborhoods, although in the nicer houses. Some whose husbands were earning as much as twenty thousand dollars a year enjoyed being able to spend freely on their homes and furnishings.

The majority of these wives had not gone to college, although a few had attended teachers' colleges, small denominational schools, or municipal junior colleges. Generally, they were no better educated than the wives in lower-middle-core or marginal. These women were not members of the AAUW or the League of Women Voters, as were many of the upper-middle-marginal wives. They were absent from the cultural and civic clubs and from college alumnae chapters. They were more often homebodies or women who preferred lodge auxiliaries and church guilds. And they did not use church membership to establish social ties with higher status women.

Lower-Middle-Marginal

The slightly inferior position of the lower-middle-marginals can be attributed to the lack of some of the symbols associated with acceptance at the lower-middle-core. These were white-collar workers whose incomes and housing fell slightly short of typical lower-middle standards, or they were middle-aged blue-collar workers who met all criteria for lower-middle status except for occupation—they fell short of the middle class ideal of a "clean office job."

The largest number of lower-middle-marginals were the social top crust, or aristocracy, of the blue-collar world. The men held jobs as railroad section foremen, cross-continental bus drivers, engine overhaul foremen for airline companies, chief electricians, linotype operators, or chief engineers for downtown business buildings. Husband and wife were usually of northern European ancestry, at least second- or third-generation Americans. They lived in the respected South Side neighborhoods and belonged to churches and clubs located there. A majority of their children at least started college. Blue-collar families of this type were readily accepted in Kansas City as part of the lower-middle class, and they were quite distant from the working class in their patterns of social participation.

Along with these blue-collar aristocrats, all of whose incomes met or exceeded the lower-middle average, another group of non-white-collar families, sometimes with lesser incomes, also seemed to belong to the lower-middle-marginals. These were families headed by mailmen, milk route drivers, barbers, firemen, police officers, shipping clerks, and express men. Kansas Citians did not usually label such families as blue-collar because the jobs were not dirty, or manual; instead they referred to them as gray-collar, white-overalls, or blue-uniform workers.

Tom and Maryland Colding were a gray-collar family. Tom delivered milk for the Allen Dairy. Before World War II and after finishing high school, he had held a job as a clerk in an auto supply store. He came back from the war determined to earn a better income, so he applied to the dairy. The occupational aspirations of his earlier years were displaced onto his sons: "You can bet your bottom dollar that they're going to get a college degree so they can have executive jobs." Thrift had been a byword with the Coldings. They bought an old house of 1920 vintage, instead of a new house in the postwar suburbs, because they got it "for a steal." With do-it-yourself vigor, they remodeled it to produce that "trim mid-twentieth-century look" advocated at that time by *American Home* magazine, and they decorated the interior in imitation of the cheerful, homey atmosphere encouraged in *Ladies Home Journal.*

Although the Colding home was in a lower-middle class neighborhood, it was one short block away from the Paseo neighborhood and placed the Coldings in a school district where many students came from lower-middle-elite families.

The Coldings were almost as active in the youth-serving organizations as Ralph and Marjorie Scott. Tom was an assistant scoutmaster and Maryland was a Cub den mother. Tom coached the junior basketball team at the Presbyterian church on the Paseo, and Maryland was a homeroom worker for the PTA. (She would like to have been a PTA officer, but she recognized that the "women who hold those offices always live across Paseo, in the better homes there.") The Coldings' social life did not extend much beyond those organizational participations, because, as Tom said, "on my income [$5,700 a year], you can't do too much and have money left over for the things that count most—our home and the boys' education." One night a month, however, they went square dancing with seven other couples from the church. Tom listed the occupations of the men in the group as assistant traffic manager of the Missouri and Rocky Mountain Railroad, accountant at Missouri-Kansas Natural Gas, office supervisor, schoolteacher, PBX installer, electrical contractor, and salesman at Auerbach's men's clothing store downtown.

A third group of lower-middle-marginals were those who might be called "frayed white-collar workers," to signify their relative poverty within the lower-middle world. These men had jobs as salesmen in neighborhood hardware stores or in auto supply houses, as bookkeepers and payroll clerks for small cleaning plants or manufacturing firms, as message routing clerks at Western Union, or as voter registration clerks for the county government. About one in three lower-middle-marginals were of this type.

Taking the lower-middle-marginals as a whole, three characteristics are worth noting. One was the money and pride invested in their homes. Their houses represented, on an average, the highest investment per dollar of income found at any of the thirteen social strata. Indeed, the lower-middle-marginals were the only group for whom the market value of their homes averaged more than double their annual incomes.

A second distinguishing feature was that the wives were usually high school graduates—their median educational level was 12.2 years of schooling, considerably more than the 8.9 years of the average working class wife. While the men were not quite as well educated as their wives, their average of 11.7 years of schooling marked them as considerably superior in education to the average working class man, for whom the median was 8.7 years. Finally, 57 per cent of the grown children of lower-middle-marginal families had attended college for a year or more, compared to 29 per cent of working class-elites.

The third characteristic that distinguished this group from the working class is that it contained the highest percentage of Protestants of any middle status group in the city. This is a reflection of the extent to which blue-collar and gray-collar families who were interacting as lower-middle class people were of old-line Yankee and Northern European ancestry, blessed as it were with an Anglo-Saxon heritage.

Lower-Middle as a Social Class

In smaller communities the lower-middle class has sometimes been characterized as the top stratum in a middle-majority world of the "little people"; in other instances it has been looked upon as the lowest stratum in the top half of society, having more in common with the upper-middle class than the upper-lower.[2] To the extent

[2] In the community studies conducted in the 1930s—Yankee City, Middletown, Deep South—the lower-middle class was described as more closely related psychologically and occupationally to the upper-middle than to the upper-lower (or working) class. But this view was reexamined after the study of Jonesville, when Warner reported that "a considerable social distance separates the upper-middle class from the levels of the common man" and frequently referred to the lower-middle class in Jonesville as "the top of the common man level." Subsequently Kahl, integrating the ideas presented by C. Wright Mills in *White Collar* (1951) and the findings from Hollingshead's work in New Haven, referred to the lower-middle class as "the top stratum of 'the little people'" (Kahl, 1957).

that Kansas City's lower-middles showed more similarity to one class than another, it was to the group above, not to the one below. This was demonstrated in many ways. Thirty-seven per cent of lower-middle people belonged to associations in which one-third or more of the members were upper-middle in status—a church, a formally organized club, or an informal clique; but only 12 per cent belonged to a group (other than a labor union) where one-third or more of the members were working class. The occupational character of the lower-middle class—with white-collar workers, professional people, and businessmen included—was more like that of the upper-middle class than the working class. Over one-third lived in neighborhoods where upper-middle people lived; but only 18 per cent lived in neighborhoods where working class people predominated. High school diplomas and college attendance prevailed in both the lower-middle and upper-middle classes but were rare among working class adults. The majority of lower- and upper-middle children attended college, but only a small percentage of working class children did so. Finally, the lower- and upper-middle classes voted Republican; the working class voted Democratic. The only respects in which this group was more like working class than upper-middle were in income and standard of housing.

All this is not to suggest that the lower-middle class was really only the lower half of one vast middle class, for it had its own self-contained interactional system, its own world of churches, grade schools, and high schools, and its own chapters of brotherhood lodges and women's auxiliaries. More than half of the lower-middle men and women in the middle-aged sample had limited formal or informal contact with either upper-middle or working class people. For these reasons, the lower-middle class in Kansas City can be described as a class unto itself, separate from the upper-middle as well as from the working class.

Within the overall social structure of Kansas City, and with the exception of the lower class—to be described in a later chapter— the lower-middle class was the least vocal and the least well-represented as a special interest group. It had few spokesmen in the councils of government; it was a bystander in the struggles between management and labor. Lower-middle class people considered upper-class leaders their representatives, but it is unreasonable to assume that this latter group served the particular needs of the lower-middle class in an effective way.

We have already mentioned some of the ways in which the lower-middle was different from the classes above and below, but the special character of lower-middle life can better be understood in light of additional facts.

Housing: In 1954 the neighborhoods of Kansas City's lower-middle class exuded an aura of the quiet, comfortable life. The streets were tree lined, the yards neatly trimmed, the homes well maintained. This was an inevitable concomitant of the attitude that home and neighborhood were the cornerstones of the good life. The basic standard for housing was one which had prevailed through the 1930s and the 1940s when most lower-middle families had only one or two children. This was a home with two or three bedrooms, one bathroom, a living room, dining room, and kitchen. Usually the house was less than thirty years old. Ninety-one per cent of middle-aged lower-middle families occupied housing at least this good. Those who did not were either marginal in status or retired couples who had formerly lived in equivalent housing. Nearly half of the middle-aged lower-middles occupied homes above this basic standard.

More than four-fifths of middle-aged lower-middle families lived in neighborhoods "on the right side of the tracks" or "in the better half of town." The others usually lived in a small enclave of middle-class housing located in a working class district. The location of their homes was important to lower-middle families, because it determined the kind of neighbors they had and the schools their children attended. Lower-middle Kansas Citians wanted to live in neighborhoods where people of markedly lower financial or social status were not present; they certainly did not want to live in neighborhoods where all classes could meet and mingle.

With the rising birth rate of the postwar years, there was a change in housing goals. By the late 1950s, younger lower-middle couples were demanding three or four bedrooms and two bathrooms as a minimum, and preferably a family room as well. A separate dining room was, at that time, not considered imperative.

A Church-Centered Class? It was commonly assumed in Kansas City that people of the lower-middle socioeconomic stratum went to church regularly, and that church participation provided the center for their social lives, exceeding fraternal lodges or private clubs in amount of attention and membership.

This assumption was only partly true. The church was indeed the center of the social lives of those families who were actively involved and, for many, a source of inspiration. The church was especially important as source of inspiration for Catholics, Baptists, Lutherans, and members of the Latter Day Saints at this status level. To members of these denominations, the social meanings of the church were often secondary to the moral and spiritual commitments. The lives of lower-middle men and women of these denominations could properly be called religion-centered, as distinguished from church-centered.

Only about 30 per cent of the lower-middle class found the church a social equivalent to the upper-middle class country club. For this 30 per cent, the social functions of week night suppers, men's clubs, bowling leagues, dances for teen-agers, and women's guilds, together with regular attendance at Sunday Services, represented their most important form of social participation.

Among the lower-middle people who attended church or at least held a membership, all but a small number did so mainly at middle-class neighborhood churches which were affiliated with the mainstream denominations—Presbyterian, Methodist, Disciples of Christ, Baptist, Lutheran, and Catholic. Only 9 per cent participated in churches in which the majority of members were working class.

Among the 37 per cent who did not attend church and the additional number who maintained only a symbolic affiliation, only a tiny fraction had rejected formal religious affiliation. Many had simply become bored with church attendance and ceased to bother once their children were grown.

The fairest assessment of the role of religion in lower-middle class life might be that for one-third—those for whom the church was of great importance—it was probably more important than for upper-middle and upper-class churchgoers. (In these higher classes, church membership and activity was often carried on principally as a symbolic assertion of gentility, or community responsibility.) Overall, the lower-middle class evidenced a great diversity in

attitudes and practices regarding religion, the church, and theo-
logical beliefs.

A Class of Joiners? It is a common belief that Americans
are joiners, and some observers have implied that this is especially
true of the lower-middle class. Kansas Citians, however, were not
inclined to picture lower-middle people in those terms. The more
common view was that most of the social life of people at that level
took place in the home with friends and neighbors, if not at church.

Our findings support the Kansas Citian's view. Middle-aged
lower-middle men averaged 1.3 club memberships (excluding labor
union memberships) and women averaged 1.0 memberships. In 60
per cent of families, neither husband nor wife belonged to more than
one formal association, including men's groups and women's guilds
at churches; and only 10 per cent of men and 4 per cent of women
were members of four or more organizations. Only 19 per cent of
lower-middle men and 8 per cent of the women were as active as
those in the upper-middle class, where both men and women averaged three memberships. In fact, most of Kansas City's joiners were
in the upper-middle and upper classes. (See Table 2, "Social Characteristics of the Five Classes," in Chapter Four.)

Joining was most prevalent among the lower-middle-elite.
Moreover, as men and women passed through middle age their
organizational activity declined. Men tended to drop out of the
lodges or business clubs they had joined when they were younger,
and women dropped out of parent and youth-serving organizations
as their children grew up.

The memberships most commonly held by lower-middle
men, outside those connected with their occupation, were in fraternal orders and church groups; only half as many were active in
those organizations, however, as upper-middle men. Church guild
membership was most common among lower-middle women, but
again, a lower proportion of lower-middle women were active in
these groups than of upper-middle women.

Respectability: Lower-middle Kansas Citians judged one
another on the type of clothing, personal grooming (a "ladylike
personal appearance"), habits of speech, choice of friends and associates, forms of parental discipline, and aspirations for children.
Families who could not pass muster on these matters were not accepted as associates by other lower-middle families.

The middle-aged families at this level showed marked stability in family life. There had been very few divorces (slightly fewer than in the upper-middle class and 30 per cent fewer than in the working class). The average number of children per woman was only 1.9 and the great concern was to be able to do well by these children. The 20 per cent of lower-middle class wives who worked for extra income were not career-oriented nor champions of the rights of women; rather, they wanted money for better homes, better clothes, long term security, and more interesting vacations.

Kahl has used the phrase *respectability* to characterize the lower-middle class in other communities (Kahl, 1957). It is appropriate to apply this phrase also to Kansas City, as long as the term is not narrowly interpreted, and as long as it is not inferred that the lower-middle holds a monopoly as compared to other classes. The respectability which the Kansas City lower-middle class seemed to cherish, and which separated it from the working class, was related to their children's schooling and the symbolic values associated with choices in housing, neighborhood, clothing, church, and associates. The lower-middle class in Kansas City might best be described as the "better-homes-and-families" class. These two things were, in the final analysis, more crucial than attending church, joining clubs, or voting Republican.

Chapter **9**

Working
Class

$\mathcal{A}$s in other communities, people in the working class comprised the largest group in the Kansas City metropolitan area. Their fellow citizens described them as "North Siders, but not slumdwellers," "people who work in factories, but aren't really poor," "the ordinary working class." These were the city's carpenters, mechanics, electricians, plumbers, toolmakers, crane operators, railroad brakemen and switchmen, millwrights, and molders, as well as the steadily employed assembly line workers.

The middle-aged families in the working class, 40 per cent of the total sample, were predominantly rural or small town in origin. Only 29 per cent had grown up in metropolitan Kansas City. As a group they were not distinguished from the lower-middle class by ethnic or religious characteristics.[1] Only 6 per cent were born outside the United States, and the great majority were fifth- or sixth-generation Americans of English, Scotch, or Irish descent, or second- and third-generation Scandinavian and German. Twelve per cent were Negro. Thus, the distinction between those in the working class and those in the higher classes of Kansas City was not so much one of family name or ancestry as of occupation, income, educa-

[1] For a description of an urban working class that is more ethnic in composition than that of Kansas City, see Glazer and Moynihan (1963).

175

tional level, living standards, ambitions, and choice of neighborhood.

Working class men and women were not nearly as well educated, for example, as those of lower-middle class, and their educational aspirations for their children were not so high. They wanted to raise their children right, and hoped to send them to college; but in reality, high school graduation was accepted as sufficient. In supporting 65 per cent of their children through high school, nevertheless, these working class parents were giving their children three and a half more years of schooling, on the average, than they had had.

Working class Kansas Citians were less club conscious and attended church less often than middle class. The typical woman at this level was not interested in organizations: she saw herself as a housewife whose first duties were to her children, husband, home, and to those of her relatives who lived nearby. Few felt themselves capable of undertaking such activities as Girl Scout leader or PTA chairman. The typical man preferred to spend his spare time watching a ball game, going fishing, or "hoisting a beer with the boys," rather than in group activities directed toward community service or self-improvement. When he joined a club, it was usually for recreation, for "getting out of the house and having fun."

One of the main aspirations of the average working class family was stability in family life and finances. Kansas Citians of this level showed less social aspiration than people at the higher levels; they were more concerned about being "away from the slums" than about being in a higher-status neighborhood as such. Their financial aspirations, however, were as great or greater than those of the lower-middle class. The typical worker was very much interested in his labor union because it contributed to his job security and to a better income. He wanted to "put something away for retirement," and in the meantime to buy as many of the symbols of modern living as possible: new and bigger cars, television sets, recreation equipment, kitchen appliances, and other laborsaving devices. Working class men and women were trying as hard as they could to "keep up with the times," as the advertisements in stores, newspapers, and television suggested. In short, the goal was to be modern, if not middle class.[2]

    [2] More recent studies of working-class families have been summarized in Shostak and Gomberg (1964). Other useful references include Berger (1960), Komarovsky (1964), and Rainwater, Coleman, and Handel (1959).

Like the classes above, the working class in Kansas City had differentiations within it. At the top was a small number of people, one of every eight working class families, who were markedly more affluent or more visible than the average. They were regarded as superior in status by the rest of their class.

In the middle were the great bulk of working class families, comprising over 25 per cent of Kansas City's total middle-aged population. Families like these gave the working class its basic character in the eyes of the wider public: they were the working-class-core.

Below them were families who were often described as "a lower level of working class—they're not doing too well financially, but you can't really call them a lower class." One of every four working class families seemed to fit this description, living in neighborhoods where the standard of housing was somewhat below that which prevailed in the better districts of the North Side. Generally these families had not had so long a history of steady work at good rates of pay as families in the working-class-core. Their status within the class was marginal and their financial status often precarious. They were the "poor but decent" members of this class.

All three groups can be regarded as members of the working class because they lived in proximity to one another in the less favored sections of the city; they were not integrated into lower-middle neighborhoods, churches, or associations; and none was so poorly housed or disreputable in behavior as to be identified with the lower class.

Working-Class-Elite

The working-class-elite provide a vivid illustration of the complexity of the concept of social class. These people had considerably higher incomes than in two social strata above them (their median income in 1954 dollars was $7,400, compared to $6,300 for the lower-middle class as a whole), yet they were not part of the lower-middle class for they did not live in its neighborhoods, participate in its church and club activities, nor send their children to its schools. Their high incomes reflected employment in the highest paid crafts, as foremen and superintendents, as union officials, as plumbing contractors, or as service station owners.

These families were content to have their houses only a few

blocks away from a factory, or in unincorporated areas along unimproved streets. They were unconcerned about the outside appearance of their houses, so long as the inside was spacious and equipped with all the latest home appliances.

Those among this elite who attended church did so in the working-class parishes on the wrong side of the tracks, where they often took leading roles as elders, deacons, or officers in the women's guilds. If they went to club meetings, it was to brotherhood lodges (Eagles, Oddfellows, Woodmen of the World) or to veterans' organizations in one of the industrial suburbs where most of the other members were factory workers.

The lack of aspiration for social advancement was attributable more to the wives than to the husbands. The women were typically eighth grade graduates, in contrast to the wives of blue-collar aristocrats in the lower-middle class who had usually completed high school. These women felt at a decided cultural disadvantage in the presence of middle-class women, and preferred to remain as they were rather than try to bridge the gap.

Nowhere is the difference between the aspirations of working-class-elite and lower-middle-marginal families more apparent than with respect to their children's educational achievements. In the former, only 29 per cent of the children attended college, and another 29 per cent did not finish high school. In the latter, 57 per cent had attended college for at least a short period of time.

Good Living: Most numerous among the working-class-elite were highly paid blue-collar families who put good living above the pursuit of social status. As they moved up the income ladder, they added to their material goods, to the fun they got out of life, and to some extent to their savings accounts, but they did not alter their basic style of life (see Chinoy, 1955). Will Schippers, a foreman at the large Vendmark plant, was an example. The Schippers had both grown up on farms in the so-called Dutch country around Orange City, Iowa. They had seen hard times until the end of the Depression, when they moved to Kansas City and Will had "lucked into this job with Vendmark." When he started, there were only twenty employees; but in 1954, there were 1,300, and Will was one of three senior foremen. Will Schippers' take-home pay was $7,200, which meant that he was at least 50 per cent better off than the average Kansas City factory worker.

The Schippers lived in a large, old, two story house just a few blocks away from the plant. The home was well maintained but was located in a slightly run-down section of the North Side. Will had personally refaced the house in 1952 to hide the original frame construction; and he had changed all the wiring in order to install air conditioning units. The kitchen contained an array of modern appliances. The pantry had been converted into a combination frozen food locker and automatic laundry. The living room, as described by an interviewer, was furnished in "standard, uninspired, comfortable manner, with its main feature a 24-inch television set." The backyard housed a double engine motor boat and a three-car garage; in the garage was a late model convertible for their youngest son. Above the garage was an apartment where each of the three oldest children had started married life.

Will was a hail-fellow-well-met, who liked to drink beer with his friends once a week at the Elks hall a few blocks away. Hilda Schippers was an overweight and good-natured housewife who was always making a cake or a pie for her children, for the church, or for a sick neighbor. Their Evangelical Reform church was located a block away, and Hilda described its members as "one big, happy family." She attended services every Sunday and "dragged Will along if he hasn't gone to the lake." At one time or another, she had held every office in the women's guild.

Only one of the Schippers' four children started college. Frank, the youngest, went to Missouri University on a basketball scholarship in 1950, but he quit, as his mother said, because "he decided he ought to help out in the Korean situation—anyway, he wasn't doing so hot in the grades department." When he was discharged from the armed services, Frank decided that life as a bachelor, with a convertible car and a good job at Vendmark, was preferable to "sweating out exams every week," and his parents did not try to change his mind. Their two older sons had both gotten good jobs at Vendmark and had not gone to college; and their daughter's husband was doing very well as an insulation contractor even though he had only finished the tenth grade.

Ethnic Leaders: Another type of working-class-elite was families exerting leadership in the neighborhood life of the Italian community in Kansas City, Missouri, or in the Polish and Hungarian districts of Kansas City, Kansas. Dominic Micelli owned a downtown barber shop where he employed five barbers, two of them his sons, and where his customers regarded him as a colorful personality, full of spicy stories which he delivered in a heavy Italian accent. He had attended school in Italy before coming to the United States at fifteen. "Nick" Micelli had lived in the same block in the Italian North End ever since he arrived in Kansas City in 1909. He now owned a three story apartment building in which he and his wife occupied two of the six flats. The building looked very old on the outside, but inside everything was "gay and comfortable, and a warm family atmosphere prevailed," according to the interviewer.

Nick's wife Rose was a central figure in the Italian community, known as "Mama Rose" by most of the boys and girls who grew up in the neighborhood. Through the years she had worked in the North End for the Red Cross and had been in charge of a community center for teen-agers. For a time she had been "permanent president" of the PTA in the neighborhood school. Rose had grown up within three blocks of her present home; she had attended the same grade school as her children, had gone to Manual High School for six months, and had then quit school and married Nick when she was sixteen. The Micellis sent their five children to the public schools because the Italian community had never had a parish school of its own. As Mrs. Micelli explained, "Not very many of the parents could afford the fees, anyway. The public school gives the children a certain amount of time off each week for religious instruction, and so the parents figure they don't need to spend the extra money sending the children to a Catholic school all day." The two older Micelli sons who worked with their father in the barber shop had finished at Manual High, then gone to barber college. The oldest child, a daughter, dropped out of high school to get married. The younger daughter went into nurse's training, greatly pleasing her mother. The youngest son was the pride and joy of the family, for after receiving a B.A. from the local Catholic college, he had enrolled in law school at Georgetown University in Washington, D.C., and was working part time in the office of Kansas City's congressman.

Mama Rose said of herself that she was dedicated to helping the children of her neighborhood. "I'm very attached to these children here. Lots of people in Kansas City won't give them a chance at a decent job because they come from 'Italian families in the hoodlum North End'—that's what the *Star* calls us—but I try to help them get a fair break. It makes me heartsick to see how they hold the faults of the father and grandfathers—and really just a few of them—against our children—it isn't right." She explained why the family stayed in the North End, despite financial ability to move elsewhere: She told of others who had moved and were unhappy, and she pointed to the wonderful community spirit she would have to leave behind. "I think there is probably a warmer feeling among the people down here than any place else in the city. Whenever there is a family that is in real need, they'll always be able to get some help from the rest of us. Some of the Italian families who have made money, well, they've let it go to their heads and they tried to move out of the Italian neighborhoods, but I think that's silly. They never seem to make friends where they move to, and most of their friends are still down here. They become unhappy because they are looking for something they can't get."[3]

Labor Leaders: A third type of working-class-elite in Kansas City was the labor union leader who lived among his men. The social position of these men illustrates again that income or occupation was not itself the measure of status in the city. Status position was heavily influenced by the clientele a man served, and this was particularly true of the labor boss. Vince Szabo, forty-one, was the United Auto Workers' representative at the Chevrolet assembly plant. He represented three thousand men, handling negotiations with the plant management regarding minor grievances such as injury claims, dismissals, or disputes over production rates. Vince and his wife Elena lived in a pleasant six room brick bungalow that was built thirty years earlier. It was by far the most expensive house in its neighborhood, an area which was somewhat too close to the growing Negro district for the "comfort" of many white families.

Elena defended the location of their home in much the same way that Rose Micelli defended hers, as a matter of principle and also of personal happiness: "People are always asking me why we bought such an expensive house in this neighborhood when we could have found one just as nice in Raytown or in one of the other nice suburbs. The answer is that my husband wants his men to know

[3] The importance to Italian-Americans of living in a neighborhood of their own has been more thoroughly examined in Gans (1963).

that he still feels he's one of them, even though they pay him a pretty good salary and we can afford nicer things than many of the men on the assembly line."

Unionism was a passionate cause with Vincent Szabo. His father had come to the United States from Serbia to escape military service and had settled in Detroit and worked in the Ford plant at River Rouge. Vince graduated from high school in Detroit in 1931. He had dreamed of going to college, but times were difficult because his father had become involved in the fight to unionize the Ford workers and had been fired. Vince managed to get in three winters of night school at Wayne University while working for the union by day.

When Vince married Elena Drakos, a strikingly attractive girl of Greek descent, she reported that "neither of our parents were very happy about our marriage, because Serbs and Greeks never liked each other and to make it worse, Vince's family is Roman Catholic and we are Orthodox. We eloped and were married first by a justice of the peace." The Szabos attended a Catholic church two blocks away from their home, where Elena worked in its Sodality and women's groups. Their children were enrolled at the St. Ignatius Academy, which served the Catholic children of the East Side factory workers. Vince had "thousands of friends through the union," but when he went to the Lake of the Ozarks to fish on weekends he went alone or with his older boy. Every fall he went to Michigan for the deer season and spent two weeks hunting with his father and two of his brothers.

The Szabos were typical of the union leadership in Kansas City. The railroad union leaders lived among their men in the Argentine district of Kansas City, Kansas, near the Santa Fe yards and roundhouses; the leaders of the packinghouse workers lived in the flats of Armourdale or on Balkan Hill; the leaders of the petroleum industry unions lived in the refinery suburb of Sugar Creek. Most of these men had homes far above average for their surroundings, but they identified with the working class. They despised the Kansas City *Star* "because it doesn't tell our side of a story fairly," and they voted Democratic both locally and nationally.

A few union leaders had achieved higher rank as legislative representatives, business agents, or executive secretaries and no longer lived among their men. Their social and business contacts were congressmen, state representatives, other union leaders, and intellectual or journalistic friends of the union movement. They were the union people most likely to be appointed to membership on the Kansas City Council of Social Agencies, the City Planning Commission, or the Mayor's Recreation Advisory Board, where they were treated as spokesmen for the working class.

The social class position of these few higher-status union leaders was an anomalous one, for few of them were completely accepted in middle class circles. Yet their world was vastly different from that of the ordinary union worker, and their positions far exceeded in importance and in remuneration those of most middle-management men. The highest ranking union leader in Kansas City, a man who was international president of the Boilermaker's Union of five hundred thousand men and vice-president of the national executive council of the American Federation of Labor, had plainly reached upper-middle status. The local newspaper once described him as "a man whose bearing suggests the generation of individualistic industrialists who rose with rare qualities of leadership to head armies of men . . . the only difference between [him] and men who run businesses is that he has a sense of mission to push the progress of other workingmen." This man was a director of one of Kansas City's banks, a member of one of its private downtown men's clubs, and served on several civic boards. Such exceptions notwithstanding, most Kansas City middle class people in 1954 could not quite forgive a union leader the fact that his power was derived from the relationship he bore to the working class and that the ends he sought appeared to be opposed to their own. He was, in a sense, "an enemy" of the middle class.

Precinct Workers: The politicians and political workers of Kansas City's North Side "Democratic Party machine" bore a relationship to the community similar to that of lower-status union leaders. They lived in working class precincts and wards where they were actively engaged in "keeping families happy between election times," "making sure no one goes hungry," "getting a break for the kid down the street who got into a little trouble with the law," and at election time, collecting the debts of gratitude they had accumulated by getting out the vote.

For fifteen years Mike and Ruth Fountain had been delivering from 90 per cent to 95 per cent of the vote in their precincts to the Democratic Party. Mike's reward was a job as deputy assistant in the Jackson County Sheriff's office; Ruth's was a job in the county auto license bureau. Their home was furnished mostly in pre-World War I furniture left them by Ruth's mother, whose husband had been one of Pendergast's ranking lieutenants back in the "good old days before reform." Their two story brick house was perched atop Goat Hill, so named because in the 1890s this was the hill where the "shanty" Irish kept their goats. The Fountain house was in the exact center of this area, which had been the center of power for the Pendergast machine in the 1920s and 1930s. One block away were small frame houses of Prairie Gothic style, all on twenty-five foot lots. While the area was not quite slum in 1954, it was below working class average. Three blocks to the south was the Mexican district, its tumbledown little homes and weedy yards looking like a patch of rural Mexico transplanted to Kansas City. Mike Fountain bossed the precincts on top of Goat Hill and on its southern slope, including the Mexican neighborhood.

The Fountains' life was wrapped up in Democratic party politics and in Goat Hill. They told the interviewer why Goat Hill in the beginning was the home of railroad men: "The railroads all had 'call boys' who'd come up from the yards and run up and down the streets yelling that the trains were ready to go and needed the crewmen to report for work. The men would hear them and get dressed, hitch their horses, and drive one another down the hill in those little carts they had." They also defended the memory of their late leader, Tom Pendergast. "He's the most wrongfully condemned man who ever went to jail from Kansas City. He did more wonderful deeds of helping out the poor people than anyone who ever lived in this town, and it wasn't bribery—it was for the humanity of the thing." Their pet hate was the Kansas City *Star*, which they called the "Tsar."

The Fountains' best friend was Jim Rafferty, president of the First Ward Club and the only nonreform politician who had managed throughout the years of "drought" (as the Fountains termed reform) to remain in the City Council. He did so as the elected representative of the northwest corner's have-not white and Negro families. Jim lived two doors up the street at the very summit of Goat Hill and was, according to the Fountains, a "well-to-do man" as a result of his various investments and interests in insurance and real estate, although Polk's Kansas City directory listed him as a beer salesman.

There were few Mike Fountains and Jim Raffertys in Kansas City in 1954, but they represented, nevertheless, a type that has been a part of all of America's larger cities. The men who presided over political machines usually grew wealthy, but remained identified with the working class. They could not get admitted to the private clubs of the upper-middle and upper classes and were not interested in the lower-middle world of respectability. Sometimes they moved to the mansion districts. But such a move did not change their social status—it only seemed to enrage their new neighbors. (One of the memories Kansas Citians still treasured with a mixture of amusement and disgust was of Boss Pendergast sitting in the front yard of his Ward Parkway mansion in his undershirt and stocking feet, puffing on a cigar, a symbol of defiance to the Republican and upper-class rich as they drove by.)

The community position of Kansas City's Democratic party politicians ran the gamut from fairly low within the working class to "Capital S Society," depending upon their social origins, the purposes and policies they espoused, and the clientele they served. There were many "Southern gentlemen Democrats," "Missouri Establishment Democrats," and "Stevensonian liberal Democrats" in the upper class. They were active in state and national politics but inactive locally. Kansas Citians regarded these Democrats in a very different light from those they called "rabble Democrats," that is, those who were identified with the working class.

Union leaders and political leaders bore the same relationship to the working class and to the wider society; both derived their support from a working class base, and to that extent always had some of their roots in that class, even though they may have risen quite high in their respective hierarchies. If they rose very much above the average working class in wealth or prominence, they became, for all practical purposes, people without a specific class position, unclassifiable because of the discrepancy between their social acceptability and their wealth or community prominence. The same was true of most entertainment and sports celebrities, and, as mentioned earlier, of racketeers. Whenever any of these men rose out of the working class to wealth and prominence without winning middle class acceptance, they moved outside the mainstream of the status structure.

Working-Class-Core

In the working-class-core, the typical family head was the "common man," the "ordinary American" who punched a time clock, made enough money to "get by, but not much more," never caused any trouble, had "three square meals" a day, was very patriotic, voted in the major elections, believed in God (but only went to church "at Christmas or Easter, or sometimes when the wife really insists") and held a union card, but otherwise was "no member of any darned club."

The typical middle-aged working class wife was a homebody, with no club meetings to go to during either day or evening. She spent her weekdays keeping house, sewing for her high school daughter or grandchild, and "writing letters to our son who is in the service." Life had been "more hectic when the children were younger, and we had to do more for them, and they messed up the house a lot more." When the children were in grade school she "went to PTA three or four times a year." Now her friends were apt to be "a neighbor lady, my sister, and a cousin who grew up with me and moved to Kansas City a few years ago." When the children were young she took them to a neighborhood church fairly regularly, but now she has dropped the habit, though still "tries to make it once a month, 'cause if I don't, I begin to feel sort of bad about it."

The typical middle-aged working class family had a settled routine of watching television in the evening, "doing some light reading" of the newspaper and a magazine or two, visiting relatives on Saturday evening, having the grown children over for dinner and a drive Sunday afternoon, and spending the rest of their spare time working on the house. The social life and horizons of the majority of these ordinary working class people in Kansas City were very different from the patterns observed among the more well-to-do working class and among lower-middle class men and women. Quite unlike the union leaders, "ethnic elite," or political workers, about half the average working class families did not have many acquaintances; unlike lower middles, they did not belong to a clique of married couples or to a square dance group. Social contacts were with children, sisters and brothers, cousins, and parents. Women sometimes found a confidante or two among other housewives in the neighborhood, and men enjoyed the companionship of fellow workmen while on the job or maybe while fishing.

This nonsocial pattern was especially typical of working class men and women in Kansas City, Missouri, where the neighborhoods were rarely dominated by a single ethnic group and did not exhibit a concentration of workers from any particular plant, trade, or industry. The neighborhoods were simply places where working class people from a variety of backgrounds and occupational roles had come together accidentally, as it were, seeking housing they could afford. The one thing uniting this class on the North East side of Kansas City in 1954 was their determination to stand against the possibility of Negro invasion. They seemed to be succeeding, for Negroes were moving with greater speed southward into sections being deserted by the middle class rather than eastward into these solidly-held working class neighborhoods.

Pleasure Seekers: About 25 per cent of the working class-core families in the middle-aged sample were more fun loving and outgoing than the typical family described above. John Meadows described a typical week in his life:

> "Fall is my favorite time of year. That's football season and all three of my boys have played on the team. I'm the kind of dad who's always out there cheering them on, and their worst critic when they get home. Every Friday night in the fall for five years now, Thelma and me have been wherever the team was. . . . Then almost every Saturday night the wife and I go to the Moose lodge. We play bingo, dance a little, and have a few drinks. Sunday has always been my day to go coon hunting. Tuesday night is Bowling League. Thursday night I stay home, and Thelma goes to a canasta club meeting with some of the girls. As you can see for yourself, we have a pretty good time. . . . Physically, I'm thicker in the middle than I used to be or ought to be—but I enjoy a good brew and a thick steak, so what the hell!"

As a heavy duty mechanic on cranes and lift trucks, John's wages were from $5,400 to $6,000 a year—"not as much as I'd like, you can bet your boots, but I've never met a man that *did* make as much as he wanted, and at least I like what I'm doing." The

Meadows' home was a forty year old stucco bungalow which "could use a paint job," according to the interviewer. Neither John or Thelma Meadows cared much about putting a lot of time or energy into their home. The interviewer described their furniture as "comfortable, but it has seen its best days."

The Meadows were not churchgoers. While John said he "believes in God and the Golden Rule," he said, "we both got fed up to our necks with religion and all those 'thou shalt nots' when we were kids; maybe that's why we don't go now." Sometimes the American working class has been stereotyped as sports-minded and boisterous like the Meadows. This is an erroneous image, mistakenly characterizing a class by its most visible members, much as the lower-middle class has been erroneously stereotyped as the "joiner" class.

Church People: Another 25 per cent of working-class-core families might be described as God-fearing and church-centered in their approach to life. Both husband and wife attended church events regularly and, with a sincere spirit of piety, "tried to live by the Bible." Eldon Roberts, his wife Ora, and their sons Ora Lee and Donald were such a family. Eldon and Ora both taught Sunday school at the Fairmont Christian Church, a small congregation of two hundred families which met in a half-finished structure the church members themselves were building. Both children sang in the choir. The Roberts always attended the Sunday morning services, and as often as possible went to the Sunday evening prayer meeting as well. Ora Roberts cooked for the Wednesday evening suppers once a month, and Eldon went faithfully every Saturday afternoon to the Men's Club meeting, which was devoted to some aspect of the construction project.

The Roberts lived in a small house, a block away from their church, in a small industrial suburb. The house was thirty years old, but still one of the best looking in the neighborhood, meticulously clean on the inside, and immaculately tidy on the outside, with new green shutters and asbestos shingles. Eldon Roberts was an inspector at the Blue Valley Sash and Door Company, overseeing the work done by twelve men on one section of the assembly line. This company was known as one of the poorest paying in the city but it had a good record of stable employment throughout the depression, and most of its employees seemed to have traded the possibility of higher wages for the advantages of long-term security. Eldon's income was about average for men in the working-class-core, totaling $4,200 in 1954. While Eldon had completed only the tenth grade in school and Ora only the eighth grade, their children were finishing high school. Eldon and Ora hoped Ora Lee could go to the National College for Christian Workers in Kansas City and that Donald could get to college on a scholarship, since his grades were "always Bs and As."

The church-centered families in the working-class-core were as concerned about their moral respectability as any lower-middle class family, and their belief in Christian dogma was generally deeper and more trusting. The churches they attended were the more dogmatic of the mainstream denominations (Baptist, Catholic, Lutheran, Methodist) or the more accepted of the off-brand churches (Church of Christ or Church of Nazarene). The congregations were almost always small enough so that any member who wanted could find a role. Most of the men taught Sunday school and served as ushers, as deacons, or members of the choir. Almost all the women did their share toward making the weekday evening suppers a success. Their churches corresponded in some ways to an extended kinship system which gave its members a sense of solidarity not only with one another but with the universal Christian community.

Older Families: The later years of middle age, from fifty to sixty-four, tended to be years of decline for many working class families and not, as in the lower-middle class, a period of stabilized good living, nor as in the upper-middle class, a period of reward. A very large number of the working class men became ill, lost their jobs and hence their incomes during these years. Many older men who once were fully employed carpenters or mechanics found themselves after age fifty-five in such jobs as apartment house janitor-managers, elevator operators, guards, salesclerks, watchmen, or part-time maintenance men—in short, working in generally less well paid, nonunionized positions.

The self-descriptions of such families were often full of "used to be's." They used to be in a church, but their friends left or they themselves left. They used to be in such lodges as the Elks, Moose, Woodmen of the World, or Oddfellows, but they had trouble paying the dues, or the organization itself had died from financial trouble. They used to have a better job, and the neighborhood they lived in used to be a lot better.

Some of these "used to be's" seemed to reflect habits of an earlier era, when perhaps the lodges were livelier than in the 1950s. Some may have reflected conditions peculiar to urban centers, for it may well be that in small towns working class people are not as socially isolated from social organizations as they are in large cities. Many, however, reflected changes in social activity brought about by declining health, declining income, and declining interest.

The decline in income and occupational status which so frequently accompanied aging for blue-collar workers meant that the typical working class family had moved into its best house when the husband was between thirty-five and thirty-nine. In the middle-aged sample, a smaller percentage occupied average working class houses in each successively older ten-year age group. This does not mean that working class families moved to poorer housing as they grew older; more commonly, they had not kept pace with the changes in their community, continuing to live in the same houses while the neighborhoods declined around them.

Henry and Viola Ruggles are an example of how aging often brought a sharp change in the living conditions and social habits of working class people. Henry Ruggles was a nights-and-Sundays elevator operator at the Second National Bank. A steady, reliable man of sixty-four, Ruggles was "just awfully happy to have landed the job" when he came to Kansas City seven years earlier from the small town of Marshall, Missouri, where he had lived most of his adult life. He planned to work as long as his health was good. The biggest drawback to the job was the poor pay; in 1954, he earned $275 a month.

In Marshall, Mr. Ruggles had been a railroad yard switch-man until the Depression. After a period on relief, he found a job as city park caretaker, then moved up to park maintenance manager by the beginning of World War II. With the manpower shortages of the war years, he became chief police officer in the downtown district. He considered this his favorite job, for it "gave me a little respect and prestige." In 1948, when he was fifty-seven, he was relieved of this responsibility and put back to park mainte-nance. His unhappiness with this demotion motivated him to move to Kansas City to look for an "inside kind of job" for his later years.

Except for the job, Henry and Viola were not happy in Kansas City, away from their friends and relatives in Marshall. They had never transferred their church membership from the Marshall Methodist. They couldn't find a church in Kansas City where they could "feel at home" and associate with "as many nice people as we had in our church back at Marshall." Henry wished he had maintained his affiliations with the Oddfellows and Modern Woodmen so that he "could meet some of those fellows here in Kansas City," but he had dropped these organizations during the early 1930s, when "times were rough and I needed all the money for the family." Viola tried to be friendly with her neighbors; but her Kansas City neighborhood didn't seem like Marshall because it had "all these cutup older houses and apartments in it."

White-Collar Workers: Not all working-class-core families were headed by blue-collar wage earners. Five per cent were self-employed craftsmen, another 5 per cent owned other types of small businesses, and 9 per cent had low paying clerical, sales, or technical white-collar jobs.

Many a working class man talked about someday having his own business and not working for a boss, but few had actually attempted it. Most of those who tried had lost their investments. They had bought small neighborhood groceries, dairy stores, amusement park concessions, or even little movie theaters. But they had not made as much money as they had hoped, so they lost patience and gave up. The most consistently successful as their own bosses were craftsmen who had become contractors of their own, and sometimes other men's, skills. All told, at least 20 per cent of the middle-aged men in the working class had at some time been self-employed, but often for just a short time. And some who were self-employed when interviewed seemed on the verge of returning to a paid job. It appeared that in the working class many of today's self-employed become tomorrow's bankruptcy petitioners and next year's employees.

Joseph Shaughnessy, owner of Joe's Place, a small beer-and-burger joint, cleared between $3,500 and $4,500 a year. Joe employed a cook, and two waitresses; his wife helped out part-time, and Joe himself was part-time cook, bartender, cashier, and host. Joe had always worked as a bartender or chef, and had long wanted to own his own business. So he jumped at the chance to buy this place when the price was inviting, believing that hard work, reasonably good food, and courtesy could make it pay. The cafe, however, was located in a changing neighborhood, prices had to be kept low, and Joe did not know how to keep costs and prices in line in order to turn a profit. Joe was now ready "to get out of this rat race" of working sixty hours a week. The appeal of a forty-hour-a-week bartender job—in which "with tips and all, I could make maybe five thousand dollars and not have the headaches"—was great.

Quite a different set of feelings characterized the shipping clerks, express messengers, salesclerks in small auto appliance stores, cashier-clerks in drugstores, unsuccessful used car salesmen, and Salvation Army workers of the working class. Leeper Wedgett, forty-eight and wearing old-fashioned steel rimmed glasses, was a white-collar member of the working class. A high school graduate, Leeper worked as a clerk in a cut rate men's clothing store and earned only $3,600 in 1954. Leeper's home was a small four room, box shaped structure across the street from a large warehouse and within walking distance of the store. In 1954 Leeper was driving a Chevrolet he had bought in 1942, the oldest car in his neighborhood; most of his neighbors, who were factory workers, bought new Chevrolets or two year old Buicks every three or four years. Members of the South Side middle class jokingly referred to families like the Wedgetts as "objects of mercy."

Like the blue-collar workers, some of the self-employed and white-collar families centered their lives in the church; others were homebodies, and others were good-times seekers. Joe Shaughnessy and his wife, for example, despite their long hours at the bar, still managed to spend one evening a week either at the Moose Lodge "having a few drinks with the old gang" or "blowing ourselves to a fancy dinner and a movie." What Joe claimed to miss most since going into his own business were the vacations he used to take at Hot Springs, Arkansas, where for two weeks every year he "had a fling at the ponies and the one-armed bandits and tried all that mineral water—you know, 99 proof!" The Wedgetts were a marked contrast. They were devout churchgoers, attending the Church of the Nazarene, whose doctrine was antisin, antifun, antimusic, anti-alcohol, antismoking, and antidancing. For Leeper and Doris Wedgett this doctrinal point of view had its advantages, for on his income they could hardly afford to indulge in any such worldly pleasures.

Working-Class-Marginal

About 10 per cent of Kansas Citians were in the category of "poor, but decent" working class, as perceived by their fellow citizens. Such people were usually semi-skilled; many had known long periods of unemployment. They lived in the poorer areas of the North Side, but not in the slums. Other Kansas Citians were inclined to speak of them as a "lower working class group" to distinguish them from the "ordinary working class" as well as to separate them from the "real lower class," the people on the bottom. The phrase "lower working class" connoted that the people of this level were considered competent to provide for themselves, were not too lazy to work, held jobs which were neither despised nor disreputable, and were all in all more akin to the families of the "ordinary working class" than to the down-and-out at the bottom of the social order. The biggest distinction between this group and working-class-core was that the latter usually owned their own homes, while these marginals were usually renters, living in the older apartment buildings, in subdivided old houses, or in very small houses.

The Volmerichs illustrate many characteristics of this group. Robert Volmerich was an oiler and greaser at the National Oil Refinery. Bob and his wife Darla lived only a few blocks from the refinery, in the unattractive industrial suburb of Sugar Creek While not a slum, Sugar Creek was considered a less than desirable place to live. The Volmerich house was typical of its neighborhood; it had clearly begun to show its age. The small front porch sagged, and the original wood siding had been replaced by a cheap asbestos covering. Bob and Darla hoped to move into a better rented house in a few years if Bob's job proved to be steadier than the others he had had since he returned from the service in 1945. In the first two years after the war when there was a shortage of automobiles, he had earned a fair wage driving a taxi. In 1949 he shifted to driving a truck for a contracting company. Finally, in 1953, he took the refinery job, which promised to be more permanent than the others.

Bob, forty-four, had been "kicking around on his own" since he was fifteen. He quit school after ninth grade because—as he looked back—"I was a smart aleck kid and thought I knew all the answers, and the way I looked at it then was that any more school would be a fat waste of time." The early depression years found him in a Civilian Conservation Corps camp; later, he was an oil-field roughneck; in World War II, he joined the army and became a jeep driver in the European theater. Bob had been divorced years ago, and Darla was his second wife. They had three sons, aged eleven, six, and five, with whom Bob spent many a summer evening playing catch in the backyard.

The Volmerichs were typical of lower working-class families with regard to club and church participation. Bob said he didn't "believe in all that heaven and hell stuff" and went to church no more than once or twice a year. Darla, however, drove two miles every Sunday to Independence to attend the small Baptist church of her childhood. She had no other formal organizational connections, and vaguely excused herself on the grounds that she couldn't "find the time, what with the kids, the house, and everything." Whenever she got away from "kids and house," it was usually to check up on her father's health or to go shopping in downtown Kansas City with her best friend from high school days. The Volmerichs rarely went out in the evening together, except to drive-in movies where they could take "our gang of boys" along.

Bob was a dues paying member of the plant union, but liked to let everyone know that "I sure wouldn't give 'em a red cent if you didn't have to, in order to hold your job." Bob's favorite recreation was to wander over to a neighborhood softball diamond on summer evenings and watch some of the fellows from the plant play ball. After the games some of the spectators and players adjourned to a nearby tavern for a few beers and verbal replay of the game. During the winter he met some of "the guys" at the same bar for "hot-stove league meetings," rehashing the previous baseball season and looking forward to the next.

Job instability was definitely a characteristic of the men at this level. One man in the sample, in the period between 1939 and 1954, was first a grocery warehouseman, then an extra railroad crewman (during the war), then a bread-wrapping machine operator, and finally a galvanizing worker. Another was first a carpenter, then an assembly line worker in a war production plant, then a maintenance man in an auto assembly plant, and finally a cafeteria janitor. Many men had driven a taxi or truck at one time or another and had worked periodically on assembly lines as the need for such hands had risen and fallen in the Kansas City area. A great number were unemployed for long periods during the Depression, and although all worked steadily during the war, a considerable portion had experienced sporadic unemployment ever since.

The income marginality of these families was more the result of this job instability than of low pay. Among working-class-marginals employed in 1954, the average income was only 10 per cent less than in the working-class-core. The fluctuations in income meant that most of these families had never been able to put much money aside, and in good times they paid off debts accumulated in hard times.

Marital instability appeared in a relatively high percentage of these families. Forty per cent of working-class-marginals in the sample were married for the second or third time, usually because the first marriage had ended in divorce but sometimes because the first partner died at a relatively early age. The comparable figure for working-class-core was 20 per cent, and the figure was lower still at all higher levels of the status hierarchy. Families like the Volmerichs were the most numerous among the working-class-marginals. Families who had been impoverished by poor health, stable unskilled workers, and immigrant families made up the rest of this group.

Poor Health: Some families slipped from average to marginal status within the working class because of a disabling injury to the husband or chronic illness in the family. Eddie Morris had earned a steady income as a pipefitter for the Missouri and Gulf Coast Railroad, until at thirty-seven an auto accident left him a semi-invalid for life. His wife Beatrice had been the family wage earner ever since. She had a job as timekeeper at a small plant a few blocks from the home. The Morrises were receiving a small amount of money from the railroad, but the main part of their income was Beatrice's wages, which totalled $2,700. Their total income, including help from one of their sons, was less than $3,600 a year, and Eddie still had sizable medical bills each year.

The Morrises lived in a five room frame house which they had been buying, but which they had been forced to sell back to the mortgage company to meet some of their bills. In 1954, they were buying it again on a longer term mortgage plan. Its condition was described as "gone downhill badly on the outside, with little care for the yard, or outside appearance; the paint is badly flaked." On the inside, the furniture was "old, but in immaculate condition; the living room has a warm lived-in atmosphere."

Life for the Morrises had been quite a struggle since the accident. The older boy, who had completed high school and married, contributed whatever he could, but they wanted him to spend most of his money on himself and his family. As Bea Morris said: "My son and his family have a future to look forward to, and Eddie and I don't; I don't want my son's life to be hurt by the problems Eddie and I have." The younger boy dropped out of school in tenth grade. In 1954 he was in the army in Japan, where he had married a Japanese girl. He was not helping his parents. The Morrises had no car, and their kitchen had none of the up-to-date worksaving devices. The newest piece of furniture was their television set. Eddie Morris said: "Television has been a godsend. If you were to ask me what the greatest invention of all time was, I'd name that little box with the eye in it."

Unskilled But Stable: Jason Skiles represented another type of "poor but decent" family. Jason was an unskilled worker who had been employed for many years by the Jackson County government to work on highway and county road repair during the summer, and on public building maintenance projects during the winter. He had never been interested in trying to get assembly line work that might pay better but offer less security. Elizabeth Skiles, his wife, worked part-time as a cafeteria helper in the school near their home. The Skiles' combined income was large enough to allow them to own a home of their own. It was located in a working class neighborhood at a safe distance from the slums and toughs. The house was neatly furnished, but was considered one of the less desirable homes in the neighborhood because it was located at the rear of its lot and had been built before the turn of the century as a small farmhouse.

The Skiles were thrifty and dutiful. They went to church regularly. Jason, one of eleven children of a very poor family, was educationally handicapped, having completed only six years of school. Elizabeth's family was also poor, but she had managed to complete eleventh grade before her father died and she was forced to go to work to support her mother. She had never stopped working, except for brief periods when her children were young. The Skiles' daughter finished high school, and their son graduated from Warrensburg Teachers' College (one of the 12 per cent of the children at this level who started college, and among the 3 per cent who finished).

"Old Country" People: One group of working-class-marginals were people of immigrant stock who lived in the "old country" enclaves of Kansas City, Kansas. Stefan and Zada Hunkeler were both born in Hungary but as young children were brought to the United States and educated in American schools. Stefan, who was in his late fifties, had lived since early childhood on Balkan Hill. Stefan had learned carpentering from his father, and when he was younger he had worked in construction crews. During the Depression work came sporadically, so his family of five children "had it rough." More recently, Stefan had been a gatekeeper at a large warehouse in Kansas City's Fairfax industrial district.

The Hunkelers lived in an old, but well kept, two story house. Built in the 1880s it occupied a very narrow lot with hardly any yard, typical of houses on Balkan Hill.

The Hunkelers did almost all their shopping in the neighborhood stores or in the downtown district of Kansas City, Kansas. They considered Kansas City, Missouri, an unfriendly foreign place. Their life was centered in their neighborhood and in St. Anthony's Catholic church, which served the area and sponsored many celebrations of Hungarian holidays and historical events.

Stefan and Zada Hunkeler often talked in Hungarian to one another, but they always tried to address their children in English and the children knew only a few words of Hungarian. Two of the grown children lived in Balkan Hill; a third had become a priest, and the other two had moved to a postwar suburb of Kansas City, where the houses were inexpensive and could be financed by GI loans. The parents were pleased that these latter two had become fully Americanized and modern in their tastes and habits; yet they were also very happy to have two of their children near them.

Some of the families on Balkan Hill were poorer than the Hunkelers, with the husband working as a laborer in the packing plants or on the railroads. Such families were considered "the down-and-out, but not disreputable" members of the lower class. On the other hand, there were many families who were better off than the Hunkelers. Some even owned considerable property and had become the dominant figures of the Hungarian community, the aristocracy of Balkan Hill, as it were.

A social class of almost identical occupational character—always 80 per cent blue-collar and gray-collar—has been singled out in every community studied by American social scientists. It was called the upper-lower class in Jonesville and Yankee City by Warner and his group and in Deep South by Gardner and Davis. However, we have labeled it *the working class* in Kansas City as a way of signifying that in its own eyes, and in the view of the wider Kansas City public, it was not a particularly lowly group as of the mid-1950s. At that point in time it had come to share with the classes above it in the major fruits of twentieth-century invention and progress. As a group it was, for the moment, doing better than just "getting by"—the phrase used by Kahl (1957) as characteristic of the American blue-collar worker's value orientation—without yet showing much evidence of wanting to "get ahead" or "move up" socially.

Chapter 10

People
at the Bottom

*W*hen the citizens of Kansas City talked about "the lowest class of people here in town," they had three main types in mind: the "poor" who lived in shacks and slums, the "bad" who were engaged in criminal or illicit activities, and the "different" who were members of minority groups not assimilated into the mainstream of Kansas City life. While minority group membership or a criminal record did not automatically condemn a person to the "lowest class," living in a slum area did. Slum living was taken as a sign of shiftlessness, laziness, low intelligence, or some other character defect which made it impossible for a man to hold a job or manage his money. Kansas Citians spoke with contempt of "people who are always on the relief rolls," and of "those people who live in public housing because they can't manage for themselves."

The "bad" were regarded with greater disdain than the poor. Professional criminals, people in illegal businesses such as narcotics peddling or prostitution, mobsters and members of the syndicate were worse than personal failures: they were described as enemies of society and threats to the moral order. Yet, while Kansas Citians were seemingly more harsh in discussing the "bad" than the "poor," the only "bad" who were relegated to the lower class were those who lived in poverty and who had not made crime

199

pay. Mobsters, jewel thieves, and call girls who lived in middle-income style were not perceived as the bottom of the social ladder; instead they were in a twilight zone, as if outside the social class structure. And middle-class people convicted of white-collar crimes such as income tax evasion, embezzlement, or crimes of passion, as well as people who had "once made a mistake" but apparently been reformed, were also exempted from relegation to lowest social status.

Mexicans, Negroes, and Italians were identified as lower class because they were different in skin color, speech, or living habits in ways that aroused either animosity or contempt in the rest of the community. "Hillbillies" were condemned because they were noticeably lacking in urban ways. The Mexican population was small and regarded more with pity than contempt. They were not only different, they were poor. And they lived in an isolated neighborhood at the foot of Goat Hill, almost completely encircled by railroad tracks. Negroes and Italians were derogated mainly on the basis of stereotypes, for it was recognized that many individuals among them were not lower class either economically or in personal standards of behavior. Thus while the latter two groups were socially disadvantaged in the larger community, being Negro or Italian did not identify a person as lower class unless this was accompanied by poverty. In the final analysis, the determining characteristic was poverty; all other characteristics were used to explain why people were poverty stricken.

The lower class constituted a group toward whom other people felt contempt, hostility, and superiority. Whether the characteristics imputed to the group were valid or not was somewhat beside the point, because the ascribed traits were those most higher-status people wanted to believe were true of people "at the bottom." When the popular criteria for lower-class status were applied to the sample, our estimate from this evidence was that only 13 per cent of Kansas City middle-aged fell into this social class group—8 per cent of the whites and 48 per cent of the Negroes. Given the overall proportions of whites and Negroes in Kansas City, the result was that almost half the lower class middle-aged were Negro.

This estimate of the size of the lower class must be viewed cautiously. For one thing, this study was conducted in 1954–55, an extremely prosperous period when unemployment for the United States as a whole was at its lowest point since World War II and the one-fifth of Americans at the lowest income levels were receiving their highest share of the national wealth.[1] Second, this estimate applies only to the middle-aged. Data on social mobility into and out of the lower class indicate that relatively more persons were identified at this level during young adulthood and again after age sixty. Furthermore the birth rate at this socioeconomic level has historically been far above average, so that in any sampling of all age groups, the excess of children gives the lower class a higher percentage of the total than when only the middle-aged are counted. (We estimated that, had all adults aged twenty-one and over been sampled, probably 16 per cent of the Kansas City population would have been placed in the lower class; had the entire population been sampled, including children, the percentage might have been 19 or 20 per cent.) A third reason for caution is that sampling and interviewing lower-class people pose special problems which probably result in their being underrepresented: many are transients and hard to locate.

Ethnic Groups

A striking difference between Kansas City's lower class and the classes above was in racial distribution and in the ethnic and regional origins of whites. Kansas Citians were predominantly whites born in the Midwest, of old Yankee or northern European stock; but this was true of only one-fifth of the lower class. Of all the middle-aged lower class in 1954, we estimated that 45 per cent were Negroes, 12 per cent "hillbillies," 7 per cent were American Indians, 6 per cent were Mexicans, 5 per cent were of southern and eastern European stock, 4 per cent were Italians, 2 per cent were Filipinos, Chinese, and Syrians. The other 19 per cent were of northern European stock, and most had been born on midwestern farms or in small towns. (This estimate was based on evidence from the middle-aged sample and on information from the 1950 census on the racial and ethnic characteristics of people who lived in slum and near-slum areas.) The concentration of Negroes

---

[1] For further discussion of this point, see Harrington (1962). The problem of poverty was not in the public eye in the 1950s; but in addition to Harrington, a number of studies of "the culture of poverty" have now appeared, including Lewis (1959 and 1961); Miller (1964); Ferman, Kornbluh, and Haber (1965); Gordon (1965); and Meissner (1966). Among significant journal articles are Roach (1962) and Miller (1964).

in the lower class was in marked contrast to the working class, which was only 12 per cent Negro, and to the lower-middle class, which was less than 2 per cent Negro. The proportion of foreign born was more than double that of the working class. "Hillbillies" were present only in the lower class. This was really a matter of definition, because anyone of rural southern or Ozark origin who managed to rise in the social structure was no longer considered a "hillbilly."

Housing and Neighborhood

Approximately half of lower class people lived in true slum level housing; the other half in substandard houses or apartments, but not of the very poorest quality. (At the time of this study there were very few public housing projects for low income families in Kansas City. By public definition public housing projects were slum units despite the fact that they were still fairly new and not truly in bad repair. Their definition as slums was a product of the types of people reputed to live in them.) Slum housing was described by interviewers in phrases such as these: "A three room shack-type dwelling; hasn't been painted in thirty years; many of the boards are rotted away on the outside." "Living quarters are located on the second floor above a cheap restaurant. The place needs repair badly; gaping holes in the wall show where plaster has fallen away." "A seventy- or eighty-year-old bungalow, probably originally a farmhouse. Still has an outside privy." This kind of housing represented the worst 7 per cent of all units occupied by middle-aged men and women in the sample (only 4 per cent by whites, but 23 per cent by Negroes). Very nearly half the people occupying such units were widows, widowers, or single; and more than 60 per cent were over fifty-five years of age.

The substandard housing was described in terms such as these: "A four room shingled house; loose floorboards on the porch; no steps or sidewalk up to the porch." "A house with one average size room and two small rooms, plus a bath. Exterior dimensions are approximately eighteen by twenty-four. Exterior has been recently painted." "Very small two story house; imitation brick siding; at least seventy or eighty years old." The housing described as substandard was similar to that which the "poor but decent" members of the working class occupied, except that generally the units were smaller and older. More important, the furnishings were poorer in appearance and fewer in quantity. Linoleum or bare wood floors were common in the living rooms; and often the houses contained only the barest necessities in furniture.

Lower-class people who occupied substandard housing were intermingled with "real slum dwellers"; 74 per cent lived in neighborhoods where the majority of their neighbors lived in slum units. This is in marked contrast to those in the working class who occupied substandard units, only 21 per cent of which were located in neighborhoods where the majority of the units were slums.

Neighborhoods where lower class people predominated were scattered throughout the metropolitan area in many little pockets and fringe areas. In addition to the decaying rooming house and apartment districts near the downtown areas of Kansas City, Missouri, and Kansas City, Kansas, there were fingers of bad housing extending along railroad tracks out from the downtown areas and around the peripheries of residential developments. Wherever there was a raw gully, an untended creek bed, or a stretch of flat river bottom land, wherever there was a factory district, an unzoned highway, or an unpaved road, there was usually a group of lower-class houses. This residential fragmentation seemed to reinforce the isolation of lower-class families from the mainstream of Kansas City life.

Income

The great majority of lower class people lived in slums and substandard housing because they could afford no better. All the single women in this class, and all the families with a male head over sixty-five, reported less than $2,400 income during 1954, many reported less than $1,200, a few, less than eight hundred dollars. Among families with a male head aged forty to sixty-four, only 20 per cent were similarly poverty stricken—that is, with incomes under $2,400—but 47 per cent reported incomes of less than three thousand dollars.

An income of $3,300 was a cutoff point of sorts between working class and lower class in our sample; the majority of persons above this point were of working class status, and below it a majority were lower class. For one-sixth of the families, lower class status could not be explained by lack of income, for these families reported $4,200 or more, often as the result of both husband and wife working. In these instances there was evidence of gross mismanagement of funds, heavy debts, or—as sometimes described—of "staggering under the load of too many children."

Two Strata?

One defect of the present study is that we did not learn what status distinctions prevailed among people perceived as being at the bottom. In following the general attitudes of Kansas Citians, we divided members of the lower class into two groups solely on the basis of their housing: the members of one group were "not quite at the bottom"; members of the other group were "slum dwellers and disreputables." When it turned out that a much higher percentage of the second group were single or widowed, and a much higher percentage were over fifty-five, it was not clear whether quality of housing was as meaningful a distinction among members of the lower class as among the wider public.

When only married couples were compared, and when age was controlled, no important differences were found between the two groups in ethnicity, community participation, or church membership. "Hillbillies" and other white ethnic groups were equally represented at both levels. There was no organized community activity in either group, except among the Mexican-Americans. Sixty-seven per cent of the better-housed and 71 per cent of the "slum dwellers" claimed church membership or attendance; and the churches attended were identical.

There was a difference in education, not for husbands but for wives. Wives of the better housed averaged 1.3 more years of schooling than the wives of "slum dwellers." Only 25 per cent of the grown children of the better housed families, and 14 per cent of the poorer housed, had completed high school—a difference which is insignificant when compared with the 57 per cent high school completion recorded by grown children in the social status group immediately above, the "poor, but decent" working class families. All these comparisons point to the conclusion that the two groups of lower class were very similar.

At the same time, the variety of personality types and life styles is at least as great in the lower class as in any of the higher classes. In fact, this is the only class group for which no single family is representative of a sizable proportion of families.

Large Families

The Cletus Turners illustrate one of the problems found at this level, the economic burden of the large family. Cletus Turner came to Kansas City during World War II to work in a war production plant. Back in the Ozarks he had farmed and raised hogs. When the war was over, Cletus worked at a series of janitorial jobs; in 1954 he was a night worker, cleaning up the cafeteria in a steel fabricating plant.

Cletus' first wife bore twelve children before she died; his second wife, Marvadelle, four; so that between them the Turners were parents to sixteen children, two of them still living at home. None of the children had graduated from high school. Cletus himself had gone to school "pret' near six years," but had only gotten through the third grade; Marvadelle completed just two grades. Neither had ever exercised their voting rights. Cletus explained: "I didn't know the men who was runnin' and couldn't understand whether what they was promisin' was good or not, so I didn't rightly figure I should stick my nose into it."

The Turners' dwelling place was four rooms cut out of an old twelve room farmhouse which had been built shortly after the Civil War. In 1954, it was crowded between a warehouse and a box factory, and six families lived in it. It was described as "in the last stages of dilapidation . . . everything is very dirty, garbage in the hallways and out in the yard; it should be declared unfit for human habitation."

The Turners did not have any friends in Kansas City. Sometimes they had supper on Saturday night with one of their married daughters who lived nearby. On Sundays, Cletus said he "just takes things real easy" and his wife "rides on the bus over to that church of hers." These were the only forms of social activity the Turners could report. Marvadelle attended the First Born Church of Holiness, which was one middle class Kansas Citians scoffed at as "one of those holy roller outfits, where they have lots of screaming and clapping and singing and rolling around in the aisles whenever someone claims he has been seized with the spirit of the Lord." Cletus refused to go with her because he "got tired of hearing them tell me about my sins."

There were approximately four thousand "hillbilly" families

in Kansas City in 1954. Most of them lived in the gulches and gullies which run down to the Blue River along Kansas City's eastern margin. Their ramshackle homes and tarpaper huts or cut up old farmhouses were on unpaved streets which followed uncertain, twisting paths from the residential plateau to the valley floor. The men worked as garbage collectors, ditchdiggers, members of road gangs, or, like Cletus Turner, as factory cleanup helpers. The older men had completed no more than three, four, or five grades of school, and their wives often less. Families were large, with six to twelve children. The children rarely went past the ninth or tenth grade in Kansas City schools and dropped out before that if they had gone to school back in the hills.

Most husbands attended church along with their wives, on Wednesday and Friday nights as well as on Sunday. They contributed a sizable share of the total membership of white Kansas City's revivalist and holy roller type churches. Family incomes ranged from $2,100 to $5,400 a year. The higher incomes were usually the result of the wife's working, often as a laundress or janitress.

"Unadjusted Redmen"

Like the "hillbillies," the men and women of American Indian descent had trouble adjusting to modern urban living. They had been the victims of the tradition of irresponsibility and dependency in which their parents and grandparents had been maintained by the American government through the latter part of the nineteenth century. John Johnson was a half-blooded Cherokee who looked back at his ancestors with pride, for his grandfather had been chief of the Cherokee nation. Still further back, Johnson was descended from the great Indian leader, John Ross, who led his people on the Trail of Tears from Georgia to Oklahoma in the 1830s, when the government required their relocation in what was then designated as Indian Territory. Johnson's father was one of the chief's younger sons; he had married a girl of Irish descent, then squandered his inheritance of oil lands when Johnny was growing up near Tahlequah, Oklahoma. Johnson's first wife was also a Cherokee. He left her when he was in the service during World War II and married a Mexican girl he met in San Diego. By the time he had returned from overseas, this marriage had also terminated. Johnson came to Kansas City to spend some time with an army buddy. He stayed on and married a waitress he met at one of the bars he and his buddy frequented; he had no children by the first two marriages, two boys by his third.

Johnny (as he called himself) claimed to be a "pretty good mechanic when I set my mind to it." He had worked at a series of auto repair shops and service stations since he got out of the army. Frequently, though, he had been out of a job and had taken much advantage (as he admitted) of the 52–20 Club of postwar fame, which enabled unemployed ex-GIs to collect twenty dollars a week for a year while looking for work. In 1954 he was employed as a helper to the night man at a filling station and said he earned $2,500 during the first nine months of the year. His work history suggested, however, that at any time he might have an argument with the boss, or "just plain get tired" of working the night shift.

Johnny and his wife lived in an apartment building—a few blocks east of the downtown district in Kansas City—which bore the distinguished name Nieuw Amsterdam. At the turn of the century this building had been a fashionable residential hotel, but in 1954 it was described as "the most interesting looking slum in Kansas City." Built originally for eighty families, it now "housed three hundred; the halls sagged and creaked, the steps outside were almost worn away." The four Johnsons occupied three rooms which were described as "surprisingly clean and adequately furnished, but they share the bath with another family."

The Johnsons had no church affiliation and no club memberships. Their friends were "the crowd at the bar where we go dancing." Johnny went to ball games with his old army buddy. By lower-class standards the Johnsons were fairly well educated. Johnny had finished tenth grade at one of the Indian schools in Oklahoma, and his wife completed nine years before she quit to get married to her first husband.

Persons of American Indian ancestry were less distinguishable from other Kansas Citians than were the "hillbillies" or the Mexicans, since most were only part Indian, did not bear Indian last names, nor have a markedly Indian appearance. They did not form a clique or neighborhood social group as did the Mexicans, and they were scattered throughout the city's slum areas and low-status residential districts. Most were described as morose and inclined toward solitary living.

Mexican-Americans

Kansas City's Mexican-American group had come to the city handicapped because they could not speak English. In most instances they seemed to have made a good adjustment to urban living and were leading honorable, if financially hard pressed, lives. The Hernandez family was typical. Jesus Hernandez was born in Mexico and came to Texas as a small boy with his parents, who worked as farm laborers. His parents never learned to speak English. Jesus completed five years of school before he started working in the fields. When he was in his late teens his parents died, and he came to Kansas City to live with an uncle. He got a job as a track maintenance laborer with the Kansas City Union Depot Company and became a member of the Brotherhood of Maintenance of Way Employees, a union with primarily Mexican membership.

At age twenty-three Jesus married Natividad Candillo, a sixteen-year-old girl in the neighborhood. Her parents had migrated from Mexico; her father was also a track maintenance worker. The Hernandezes had five children, all of whom were given American names: Frank, Jerry, Ralph, Mary, and Carol. The oldest boy, Frank, made a name for himself by winning a Golden Gloves boxing championship three years in succession, one year reaching the national semifinals. He finished high school and joined the marine corps where his boxing skill again drew considerable attention, judging from the press clippings his father kept in a metal box in the bedroom. The second boy, Jerry, quit school after ninth grade and tried unsuccessfully to enlist in the Marines. At seventeen he seemed to be "just loafing around" with a group of other jobless youth in the neighborhood. This worried his parents, who were afraid of the trouble he might get into.

The Hernandezes' home was the lower floor of a very old brick, two-flat building. Mrs. Hernandez' sister and brother-in-law lived on the second floor. All the furniture was very old and well worn except for the recently purchased television set. Inside, the home was relatively neat and clean; but outside, the porch railing was broken, and much of the front yard was overgrown with weeds and cornflowers. The most treasured objects in the Hernandezes' home beyond the television set and the box of clippings were a plaster statue of the Virgin Mary, a picture of Christ, and a metallic crucifix. Mr. and Mrs. Hernandez attended mass regularly at the Mexican parish church. This church served as a community center, and provided the Hernandezes and other families in the neighborhood with their main social experiences outside the home and the circle of relatives.

The children of the Mexican community often finished high school. In fact, among children of the lower class, the Mexican boys and girls had a far better than average record of school completion. Several boys had gained recognition in high school athletics; for the brighter and more ambitious, this provided a start up the social ladder. A larger number who had not distinguished themselves scholastically or athletically had become, like Jerry Hernandez, idle street youth. There were fewer opportunities for the girls in Mexican families to achieve in school, and they tended to follow their mothers' paths of early marriage.

Most adult Mexican men were employed by the railroads or at the lowest skill level in factories or packing plants. Very few of the women worked outside the home. The family incomes were rarely over $3,600. There were four, five, or six children in most families. Their homes were very old, small wooden bungalows or brick two-flats which needed repair. The yards looked quite rural to middle class city dwellers. Kansas City's Mexican families were determined to be "good Americans," and the great majority of adults stayed out of trouble. In the early 1950s whatever crime could be traced to Mexican-Americans was mainly perpetrated by the young men between fifteen and twenty-five who were out of school, unmarried, and jobless; these boys were the despair of their parents. The parents were very religious, attending either the Guadalupe Catholic church or the Mexican Baptist, both in the neighborhood. Some of the men with better educations were members of The Mexican Cultural Union, and many of the women claimed membership in a church sodality group. There was a strong sense of community among these families, unlike the "hillbillies" or the American Indians.

Other Ethnic Groups

In addition to the Mexicans, another one-sixth of the middle-aged people of the lower class had immigrated to the United States or were first-generation Americans. A few had come from the British Isles or Canada and were at the bottom for reasons other than ethnic origin; some were German, French, or Scandinavian in ancestry. Some of the older Italians of the North End, especially those who had come to the United States as adults, had remained poor and unassimilated; and some of their children had (unlike the Micelli family) failed to rise to working class level. The same was true of some of the Polish, Russian, and Hungarian families of Balkan Hill in Kansas City, Kansas.

Only one ethnic group of European origin was still predominantly lower class in 1954. This was a tiny community of about two hundred Belgian families who lived together in the North Bottoms along the Missouri river and were truck farmers. They were all very poor and were hardly visible to most Kansas Citians.

There were no Chinatown or Little Tokyo neighborhoods in Kansas City, but there were some two hundred families of Chinese and Japanese origin and another two hundred from the Philippines and Hawaii. Most of these people were at the bottom because they worked as gardeners, greenhouse and nursery laborers, or in the kitchens of railroads, hotels, and cafeterias. A few had obtained better jobs, but not many were independent enterprisers—with laundries or restaurants of their own—as is the case in cities with larger Far Eastern populations. Finally, a scattering of persons from Near Eastern countries—Turkey, Syria, Lebanon—were in the lower class. (Most Lebanese and Syrians in Kansas City were, like the Greeks, moderately prosperous entrepreneurs. The Greeks owned restaurants, and the Lebanese and Syrians owned luxury goods importing businesses. These families were not, of course, lower class; and a number of them lived in mansions in older areas of the city.)

Midwesterners

Almost one of five lower class families was a white, old line American, product of a midwest farm or small town, or occasionally of Kansas City itself. The handicaps of these families were personal rather than cultural—character defects, low mental ability, or physical deformities. The life history of Jed Stigler, however, shows how a man born with no serious handicaps can nevertheless wind up in the lower class of a large city. The son of a carnival concessionaire, Jed Stigler spent the first eight years of his life on the road. At thirteen, after completing four grades of school, he "ran away from home for good." He drifted out to California and during thirty years there, "went through three wives and lots more jobs." He recalled becoming "a real heavy drinker when I was about twenty-two and learned that my first wife was playing around on me." From then until 1946 he "drove a truck whenever I was sober, was a darned bum whenever I was drunk, and married two more women."

In 1946 he happened to stop in Kansas City and met his present wife when he took some shirts into a laundry where she was working. A year later he married her and moved to Kansas City. Since then he has stopped drinking, except for "a bottle of beer every so often when I'm watching TV and it's about bedtime." Jed and Shirley had been married seven years, and Jed was working sixty hours a week. Forty of them he drove a big "semi" for one of the local trucking firms, and the other twenty he spent at a branch dry cleaning shop he and his wife had begun to manage the previous year. The shop was on the edge of the downtown district, only one street south of Kansas City's skid row. Most of the customers were men and women who lived in nearby transient hotels.

Jed had fathered "five children I know of," none by Shirley. The youngest, the only one with whom he was in contact, was fifteen and already married. Jed said, "I'm probably a grandfather to a lot of kids out there in California—I'm not going to go lookin' them up, though, and I hope they don't find me. I want to let bygones be bygones."

Jed credited Shirley with "making a new man of me." They maintained a running battle, however, over his attitude toward religion. Jed said he had "no use for the Bible—I just don't understand it, and what all those preachers say don't make sense to me; I don't believe it." In contrast, Shirley was certain that "there's God's truth in the Bible" and attended services at a Church of God in Christ. She admitted having changed churches about every two or three years, trying to find one which would give her "satisfaction"

that "they have the truth." All the churches she had tried were—
like the present one—in the evangelistic, fundamentalist tradition.

The Stiglers did not claim any friends or club memberships
in Kansas City. Jed described his attitude toward clubs, parties, and
friends as follows: "I don't like them. I never have been one to run
around in a bunch. I like to keep sort of to myself—that way you
stay out of trouble and don't make enemies." Shirley was much the
same way; she had always been "suspicious of people" she said, and
"would just as soon that no one comes around to bother me." She
had "never been one for visiting with other women—it's all gossip
and poison and doing other people harm."

One-third of the old line midwestern white Americans in
the lower class and 10 per cent of other lower class people were
physically handicapped—blind, deaf, one-armed, or otherwise de-
formed since birth or from injury. This frequency was six times
greater than among any other social class. Approximately one-tenth
of the lower class families did not belong in the slums on the basis
of parental origin, educational level, or income. For this group,
some traumatic past event had seemed to constitute a blow from
which they never recovered; for some, alcoholism was involved.

Marty and Lucy Caruthers are an example. In the summer
of 1954 Marty was working as a welder and reported an income
of over three hundred dollars a month. Both Marty and Lucy had
grown up in Kansas City as fifth and sixth generation Americans
of Scottish-English descent. Marty had completed ten grades of
school and one year of trade school education in welding; Lucy had
finished the ninth grade. Yet slumdwellers they were, living in "a
wretched little four room shack that has its toilet in an outside
privy." In this case, alcoholism was the problem. Marty had had
long periods of unemployment compounded by extended stays in
hospitals and state sanitariums, during which Lucy worked as a
laundress or maid and tried to keep their two children in school. It
was only for the year prior to the interview that Marty had held a
job for twelve straight months.

Single, Widowed, and Divorced

One out of every five persons in the lower class was living
alone in 1954, almost double the frequency in any other class. The
widows and divorced women who lived in slum apartments and

little run-down houses at the edge of the city were a particularly defeated and apathetic group.

Somewhat more cheerful than most of these women was Mrs. Hazel Sanders, born in Kansas City, daughter of a Welsh immigrant. In Wales her father and grandfather had worked in the collieries. After arriving in the United States, her father had worked at "whatever job he could find, most usually on the streets or hard roads, repair sort of work." As a little girl, Hazel had a "hard time in school" and did not go past the fourth grade.

At sixteen she married Clipper Sanders, nine years her senior. Hazel remembers proudly that "Clipper was a good provider," by which she meant that he almost always had a job, kept a roof over their heads, and food on the table. Clipper, like her father, worked at a variety of occupations: hodcarrier, cement finisher, coal hauler, and freight loader for the railroad. When he died at fifty, he left her with seven children and a four room house he had put together out of reject lumber, shingles, plywood, and scraps of tin. In 1954 Hazel still lived in this house, with her youngest and only unmarried son. It was located in the North Bottoms, which is on the south side of the Missouri River, in the valley floor. This is one of the city's most sparsely settled areas, and subject to floods. Hazel's house was described as a "makeshift cottage in a bad state of disrepair, with the interior very dirty."

Hazel worked as a dishwasher at a grade school cafeteria; her son worked in a laundry and dry cleaning plant as a loader on the delivery trucks, and gave his mother some rent and food money. This brought her income up to more than one hundred dollars a month. Some months, when she got babysitting jobs for the evening, it was more. This son, like Mrs. Sanders' other six children, did not go past eighth grade in school. Hazel Sanders referred to herself as a member of Christ Episcopal, one of Kansas City's Society-type churches. She started going to this church, located in the downtown area, after her husband died, because her mother had taken her there a few times as a little girl and she remembered "how good I would feel when I was sitting there beside mother in church—all troubles seemed to go away." She would like to be invited into church activities, such as preparing lunches for the ladies' guild meetings or for one of the fundraising socials, but she had never been asked. Her explanation was that, "I'm not in Society, you know."

Women younger than Mrs. Sanders who lived in the slums and had growing children at home were usually recipients of aid-to-dependent-children grants; some of the older women reported themselves on other forms of public assistance. Many were cared for by social welfare agencies, and some were apparently beneficiaries of private donations from well-to-do families. A few, like Mrs. Sanders, proudly denied being "on charity" and insisted they were managing on their own resources.

One of the single men of this class, Pete Kowalcyzk, was an "urban hermit." Pete lived in a little tin-covered hut, just one large room with bed, chair, table, potbellied stove, sink, old wooden ice box, and a pair of coal-oil lamps. There was no street address except "Howarth Road," which is little more than a rutted path paralleling the banks of the Missouri River. The hut was not connected by electricity or telephone or gas line or water pipe to the city. Pete was fifty-eight and had lived in this hut ever since the Depression—almost twenty years. Pete never had a regular job in all those years. He kept alive, and off relief, by fishing and selling his catch to a local fishdealer. Indeed, fishing was all that Pete had done since 1930 for either fun or money. He denied having any friends, claiming he liked to "live off to myself, away from people, as much as they'll let me."

Before 1930 Pete had been married and had a son. His wife left him and his son was killed in the Second World War. Even when married, he never had a regular job for more than a few months at a time. In his younger days he sometimes worked at one of the packing houses, but he could never stick at the job for very long because "I just don't like workin' for nobody." Pete's parents were Polish immigrants who came to Kansas City, Kansas, before Pete was born. His father was a bricklayer and packinghouse worker. Pete quit school in 1908, when he was twelve years old and still in third grade. "All I wanted to do then was go fishing—it made my old man pretty sore; he was always getting me jobs at the packinghouse, and I'd work a few weeks, then I'd just quit and go fishing." In 1954 he reported that his money income for the preceding twelve months had been "somewhere around six hundred dollars."

Pete Kowalcyzk was an exceptional case, not only for being a recluse but also because he was so willing to acknowledge lack of ambition. Almost all other lower class men described themselves as having tried hard at one time or another to improve their job and blamed their defeats on outside forces—accidents, ill health, or other people who had worked against them in some mysterious fashion.

A Class of Common Laborers?

In addition to housing and neighborhood, and racial and ethnic origin, the lower class in Kansas City was differentiated in various ways from the groups above them in the status hierarchy.

With regard to employment, among the forty to sixty-four-year-old lower class men in the sample, 6 per cent were unemployed and looking for work; 13 per cent were retired because of ill health or were temporarily out of work (and expecting to return to their jobs); 45 per cent were employed in unskilled jobs, 23 per cent in semi-skilled, and 13 per cent in skilled. The 6 per cent unemployed was relatively low, because, as already mentioned, 1954 was an unusually prosperous period in the Kansas City economy. The figure is to be compared to the 1.5 per cent unemployed among the men classified as working class (whether working-class-elite, -core, or -marginal). The number of lower-class men retired because of ill health was two or three times higher than in other classes (for example, the figure was 5 per cent in the working-class group).

All told, 55 per cent of lower class men fit the common conception of this class as a group composed of common laborers, the unemployed, and men retired from unskilled jobs. They worked for city street and water departments, in general repair and maintenance work, on heavy construction gangs, or for business and industry as night janitors, porters, railroad laborers, and deliverymen. Some were garbage collectors, trash haulers, floor sweepers, hodcarriers. Most of the women were employed in domestic service or as hotel maids, as operatives in laundries and cleaning establishments or cafeteria helpers.

Employment as a common laborer did not inevitably place a Kansas City man or woman in the lower class: one out of every four persons so employed was of working class, not lower class status, because he maintained a decent standard of housing, lived in a respectable neighborhood, and associated with average working class people. By the same token, 45 per cent of lower class men worked at jobs above the unskilled level.

A Class of Poorly Educated?

The typical lower class individual in the middle-aged sample was not markedly disadvantaged in education in comparison with working class people. On the average he had only one and a half years less schooling and 20 per cent had gone further than the eighth grade, which was average for the working class. Only 15 per cent could be regarded as seriously handicapped because they had completed less than four years of schooling. Only 7 per cent could neither read nor write English.

The grown children (born from 1910 to 1935) of parents in the sample were better educated than their parents but were more disadvantaged with respect to their contemporaries than their parents had been. The average adult child had dropped out of school before completing the tenth grade, and only 19 per cent had graduated from high school. This was in marked contrast to the children of working class families, 65 per cent of whom had finished high school. Lower class children had thus compounded the disadvantage of starting at the lowest socioeconomic level.

A Class of Disreputables?

Kansas Citians widely imputed criminality and immorality to the people at the bottom, as well as poverty and illiteracy. Using our sample survey and self-report interview methods, these accusations were difficult to prove or disprove. Of the eighty-three lower-class families in the sample, only one reported a family member in prison; only two men acknowledged an illegitimate child; none indicated that they were not legally married; and none recounted a previous common-law marriage. Extramarital relationships frequently were reported for ex-husbands or ex-wives, but rarely for the self. Alcoholism or another type of trouble was reported when the individual now felt proud that he had overcome it.

The great majority of lower class men and women sounded in interviews like the soul of honor, integrity, industry, and decency. They presented themselves as moral and respectable people, frequently sounding more middle class in these respects than middle-class respondents. It was clear that lower class people knew the prevailing value system of Kansas City and presented themselves as sharing these values, particularly when interviewed by persons who looked middle class.

To differentiate between reputation and fact with regard to the frequency of criminal or immoral acts, careful analysis of police, hospital, and welfare agency records would be required, a task we did not undertake in the present study. Newspaper accounts, while often helpful, can be misleading with regard to incidence, for they tend to emphasize the dramatic. One fact that emerged from examination of Kansas City newspapers, however, was that much of the immorality and criminality imputed to slum dwellers occurred outside the slums. Addresses given for persons arrested in connection with major thefts, prostitution, rape, forgery, kidnaping, and for those persons described as having criminal records, were not concentrated in slum areas but were scattered throughout the city, usually in areas of high transiency and declining neighborhoods, but by no means in the city's worst neighborhoods.

The one respect in which lower class people in our sample approximated the public imputation of "lack of standards" was in their record of marital instability and what Kansas Citians often called overbreeding. Divorce and multiple marriages were the rule rather than the exception—in marked contrast to the other social classes. In the middle-aged sample (with most women beyond the childbearing stage), the average lower class woman had borne 4.8 children, as compared with 2.6 for working class, 1.9 for lower-middle, 1.7 for upper-middle, and 2.1 for upper class.

Social Isolation

The lower-class middle-aged men and women in the sample were almost totally isolated from Kansas City's large array of social clubs and formal organizations. Only 3 per cent claimed any memberships beyond those in a labor union as required by their jobs. These were women in altar societies or ladies' missionary guilds, and men in ethnic clubs such as the Mexican Cultural Union or the Italian-American Club. Even labor union memberships were fewer at this class level than in the working class, since many of the men were not employed or were in nonunionized occupations.

Both the men and women of the lower class exhibited distrust of other people and a reluctance to establish friendships outside their circle of relatives. This attitude seemed prevalent except among those who lived within a tight knit ethnic neighborhood such as the Mexican district. Many lower-class people commented to the interviewer that they "don't bother with friends." For example: "I don't go bothering people and they leave me alone," or "it just seems that I don't like people—I don't like to be around them much, and I wouldn't belong to anything even if someone asked me." Except for the ethnically integrated, lower-class families seemed relatively isolated from families above them on the social ladder and also from other lower-class families.

Added to these impressions was the fact that in Kansas City there were far more lower-class people who had migrated from other communities than was true of other social class groups. Only 19 per cent of lower-class men and women, whether white or Negro, had been reared in the Kansas City area, as compared to 35 to 40 per cent in the other social classes. Lower-class people were isolated in yet another way. A very large percentage worked at odd and irregular hours—at night, or on weekends—a fact which seemed to contribute to the sense of marginality.

Religious Life

Whether or not in compensation for their relative social isolation, many lower class Kansas Citians seemed to seek a close relationship with the divinity. Eighty per cent of lower-class Negroes and 69 per cent of lower-class whites reported church membership or regular church attendance, a higher proportion than in the working class or in the lower-middle class. Of the church-going whites, one-third were Catholic and two-thirds were Protestant. Almost all the latter were affiliated with sects and churches scorned by higher-status Kansas Citians—the Assembly of God, Freewill Baptist, Church of God in Christ, Church of God of the Prophecy. The Full Gospel Tabernacle, Beams of Light, Church of Faith, Pilgrim Holiness, Foursquare Gospel, and Jehovah's Witness. Many of these were very tiny churches, housed in tents erected on vacant lots or in abandoned stores (the so-called storefront churches).

Among lower-class people four different patterns of religious attitudes and activities were evident. In one, religion and church were viewed as an escape from the realities of earthbound misery, and heaven was looked to as the promise of future happiness. This was the pattern found among many "hillbilly" families and among women of all cultural and ethnic origins. A second pattern, found among Italian, Mexican, and Polish Catholics, was the use of the church not only as a religious center but as a social center and as a tie to the mother country and its customs.

A third pattern, found mostly among men, was bitterness against religion and against churches. This attitude was common among Catholic men who had defied the church by marrying outside it or by contracting second and third marriages. It was also frequent among men of Protestant origin who were bitter about their low socioeconomic status and who had specific objection to the way they had been treated by a particular minister or churchman in the past.

The fourth pattern, less common than the others, was shame and guilt over being "not good enough" to go to church: too poor to have proper clothing, too poor to play an acceptable role, or too poor even to attend. This attitude was found mainly among Protestants who had been raised in a mainstream denomination—Presbyterian, Methodist, Episcopalian, or Christian—and who had been downwardly mobile. One woman said, "My husband and I would go, because we were raised good Baptists, but we don't have enough good clothes to wear—so we read the Bible every night and listen to radio services. I feel we are doing our best to be good Christians and hope we don't have to go to church to prove it."

Thus in religious behavior, no less than in other ways, many lower-class people in Kansas City tended to isolate themselves from the mainstream of working-class life and from generally accepted social patterns.

Chapter 11 ❦❦❦❦❦❦❦❦❦

Social Mobility
in Kansas City

𝒮tudies of social mobility for the most part have dealt with single indices of status, such as occupation or educational level (Rogoff, 1953; Jackson and Crockett, 1964; Duncan, 1965; see also Lipset and Bendix, 1959). In the present study, various dimensions of status have been combined in assessing the social positions of parents and children and in estimating the quantity and direction of social mobility occurring in American society. The present chapter deals first with the problems of measuring intergenerational mobility, then with several other questions: How is social mobility related to chronological age? What life experiences have been associated with mobility or with stability? What is the relative frequency of various routes or pathways of mobility?

Intergenerational Mobility

The most critical problem in studying intergenerational mobility is that of judging the class status of individuals and their parents at previous points in time.[1] Even when the information available can be assumed to be valid, there is the question of

---

[1] To measure status in previous generations by using more than one variable poses great problems, but the advantages are spelled out by Bloombaum (1964). See also Allingham (1967).

whether present-day criteria of social status are applicable to prior decades. For example, with the rise in real income that has occurred at all levels of the society from the 1920s on, working-class families in 1955 enjoyed a much higher standard of living than did a middle-class family of the 1920s. Similarly, the significance of a given educational level has changed from generation to generation. Indices of status position shift with time, and the indices must be modified if they are to be applied to previous eras.

Joseph Kahl, in evaluating research on the American class structure, takes the pessimistic view that our inability to reconstruct the standards of earlier periods makes it impossible to study social class mobility. He says: "The relative values . . . do not remain stable from one generation to the next. For example, a high school education would be worth much more in 1920 than in 1950, but we do not know how much more. . . . Furthermore, it would be impossible to get adequate information about the older generation. . . . For instance, how can one find out how a man's father identified himself, or who his friends were?" (Kahl, 1957, p. 252).

Quite obviously community evaluations of status dimensions cannot be obtained for parental generations, nor even from respondents at earlier stages in their own lives. Earlier studies of community structure can, however, be utilized as one source of data. Census data on the distribution of occupational, educational, and ethnic characteristics are also useful for the decades both before and after the 1930s. Given such resources, we can estimate the evaluations placed upon these characteristics, and we can estimate the social status of individuals who possessed various combinations of these characteristics.

Two assumptions are involved. The first is that the social status structure in America has rested throughout the past fifty years upon much the same occupational base. Despite the fact that the dichotomy between white-collar and blue-collar groups has been blurred since the 1920s, and despite a burgeoning working class and a shrinking lower class, we can nevertheless speak of a continuing upper-middle level of prosperous business entrepreneurs, managers, and professionals; a lower-middle level of white-collar workers, small businessmen, and highly skilled craftsmen; a working class of blue-collar workers; and a lower class of unskilled laborers. Each of these four status levels is defined primarily by the occupations of its members, just as was true in earlier decades. Furthermore, the public evaluation placed upon various occupations has remained relatively unchanged over the past four decades (see Hodge, Siegel, and Rossi, 1964).

The second assumption is that an individual's social status position a generation ago—while determined by the total patterning of social characteristics, including educational background, associations, religious affiliation, and ethnic identity—rested primarily on his occupation and his economic standard of living, as has continued to be true.

Inherited Social Status: Intergenerational social mobility is measured by comparing the status position of the adult with that of his parents. Although there are several alternatives, we chose to assess parental status at that point in time when the particular child with whom the parents are being compared reached adulthood. The social status a child inherits from his parents has thus been defined here as that which the parent held during the child's adolescence, just before the child was launched into his own adult career. This concept of inherited social status is illustrated in the case of Chet Rodewig.

Chet Rodewig's father was an oil well driller who experienced a dramatic up-and-down occupational career. During Chet's earliest years his family was on the brink of starvation several times, but during his adolescence his father was at a peak of financial and social success. Chet was sent to a fashionable university and joined one of the better fraternities. Thus we can say that he was launched into adulthood from an upper-middle status platform, a fact that remained unchanged even though ten years later, in the Depression of the 1930s, his father had been reduced to lower-middle status.

The judgments of a respondent's inherited status were made, of necessity, on the basis of the data provided by the respondent himself regarding occupational status, economic well being, educational backgrounds, ethnic identities, and religious affiliations of his parents. Respondents were questioned regarding the father's typical job as well as the father's best job. Each respondent was also asked, "Are you as well off as your parents were at the same age?" An additional bit of information which was sometimes helpful in classifying parents was the number of children born into these parental families. While we have relatively complete data on these points, it is evident that our evaluations of parental status involved greater sub-jectivity than did the status assignments of the respondents them-selves.

A classification procedure was adopted which relied most heavily upon the ratings given to parental occupation and economic well being. Based upon these ratings, the parental status assignment was modified whenever the educational attainments were sharply contradictory, or whenever ethnic identity or religious affiliation appeared to have been a major handicap or asset. A seven-point scale was employed in rating parents on occupation and economic well being. The seven points bore the same social significance as did the seven points in the Index of Kansas City Status described earlier. That is, there was a point corresponding to upper-class status, an-other for upper-middle status, and so on. For example, if a respon-dent's father had been a proprietor of a blacksmith shop (a re-putedly lower-middle occupation in the early part of this century), the parents were characterized as lower-middle—unless they were first generation immigrants, or backwoods rural Americans, in which case they were placed in the working class.

Characteristics of Parental Groups: The occupational character of the urban segments of the upper-middle and lower classes is quite similar for both generations. For example, 73 per cent of the urban upper-middle fathers were businessmen—owners, managers, or executives; for the sons, the corresponding figure was 78 per cent. The biggest alteration had come with the decline in self-employment among middle-class businessmen. In the parental gen-eration, 69 per cent of the upper-middle and upper-class business-men owned their own businesses, as did 56 per cent of the lower-middle businessmen. In the sons, however, these percentages had dropped to 37 and 15, respectively.

The societywide advance in educational levels is reflected in the comparison between median years of schooling for each status group in the two generations. The upper-class fathers averaged one year of college, upper-class sons, four years of college. Educational advances for other groups were similar; the median for upper-middle had risen from twelfth grade to two years of college; for lower-middle, it had jumped from eighth grade to twelfth grade; for working class, from sixth grade to eighth; and for lower class, from third to seventh grade. In short, in the mid-1950s, adults in each social level had spent as many years in school as had the previous generation of the next higher status level.[2]

Table 7 shows the occupational, educational, and rural-urban characteristics for the four parental groups. (The upper-class group, since there are so few in the sample, has been included with the upper-middles in this table.) The rural and small-town origins of middle-aged adults in Kansas City can be seen from the table. The large majority of "other urban" parents lived in small communities, mostly in Missouri, Kansas, and Iowa. Four-fifths of all parents were born in the United States.

Rates: From the Kansas City sample we were able to make estimates for 604 cases of social status at two points in their life cycle: late adolescence (inherited social status), and current age. For reasons discussed in the appendix, this sample was not representative. Upper-middle and lower classes were overrepresented, and Negroes were overrepresented. Accordingly, in order to make more accurate estimates of rates of mobility, the sample was altered in two ways.

First, Negroes were separated from whites. Negroes had faced very different problems in accomplishing social mobility. For example, discriminations in occupational opportunity had forced them into lower level jobs and had automatically prevented most of them from rising out of the lower class, as indicated by the fact that 40 per cent of the Negro sample—in contrast to 5 per cent of the white—were identified as having been lower class throughout their lives. While the sample of Negroes was relatively small ($N = 109$), differences in rates of mobility between the two racial groups for larger samples can be estimated from our finding that over two-thirds of the Negroes had been socially stable as compared to only half the whites. The percentages of stable, upwardly mobile, and downwardly mobile were 69, 23, and 8 for Negroes as compared with 51, 36, and 13 for whites. Because Negro mobility patterns were so different from those of whites, Negro cases were omitted from subsequent analyses.

Second, the data from the 495 white cases were projected

---

[2] Our evidence indicates that the children of our respondents were repeating this trend, with the typical upper-middle son or daughter graduating from college, those from lower-middle families attending college one or two years, and working-class children graduating from high school.

Table 7. CHARACTERISTICS OF FOUR PARENTAL GROUPS[a]

	Upper-middle[b] (N = 68)	Lower-middle (N = 147)	Working class (N = 195)	Lower class (N = 85)	Total (N = 495)
			Per Cent		
Occupation:					
Businessmen (owners and employees)	68	41	5	—	24
Professionals	25	5	—	—	5
Laborers and blue-collar workers	—	28	55	62	40
Farmers	7	26	40	33	31
TOTAL	100	100	100	100	100
Education:					
College (one or more years)	34	9	—	—	7
High school (one or more years)	50	34	8	5	23
Grades 4–8	16	57	73	45	55
Grades 0–3	—	—	19	50	15
TOTAL	100	100	100	100	100
Place of residence:					
Kansas City	42	30	24	25	29
Other urban	51	44	36	37	40
Rural	7	26	40	38	31
TOTAL	100	100	100	100	100

[a] For white men and women only.
[b] Includes the few upper-class cases.

onto a hypothetical population properly weighted with regard to status distribution.[3] Table 8 presents our estimate of the inherited social statuses that would be found among a representative sample of one thousand white middle-aged Kansas City residents. It is from Table 8 that estimated rates of social mobility have been made in the sections to follow.

Approximately 51 per cent of Kansas City's adult white population in the forty to seventy age group were identified with the same social class as that with which they were identified as adolescents. That is, half have been socially stable; 36 per cent have been upwardly mobile; and 13 per cent have been downwardly mobile. It should be noted that, as frequent as social mobility seems to be, the instances of dramatic upward and downward moves were exceedingly rare. Only 4.5 per cent had increased their status by more than one level, and less than one per cent had fallen two steps.

From the evidence given in Table 8 it is estimated that only 39 per cent of the parents of these white middle-aged Kansas Citians were identified with the middle or upper classes, compared to 52 per cent of their now-adult children. In general, Kansas City upper status levels include many who have been upwardly mobile, while the lower status levels are primarily composed of people who have been more or less stable. With the exception of the upper class, the mobility patterns consistently point in the same direction. That is, increasingly large proportions of each higher social class are made up of individuals who have been upwardly mobile, while increasingly large proportions of each lower class are composed of people who have been downwardly mobile.

[3] We took a projected population of one thousand white adults aged forty to sixty-nine. In such a population, if our estimates of the class distribution were correct, there would have been 21 in the upper class, 131 upper-middle, 366 lower-middle, 400 working class, and 82 lower class. In our sample of 495 cases, there were 28 upper, 89 upper-middle, 159 lower-middle, 166 working, and 53 lower class. The mobility data for each class group were projected from the actual sample onto the hypothetical population. For example, among the 159 lower-middle cases in the sample, 15 had inherited upper-middle status and had been downwardly mobile; 71 were originally lower-middle and had remained stable there; 64 had moved up from working-class origins; and 9 had moved up from lower-class origins. When these data were projected onto a hypothetical lower-middle group of 366 cases, we estimated that 163 of these 366 were socially stable, that 147 of them had moved up from the working-class level, and so on.

Table 8. Inherited and Adult Social Status in a Projected Sample of 1,000 Middle-Aged White Persons

Inherited Status	Number at each social level in 1955					
	Upper	Upper Middle	Lower Middle	Working Class	Lower Class	Total
Upper Strata:						
Upper[a]	10	5	—	—	—	15
Upper Middle	8	42	35	7	—	92
Lower Strata:						
Lower Middle	2	63	163	55	2	285
Working Class	1	19	147	239	23	429
Lower Class	—	2	21	99	57	179
TOTAL	21	131	366	400	82	1,000

Total, upwardly mobile .... 36 per cent
Total, stable .... 51 per cent
Total, downwardly mobile .... 13 per cent

[a] These projections of mobility into and out of the upper class are based on data from the special study of the upper class as well as from interviews with upper status respondents; this provided data on 2,270 middle-age families currently of upper status, plus another large number of families and individuals formerly of that status. Of the total number who had been at the upper-class level as adolescents, 69 per cent had remained at the same level, while the other 31 per cent had been downwardly mobile (in a few cases even down to the working class).

The apparent exception of the upper-class group serves to emphasize the separation of this group from the upper-middle. As shown in Table 9, the staying power of the upper class (the extent to which people do not move out of or into the class) is far beyond that of the upper-middle. The upper class defied the general rule that successively higher strata recruited increasingly large percentages of their members from individuals born into lower social strata. The upper-class group in Kansas City seems to have been a difficult class to move into—perhaps because its members exercised greater selectivity in "admission policy" through their clubs and their informal patterns of social acceptance and ostracism (as described in Chapter Six). In contrast, an upper-middle position seems to have been a precarious one, as witnessed by the fact that almost half of those born into this stratum had dropped to a lower status position by their middle-adult years. At the same time, as compared to the upper class, far fewer social barriers seem to have been erected around this group to block the entrance of new applicants. The upper-middle level had been reached by many newcomers who had demonstrated—by their professional and financial successes—their right to status positions above the common man level. All in all, this stratum experienced the greatest turnover from generation to generation. If the findings from this sample can be generalized, the upper-middle level stands as a reasonable goal for many socially ambitious Americans—it can be reached from almost any class of origin.

Status at the working-class level is perhaps easiest of all to maintain. Given average capacities and no dramatic misfortunes, most persons can maintain this status with only ordinary effort. To advance into or to retain lower-middle status, on the other hand, the breadwinner of the family must possess competence at either sales work or clerical tasks or must develop a high level of mechanical-technical skill.

Meanwhile, decline to or maintenance of lower-class status seemed to involve characteristics of quite another type, because more than half of the white children born in the lower class had risen out of it. Apparently some extraordinary debilitation, personal disorganization or incompetence was required for an individual to stay at this lowest level, particularly if no handicap of ethnic identity was involved.

Table 9.   STAYING POWER OF THE FIVE SOCIAL STATUS GROUPS[a]

Current Social Level	Always at Same Level	Only as Children	Only as Middle-aged Adults	Total
		Per Cent		
Upper Strata:				
Upper	39	19	42	100
Upper Middle	23	28	49	100
Lower Strata:				
Lower Middle	33	25	42	100
Working Class	41	32	27	100
Lower Class	28	60	12	100

[a] Percentages based on projected sample of 1,000. This table is to be read this way: Of the projected 181 persons in 1,000 who are currently upper-middle class or inherited that status and since moved up or down from it, only 42 (or 23 per cent) have stayed in the class at both measured points, adolescence and current age; 49 (or 28 per cent) who were in the upper-middle class as adolescents have since moved up or down out of the class; and 89 (or 49 per cent) have been in this class only as adults.

Place of Origin: It is often suggested that people who move about from one place to another are thus reflecting greater motivation to change their social status than is true of those who remain in the same locality. To check the relationship between geographic and social mobility, the sample of adults was classified into three categories according to place of residence during adolescence: Kansas City and its satellite communities, other urban or small-town locales, and farms. The percentages of socially stable in each group were 56, 45, and 53 respectively. These differences were small, but they support the hypothesis that there is a positive relationship between social and geographic mobility: Those who originated in Kansas City had been socially stable somewhat more often than those who had moved from other towns; and of persons who had moved into Kansas City, the farm-born were not so frequently upwardly mobile as were the city- or town-born. There were differences, however, by social class of origin. Those who had

Table 10. GEOGRAPHIC ORIGIN OF UPWARD MOBILITY

| Inherited Status | Origin | | |
| | Kansas City | Other Urban | Farm |
		Per Cent	
Upper Middle	12[a]	18	—
Lower Middle	17	28	32
Working	38	45	29
Lower Class	64	82	52

[a] This table is to be read as follows: Of those originating in upper-middle Kansas City families, 12 per cent were upwardly mobile.

come from rural lower-class families had much less often climbed up into the middle classes than had those who were city-born lower-class. On the other hand, those with lower-middle farm origins had been upwardly mobile somewhat more frequently than those of lower-middle urban origins. These data are shown in Table 10.

There are several factors involved in the different rates of upward mobility in these various groups. First, farm mechanization probably contributed to the movement from farms into the city of many lower-class people who were seeking employment rather than an improvement in social status. Second, rural-born lower-class people were generally less educated and more folkish in their behavior than were people born in the city. Many had been relatively unable to adapt to the requirements of urban living and had remained isolated from the ongoing stream of urban life. (These people were known in Kansas City as "hillbillies.") The upward mobility of farm-born middle-class people into the upper-middle level reflects a different set of factors. Urban life probably attracts farm-born middle-class individuals whose drives or talents press them toward occupational roles that require an urban setting. Considering these various phenomena, it appears that while geographic movement facilitates social mobility, and sometimes may be necessary, it is neither *sine qua non* nor guarantee of mobiilty.

Age: Social status changes continue to occur throughout adulthood. Accordingly, the rates of social mobility among adults of a particular sample are relative to the age distribution of that sample. That is, the quantity and direction of intergenerational mobility varies according to the age-period at which the comparisons between offspring and parent are made.

When our sample was divided by age into forty to forty-nine, fifty to fifty-nine, and sixty to sixty-nine, intergenerational mobility rates varied as shown in Table 11. In that table another age category has been added, young adulthood, based upon additional data gathered on eighty-seven men whose social mobility patterns had been studied in more detail than for the remaining cases.

The table shows that the further an individual had moved in age from the time he left the parental household, the less likely he was to still be in the same status as that of his parents. In general the life period in which upward intergenerational mobility was most common was early adulthood. Once age forty was reached, the frequency of upward mobility dropped off sharply. (In the upper class, however, the percentage upwardly mobile into the class increased throughout adulthood, until at least late middle age. Only 42 per cent of upper-class members in the forty to forty-four age group—

Table 11. Changes in Mobility Rates by Age

Inter-generational Pattern[a]	Age of Respondents			All age groups	When *R*s were aged 25–29[b]
	40–49	50–59	60–69		
			Per Cent		
Stable	55	51	48	51	67
Upwardly Mobile	34	37	35	36	22
Downwardly Mobile	11	12	17	13	11
TOTAL	100	100	100	100	100

[a] The table is to be read as follows: In comparing the social status of respondents aged forty to forty-nine with the social status of their parents (as determined for the period of the respondent's late adolescence), 55 per cent were found to have remained at the same social level.

[b] Estimates projected from detailed life history data available for eighty-seven men in the sample.

but 67 per cent of those in the sixty-five to sixty-nine group—had moved up into the class from lower origins.) After the mid-fifties, when status losses had become more frequent than status gains, a few individuals who earlier moved above their parents had moved back down again, and others who earlier had been stable had now fallen into the downward mobile category.

Mobility During Adulthood

For investigation of the social and psychological processes associated with mobility at various stages of adulthood, a special set of data were available from a sample of eighty-seven middle-aged men. These men had been interviewed at length about their occupational histories and their social experiences with regard to schooling, marriage, and club memberships. Status assessments were made for two earlier periods of their adult lives, the late twenties and the early forties.

The earlier of these two ages was chosen on grounds that by age twenty-seven or twenty-eight, most men were settled into their careers, even young professionals; and the majority had married and had had children of their own. By the late twenties, then, most men may be said to have established social status positions in their own right. The early forties was chosen as the second age period, on grounds that by that age most of the major changes in a man's status will have occurred. It is usually said that the occupational destiny of a white-collar worker is sealed by the time he is forty-five. By then it has usually become clear whether he will ever reach the managerial or executive echelons, or whether instead he will have settled onto a plateau, along which further gains will primarily be increases in income based upon seniority.

In determining the status of these eighty-seven men at earlier points in their lives, the principal evidence was the respondent's report of his occupational status at these previous periods. (As part of the career history, each man had been asked to compare the various jobs he had held, the remuneration received, and the status accorded him.) Additional evidence on the standard of living was obtained by asking each man also to describe the relative merits of the houses and the neighborhoods in which he had lived at previous points in time.

A special problem arose in basing the status assessments for young men upon occupational and economic indexes. The occupations had to be evaluated for implied future potential as well as already demonstrated accomplishment. No man in the sample had attained an upper-middle-marginal post by the time he was twenty-seven or twenty-eight; the success of any given professional career was still undetermined; and in fact, the job titles held by most young men of upper-middle status were identical with those held by many young men of lower-middle status. So too, the housing of young adults had to be evaluated in light of the chronological age of the inhabitants. It appeared, for example, that most lower-middle adults had lived in their late twenties—because of their relatively lower incomes at this point—in housing comparable to that occupied by middle-aged working-class people. Accordingly in rating young adults, their potential status as well as characteristics of the moment was given careful attention. Among factors taken into account were family background and, in particular, level and style of education. When estimating the status of men in their mid-forties, all their attributes were profiled according to the Index of Kansas City Status; then judgments were rendered on the basis of this profile.

The course of individual mobility through adulthood cannot be understood without taking account of the fact that there is a societywide excess of upward over downward mobility which prevails among men in all the age groups below the fifties. Indirect evidence on this point was provided within this limited sample. When the eighty-seven cases were used, they were found to be distributed at four successive age periods in the manner shown in Table 12. Of the eighty-seven men, approximately 10 per cent had been identified with the two upper strata when they left their parental homes; by the early forties, however, the figure was 15 per cent. Meanwhile, at the two lower levels, the proportion had dropped with age from 62 per cent to 48 per cent. Table 10 shows also that a sizable proportion of these men experienced upward mobility during their early adult years, but that the amount of mobility dropped off sharply after middle adulthood.

The total amount of upward or downward mobility cannot be estimated simply by adding the percentages of those who have been mobile during successive age intervals, for at any age period a certain amount of earlier mobility is cancelled out, and a small

Table 12. SOCIAL STATUS AT FOUR PERIODS OF ADULTHOOD[a]

	Late adolescence (inherited status)	Age 25–30	Age 40–44	Age 55–69
	Per Cent			
Upper Class	2	2	3	4
Upper Middle	8	9	11	13
Lower Middle	28	33	38	34
Working Class	44	42	41	38
Lower Class	18	14	7	11
TOTAL	100	100	100	100

[a] This table is not statistically weighted toward a representative sample; these percentages refer directly to the eighty-seven men sampled, only forty-seven of whom were fifty-five years of age or older.

amount is enlarged upon by persons moving further up or down the scale. In the present sample, the upward mobility of one-third of those who advanced between ages eighteen and twenty-seven was cancelled out between ages twenty-seven and forty-five by a retreat to the original status level, while 19 per cent of those who achieved upward mobility in the first period continued to advance during the second period.

The course of social mobility, once launched upward, does not always continue upward, nor is the course necessarily irreversible once it has begun in a downward direction. A great deal of intergenerational social mobility may be concealed when rates of mobility are based on measurements taken at any one point in time. Only 35 per cent of the middle-aged men in our sample had experienced lifelong social stability, even though at any one time, in comparing a man's status with that of his parents (when he himself was in late adolescence), the lowest proportion would have appeared to be 46 per cent.

Adolescence to Early Adulthood: It has usually been assumed that education is the principal key to a man's social status during his early adult years, and that unless he has secured more education than is typical for his class of origin it is unlikely that he can move up the social scale in the early phases of his career. It would appear from our evidence that this assumption is well founded, even though our measure of status was itself based partly upon level of education, so that the two measures cannot be entirely separated. At the same time, the ratings of social status, even in young adulthood, are to some extent independent of educational level, as is illustrated in the following cases.

French Gilbert came from a lower-middle family and had attended a teachers' college located in his home town of Warrensburg, Missouri. He had completed his training and was teaching in a rural community during his late twenties. He had married a girl of similar status who had attended the same college for a year. Even though both had attended college and he was a teacher, they could not be said to have moved beyond the lower-middle level.

On the other hand, Harry Briskobie, a salesman, had been a working-class boy who quit school at tenth grade (see Chapter Eight). He had moved into Kansas City and had acquired his present sales route by the time he was twenty-five. His wife was a high school graduate, the daughter of a lower-middle class grocer. Thus, despite his relatively low educational level, Harry Briskobie had become clearly identified as lower-middle by his late twenties.

Jerome Sullivan's father was a successful Irish immigrant railroad contractor who had achieved lower-middle status. Mr. Sullivan believed in the virtues of hard work, and urged Jerome to quit school after the eleventh grade and to take a job as board-marker in a brokerage house. Before young Sullivan was twenty he had moved to a bookkeeper's position with the brokerage firm; at twenty-four he had become a customer's man; and at thirty he was named the Kansas City representative for a prominent New York investment firm. Meanwhile, he had married the college-graduate daughter of a prosperous Irish-Catholic bank official. The Sullivans were definitely in Kansas City's young upper-middle group by the time Jerome was twenty-eight.

In these cases, social mobility or lack of it occurred in early adulthood despite incongruent educational level. Still, these cases were more the exception than the rule. Among the young men who had acquired the educational advantages associated with a higher status level, almost half had translated these educational assets into social status gains by the time they had reached their late twenties, and none had declined in status. Of those whose educational levels were typical for members of their class, 13 per cent had gained in status and 10 per cent had declined. Of those whose educational levels were below average for their group, half had lost social status. Analysis of all the data led to the conclusion that lack of extra education more seriously limited the chances for upward mobility during early adulthood than had extra educational accomplishment insured it.

Educational accomplishment alone was not sufficient to produce a change in social status during early adulthood, as shown by the fact that only half the young men from lower status levels who had attended college had reached the upper-middle level—and each of these men had married upper-middle girls or else had acquired unusually favorable reputations in their business organizations. Similarly, only half of the youth from the two lower levels who had graduated from high school had moved up into the lower-middle level. The differences between those who did and those who did not move up the social scale by their late twenties were usually found in the educational and social status of their wives as well as in the kinds of jobs they themselves secured.

Upward mobility from the lower class during early adulthood appeared to be easier to achieve than from any other level. Once again, however, educational advantages were not prerequisites. Stable character, hard work, thrift, and the acquisition of a medium-level manual skill seemed to be the requirements—and fifty per cent of the sons of lower-class origin had passed those tests for admission into higher social levels by their late twenties.

The almost exclusive route for upward mobility into the upper class during the early adult years is illustrated in the case of Fletcher Sartain; he married up (see Chapter Six). Sartain was prepared for this accomplishment in the best possible way, for he had obtained a prestige education. It was by virtue of the fraternity connections he established during his years at Tulane University that he happened to be present at a party in one of New Orleans' most fashionable Garden District homes, and there met the upper-class Kansas City girl who became his wife.

In summary, the 22 per cent of men in our sample who exhibited upward mobility in this first period of adulthood was composed of 12 per cent who accomplished the upward move with the aid of education and 10 per cent who managed it without such educational advantages. Among the 11 per cent who exhibited downward mobility, all but 2 per cent initiated this movement by failure in the realm of education.

Early Adulthood to Mid-Forties: The fifteen to twenty years between young adulthood and middle age was the period when the greatest amount of social mobility occurred in this sample. Thirty-six per cent of the men at age forty-five were in a different social class than at age twenty-seven, with 24 per cent having moved up, and 12 per cent down.

Although it is commonly assumed that the prime route for mobility during this period is found in the man's occupational achievement, the relationship between occupational achievement and social mobility was not a simple one. The nature of the relationship is greatly confused by the fact that occupational success during this period of adulthood is much more prevalent than is upward mobility. At least 70 per cent of the men in our sample felt that they had greatly improved their standard of living as they had progressed from early to middle adulthood—improved, that is, beyond the general rise in living standards which characterized the American society as a whole. These men pointed to the fact that they were living in much better houses during their middle forties than those they had occupied during their late twenties; that they had moved to more desirable neighborhoods; that they owned more material goods; and that their bank accounts were larger. In all these ways, they believed they were better off at age forty-five than they had been at twenty-seven.

According to our ratings, 48 per cent of these men had improved their occupational positions—they had clearly advanced in the job hierarchy and they were being remunerated at a much higher rate (after correcting for the changing value of the dollar). Yet in only half these instances had occupational success led to social status gains. Much of this occupational and economic success was nothing more than the benefits of seniority. Because it is the normal course of events in our society for a man to advance up the occupational ladder as he approaches his middle forties, occupational status is age-graded, and the social status significance of a man's occupation is relative to his chronological age. In a very real sense the occupational failures are not only those who go downhill but also those who do not advance upward at the normal rate. It is therefore the men who exceed or fall behind the *average* increase in occupational status who experience social mobility.

For example, almost all the young men who were placed in upper-middle levels during their late twenties either held jobs at junior management ranks or were struggling young businessmen and professionals (lawyers, physicians, teachers) who had just begun their careers. In this category were Warren Knight, a rising young salesman for Valley Steel; Ned Clay, advertising artist for a leading department store; Durward Gregory, managerial trainee at the same department store; David Austin, insurance company personnel department assistant; Paul Wellman, high school journalism teacher; and Walter Hallstrom, founder-builder of a radio manufacturing firm. By their early forties, these men were split widely in their occupational accomplishments and social status. Walter Hallstrom was in the process of scoring one of the nation's most impressive business successes, had already climbed up to Level III of Kansas City's non-Capital S upper class, and was destined to go still further; Warren Knight had become, through social connections established in his young manhood, a successful executive in one of Kansas City's medium sized businesses and was on the same social plane as Walter Hallstrom but not likely to go further; Durward Gregory had progressed faster than anticipated to a semi-executive position in Kansas City's top-ranked department store and was recognized as part of the upper-middle-elite, with a real chance for advancement in his next ten years into Level IV of the upper class; David Austin had proceeded in the normal course and at a normal rate to becoming personnel manager for his company and was an upper-middle-core member, while Ned Clay and Paul Wellman had remained at the same occupational level or gone somewhat downhill and hence were part of the upper-middle-marginal social world.

These patterns of occupational and social mobility were repeated among men who in their early twenties were at the lower-middle class level. Samuel Levy, for example, achieved a marked occupational success, rising from shoe salesman at Teller and Sons to prosperous owner of Teller-Levy. This occupational success was in turn translated into social mobility: he had been accepted into membership at the Idlewild Country Club, and he lived in a big house in the Country Club area. Jack Whittier, on the other hand, who had been an inventory clerk at Westinghouse Electric and had become a top salesman in the Kansas City area, is an example of a man who had achieved typical occupational success without reaping any social class mobility; he had reached lower-middle elite.

When mobility was accomplished from working class to lower middle in the period from early adulthood to mid-forties, it rarely involved transition from a blue-collar to a white-collar job. Almost invariably this mobility was achieved instead by success within the blue-collar hierarchy—by attaining the level of foreman or shop supervisor or by becoming a contractor—and by translating such occupational success into middle-class housing and living habits. Doug Troast, a railroad engineer, was one such example; in moving up from an early-adulthood identification with the working class, Troast was joined by many other blue-collar workers who used their pay increases to move into middle-class houses, neighborhoods, and associations. Thus, the occupational composition of the lower-middle class was drastically altered between the two age periods: in young adulthood, only 6 per cent of the lower-middles were in blue- or gray-collar jobs; by middle adulthood, it was 38 per cent.

Almost all the working-class men who remained stable during these years of their lives reported considerable increases in their living standards and housing conditions. They credited this improvement to the general increase in well-being of the working class, to union organization, and to the gains that automatically came with job seniority.

In the period from early to middle adulthood, mobility up and down between working and lower classes was directly related to economic standing, but the latter was in turn a product of personal stability. For instance, Robert Volmerich's rise into the working class came as a result of his marriage and the fact that he returned from Army service an emotionally steadied man. Jed Stigler remained in the lower class, despite many opportunities for remunerative employment, because he had developed an alcohol problem.

In illustrating the relationship of occupational and social mobility between early and middle adulthood, the conclusion seems warranted that occupational success between the late twenties and middle forties is no guarantee of upward social mobility, even though it is a very important aid. As a man moves through his thirties into his middle forties, changes in life style must accompany improvements in occupational status if the latter are to be translated into social mobility.

Mid-Forties to Sixties: In contrast to the earlier periods, little social mobility occurred during later adulthood. Ninety-one per cent of the men in this sample remained stable in status position through the years from forty-five to seventy. Furthermore, whatever mobility occurred usually proceeded in the direction opposite that of earlier years. Only 2 per cent of the men moved upward during this period, while 7 per cent moved downward.

The changes that occurred could be traced to occupational mobility, which in turn most often reflected decline in physical or mental health. Occupational mobility itself was less frequent than during the early period. Sixty per cent of the men had changed in occupational status between early and middle adulthood, but only 35 per cent changed between middle and late adulthood. Many of the latter changes, furthermore, were too slight to be scored as changes on our occupational and economic scales. One-tenth of the men believed they had improved their status; they had risen to higher positions within their organizations, or, as independent entrepreneurs, they had prospered more in the 1940s and 1950s than in the 1930s. Yet 25 per cent believed they were not doing as well as when they were in their middle forties. The latter were primarily men with specific health problems; or they were blue-collar workers suffering from declining physical vigor.

Among the older men who believed their occupational and economic status had improved since they were forty-five, only one in five could be said to have achieved upward mobility in consequence of these economic improvements. One such instance was that of Thomas McNally. Thomas McNally, born a poor Irish boy on Goat Hill, established a trucking business that grew enormously as he moved through his fifties into his early sixties. Until his middle forties, McNally had concentrated all his energies on building his business, but during his fifties, as the community recognized his economic success, he took on many leadership roles in civic enterprises. He became a widely recognized leader of the Catholic elite in Emerald Hills, and at fifty-eight he joined the Tavern and Trail Club.

The upward mobility of Thomas McNally from upper-middle to upper class illustrates the type of mobility characteristic of this age period. In instances of great business success, movement into the upper class is often delayed until the men reach these later years, when simultaneously their children are becoming visible in the city's younger leadership, and the parents begin to take on an image as founders of dynasties.

Upward mobility from the lower-middle to the upper-middle class occurs during this age period under somewhat similar circumstances. Many ministers, schoolteachers, hospital or social service administrators are appointed to executive positions in their fields only after they have passed their middle forties. The same occurs among businessmen, both owners and employees. There are also some whose occupational status was sufficient for higher social status before the age of forty-five, but who did not, until their later years, change social club and church identifications and make the appropriate residential moves to qualify them for upper-middle class membership.

Upward mobility in the age range of the fifties and sixties was largely confined to the middle and upper classes. A very few blue-collar workers advanced in their occupations during these years —some of those who had been at the foreman level moved up to being foreman supervisors or works superintendents, for instance— but such occupational advances were seldom of significance in terms of social mobility.

All the downward social mobility, and most of the downward occupational and economic mobility, was found at lower status levels. As indicated earlier, much of this downward movement is directly traceable to health problems. Many of the carpenters, plumbers, painters, and electricians who had worked all their lives for independent contractors found themselves during their late fifties and early sixties unable to work as many hours as before. Even those without health problems found that contractors called upon them less often than upon younger men, apparently because they felt the older men had slowed down in productive capacities. Most of these gradual changes did not result in downward class mobility, even though it meant decreased income and somewhat lowered standards of living. The few men who did lose social status during these later years were those who had suffered serious accidents or who had became demoralized by one or another traumatic event and had undergone changes in life style. For example, a roofing foreman had been disabled in an accident, and his wife had to work as a laundress to support the family. Apparently this couple was demoralized by this turn of events, because when interviewed they were living in a slum apartment, were spending many of their evenings at the nearby bar, and spoke continuously of their better days before the accident.

Accidents or health difficulties did not seem to have such serious effects on upper-middle class men, most of whom had prepared themselves for such eventualities through investment or savings program. The wives of white-collar workers had usually obtained work as salesclerks or secretaries, and had managed to maintain their families at the same general status level, although in straitened circumstances.

Occupational and economic declines were often magnified by the decline in housing witnessed among these older families. Most lower-middle or lower-class families had remained in their older houses located in neighborhoods of declining social reputation, so that the community's evaluation of their housing usually placed them below the average for their class. Similarly, many upper and upper-middle class couples, as they had grown older, voluntarily reduced the status value of their housing by abandoning their large houses for apartments in fashionable buildings or for smaller modern houses. Although such changes in housing do not in themselves constitute loss of social status, they represent a loss in the surface credentials of status for many older couples who often find this difficult to tolerate.

Course: The foregoing discussion has indicated the principal routes of social mobility as they appear at three different stages of adulthood. Education, marriage, and occupation are intertwined in the earliest years when sons leave their parental homes and begin their own careers. Subsequent occupational success must be translated into other changes in life style—in neighborhood, in church membership, in clubs and associations—if social class mobility is to be realized during the middle and later adult years.

Perhaps the most important conclusion which emerged from

examining the relationship between occupational and social mobility is that a great deal of occupational mobility—that is, the steady improvement in occupational and economic status that occurred as men moved from young adulthood to their late forties or early fifties—represents merely the typical age-related sequence of events in urban American society. Thus, upward mobility required dramatic, above-average increases in occupational and economic standing.

Another fact that merits reiteration is that upward mobility, once launched, is not necessarily a smooth or consistent upward path; nor is downward mobility an irreversible process. Many careers reflected a series of up-and-down movements. Only one-third (36 per cent of the sample) of Kansas City's middle-aged men had remained stable in terms of inherited class positions throughout their adult years. The cases of Charles Parker and Jim Barstough are illustrations of the varied career lines that characterized this sample.

Charles Parker's father and mother were both college graduates, at a time when only 1 or 2 per cent of Americans attained such an educational level. The father owned a five-town telephone company in central Missouri. The family was clearly upper-middle class. Charles quit college after only one year, then further disappointed his parents by marrying a girl of whom they did not approve. Charles and his young bride left Missouri for Wyoming where they rented a small ranch. They had financial difficulties, then marital problems, and the marriage ended in divorce. At twenty-nine Charles returned to Kansas City where, through his father's connections, he found a job as farm appraiser for a mortgage company.

By then he was a changed young man, determined not to be the "only dead twig on my family's tree." Parker worked very hard to recover his lost status. He turned out to be a good judge of land and did well for his company. In his late forties he established a farm mortgage business of his own which prospered. He married again, this time his wife was a college graduate. At sixty-five, Charles Parker's income was well over twenty thousand dollars a year. He and his wife were members of the Shawnee View Country Club. They were well-established members of Kansas City's upper-middle class.

Jim Barstough's career was less fortunate. Born on a farm, he married a lower-middle class storekeeper's daughter, and took over the store at twenty-five when his father-in-law died. He ran the store well, with his wife's assistance, but the depression of the early 1920s hit, first the farmers of his region, and then the businessmen. His wife divorced him, and he returned to his father's farm. This too went under in the early 1930s, and at forty-two he moved back into town and found a job with the WPA.

The financial and marital disasters seemed to be psychological blows from which Jim could not recover. In the early 1940s he was working in a Kansas City war plant and was married to a young wife of lower-class background. In the middle 1950s he was living in a shack along a rural Jackson County road, scratching jobs for a week or so whenever he really needed money. He was apparently drinking heavily between jobs, and his wife had left him. Thus, Jim Barstough wound up on the bottom rung of the social ladder in his later years.

Factors of Social Mobility

Occupation: The principal factor in intergenerational social mobility was quite obviously occupational-economic status, as has been made clear in the previous section. Occupational mobility, however, was more nearly a prerequisite than a guarantor of intergenerational social mobility. For example, 91 per cent of the men who had been upwardly mobile also ranked higher on the occupational and economic scales than did their parents. Yet when these relationships were viewed from another perspective, it was found that, of those who had improved upon the occupational levels of their parents, only 69 per cent had managed to climb in social status. Similarly, of the men with jobs at lower levels than their fathers, only 44 per cent were at lower social status levels. Table 13 shows the relationships between occupational and social mobility.

These relationships lead to two generalizations about social mobility: First, sons usually retain the same social class positions as those of their fathers, even though they move upward or downward from their fathers' occupational levels. Only when occupational differences were dramatic did they produce differences in social status. (This was seen most clearly in respondents whose occupational positions were midway between typical upper-middle and lower-middle. In this group, almost all those who—because of their religious and social affiliations and their educational backgrounds— fell in the upper-middle class were themselves the sons of upper-middle class families or had married the daughters of upper-middle families. On the other hand, most of this group who fell in the lower-middle class proved—on inspection of their parental status— to have originated in the lower-middle class.)

Table 13.   OCCUPATION, EDUCATION, AND SOCIAL MOBILITY

	Social status of sons compared with that of fathers			
	Upwardly Mobile	Stable	Downwardly Mobile	Total
	Per Cent			
Occupational Level:				
Sons higher than fathers	69	31	—	100
Sons equal to fathers	11	86	3	100
Sons lower than fathers	—	56	44	100
Educational Level:				
Above average for class of origin	58	39	3	100
Average for class of origin	27	56	17	100
Below average for class of origin	12	54	34	100

The corollary generalization is that social mobility can proceed despite occupational stability. Of sons who were equal to their parents occupationally, 11 per cent had managed upward social mobility. These men illustrate the concept of second-generation consolidation, whereby the occupational and economic gains made by parents may result in upward mobility for their children rather than for themselves. This consolidation most frequently was achieved by sons of fairly prosperous blue-collar fathers, fathers who often encouraged their sons to become white-collar workers so that they would have a chance for the big executive positions. Some of these sons, although they never got beyond the lowest levels of the white-collar hierarchy, became identified with the lower-middle rather than the working class.

The number of cases of second-generation consolidation was very small; it would no doubt have been much larger had this study been conducted in a community with a large ethnic population. Rarely do immigrant parents achieve the status to which their economic success entitles them, since they usually retain the social taints of foreign accents and ethnic customs. Their children, how-ever, in forsaking these customs, often move into a higher social status level than their parents without having to outdo their fathers in occupational and economic accomplishments. These phenomena are reminders of the essentially social character of the social classes, and demonstrate once again why it is that occupational status does not precisely determine social status.

Education: The role of education in social mobility during early adulthood was discussed earlier. It can be said further, how-ever, that educational achievement does not appear to be as effec-tive as occupational achievement in producing changes in social status. Almost everyone has had more schooling than his parents, partly due to the ambitions of parents for their children.

In this analysis the respondents were divided into three groups: those who went to school longer than the average for their class of origin; those who were average; and those who quit school earlier than average for their social class. Table 13 shows that edu-cational level was less related to social mobility than was occupa-tional level. Education helped many men to launch careers of greater potential status than those of their fathers, but it did not guarantee that this potential would be realized. At the same time, many men managed to get ahead occupationally without educa-tional advantages.

In general, the direction of educational level—either above or below average for class of origin—was more important in pre-dicting an individual's ultimate status than was the absolute educa-tional level achieved. The man born into a working class family who completed the eleventh grade and thus exceeded the average educa-tion for his class of origin was more frequently a member of the lower-middle class in adulthood than was the lower-middle class man who, although he, too, completed the eleventh grade, fell below the average for his social class of origin. What seems to be important is the set toward mobility mainfested in these cases—the ambition to better oneself and the self-discipline to act upon this ambition. The relationship between educational level and social status is most marked during early adulthood; it declines thereafter as occupational achievement becomes ever more important in determining social status.

Marriage: Thus far we have referred only casually to the choice of marital partner as a factor in social mobility. Our data on marriage and mobility are limited, since they are based on only 105 couples for whom we had data on class of origin from both husband and wife. Nevertheless, two generalizations emerge: first, no more than half of these marriages had been contracted between social equals—that is, man and wife rated as same class of origin; 48 per cent had been contracted across social class lines. Among the latter, all but 4 per cent united men and women from immediately adjacent social levels. Thus, even though the odds were fifty-fifty that a man or woman would marry up or down the social ladder, it was extremely infrequent that a marriage bridged a wide difference in the social origins of the marital partners. (Many of the marriages across class lines occurred after one or the other partners had already partially crossed the class line through occupational or educational mobility.)

Second, a cross-class marriage increased an individual's chances for further social mobility at later ages. In marriages between social equals: 35 per cent of these couples achieved higher status by middle or late adulthood than their class of origin; 56 per cent remained stable through middle and later adulthood; and 9 per cent dropped to a lower status than that which they had inherited. In marriages between individuals from different classes: 16 per cent of these couples, by middle or late adulthood, had achieved a social class position higher than either partner had inherited; 54 per cent consolidated their status at the level of the originally higher partner; and 30 per cent involved a loss of status for one of the marital partners, but none involved a loss for both partners. Thus, 56 per cent of the men and women involved in equal marriages, but only 42 per cent of those involved in cross-class marriages, remained socially stable.

When these data were compared with the data on educational and occupational levels, marriage into a higher class level appeared to be as excellent a guarantee against downward mobility as was upward occupational mobility or more-than-average educational achievement.

The number of cases was too small to warrant the conclusion that women were more likely to marry up the social ladder than were men, although in this sample 53 per cent of the cross-class marriages were ones in which the women had married up.[4] The evidence from the unmarried men and women in the sample suggested that women were more likely than men to remain single if they could not marry at least a social equal. Only 11 per cent of all the women in this sample were downwardly mobile as compared with 15 per cent of the men, a difference that can be traced almost entirely to the single men and women. The majority of single men in this sample—bachelors, divorced men, and widowers—had been downwardly mobile. Of the single women—spinsters, divorcees, and widows—only a small number had been downwardly mobile. For single women, the more interesting fact was that many had converged upon the lower-middle class, whether originating at higher or lower levels. A large number of never-married women who originated in the middle classes had all been retained within the lower-middle class. Their ranks had been increased by an influx of single women born into the lower classes who had ascended into the lower-middle class as a consequence of having chosen to pursue such white-collar occupations as schoolteacher, salesclerk, or secretary.

Changes in Life Style: Throughout our discussion of mobility we have emphasized the necessity of changes in life style—that is, changes in the associational patterns, in church affiliations, in choice of residential neighborhoods—if gains in occupation, education, or marriage to a higher status partner were to be translated into social class mobility. Without such changes in life style, social mobility did not occur.

It has been widely hypothesized that changes in occupational-economic levels almost invariably precede other changes in

[4] There is evidence from other studies that to a slight degree women are more likely than men to marry up. See Hollingshead (1950); Zick (1968); and Ellis and Lane (1963).

life style. This belief is perhaps based largely on observation of behavior among the nouveau riche, whose social and cultural accomplishments have usually lagged behind their occupational and
economic achievements. From these observations it has been assumed that the same was true at lower social levels, that those
families within any class who displayed the highest consumption
standards were most likely to have been upwardly mobile into the
class and were being held back from further social advance by their
lack of social skills or cultural attributes. Certainly, there are such
cases within each status level. However, there are other families
at each level who have above average consumption standards but
who have not been upwardly mobile into the class—they have lived
their lives in the same class and have no particular wish to attempt
upward mobility, even though they possess the necessary economic
resources.

Sometimes changes in associational pattern precedes occupational and economic gains. There are many modestly paid blue-
collar families in the sample who moved into middle-class neighborhoods and joined middle-class associations and churches without
having achieved a middle-class occupation or income level. Determined to be identified with what they considered the decency and
respectability of the lower-middle stratum, these families used their
limited financial resources for this purpose.

It must be concluded, then, that the consumption-before-
culture hypothesis is applicable to some, but by no means to all,
cases of social mobility in this sample. Many different channels of
mobility were in evidence. Some families were moving up in social
status despite the lack of supporting occupational and economic
mobility; others were losing status, not because of occupational loss,
but because their behavior was not favorably judged by the community (this was particularly true in cases of marital instability,
retreat from social interaction, and unwise use of leisure or money).
Apparently many paths are open for the expression of mobility
drives, with the nature of the particular route varying according to
the talents and training of the individual.

Part Three

Nationwide Status Structure

Chapter 12

Social Classes Across the Nation, 1925-1960

$\mathscr{I}$n previous chapters we have shown that a large American city can be described as a social class structure composed of groups ranked in a status hierarchy. In the present chapter we ask how the class groupings delineated within the metropolitan area of Kansas City compare with those described by previous investigators in other towns and cities. How do the social classes compare in size and with regard to basic socioeconomic characteristics? To what extent is one justified in speaking of a nationwide status system in which the different classes identified are similar from community to community?

A Comparison of Eight Communities

To this end, seven other communities have been selected for comparison. The communities are self-contained (that is, they are not suburbs or satellites of big cities); their status structures as a whole have been the focus of study (rather than discrete parts of the structure) and have been described in considerable detail by their respective investigators. They are grouped here according to the methods used by the investigator:

The first group consists of small communities studied by the method of evaluated participation (including systematic clique

analyses) and by extensive interviewing of community residents
regarding their views of the status system and their rankings of
fellow citizens. Using these procedures, all adult members of the
community were placed into status groups, which were then examined for socioeconomic characteristics and cultural and associational patterns. Newburyport, Massachusetts, a community of seventeen thousand, was studied by Warner and Lunt early in the 1930s
(Warner and Lunt, 1941); Morris, Illinois, a town of six thousand,
was studied in the early and middle 1940s by Warner and a team
of researchers from the University of Chicago (Warner et al., 1949;
Warner, Meeker, and Eells, 1949; and Hollingshead, 1949); and
Statesboro, Georgia, a college town of about seven thousand, was
studied by Bevode C. McCall in the late 1940s and early 1950s
(McCall, 1954).

The second group consists of communities studied on the
basis of interviews with a wide variety of community residents, observations of community interaction patterns, and documentary
data of various types. The investigators have analyzed the status
structure without making use of systematic clique analysis or cross-
sectional samples, and they have provided no quantitative description of class size or of the social characteristics of the various class
groups. Muncie, Indiana, was studied twice by the Lynds, first in
1925 when it had a population of thirty-five thousand, and again in
1935 when it had grown to fifty thousand (Lynd and Lynd, 1929;
Lynd and Lynd, 1937); Natchez, Mississippi, a community of thirteen thousand, was studied in the middle and late 1930s by Allison
Davis and the Gardners (Davis, Gardner, and Gardner, 1941).

The third group consists of large cities examined only by the
use of cross-sectional samples, without interviewing for community
attitudes or clique analyses; in the studies of these cities classifica-
tions were made according to scores on one or another index of
social characteristics. In these studies, the investigator applied prior
conceptual frameworks derived from studies of small towns. New
Haven, Connecticut, a metropolitan area of approximately 250,000,
was studied by Hollingshead and associates in the early 1950s
(Hollingshead and Redlich, 1958); Chicago, Illinois, was studied
by Pierre Martineau for the *Chicago Tribune* in 1955–56 and by
Simmons and Associates for the *Chicago Sun-Times* in 1960. In
these studies the entire metropolitan area was sampled, embracing

a population exceeding five million (Martineau, 1957; Simmons, 1960).

The number of social classes described in these eight communities, including Kansas City, has been either five or six (with the exception of the Lynds' first analysis of Middletown in 1925). This difference appears to be partially a product of the investigator's methods and research approach. But the geographic location, population size, ethnic composition, age, and historical development of the community are more significant in producing the difference. Those communities in which six classes have been identified are older than the others and located on the Eastern seaboard or in the Deep South, where a differentiation has been made within the upper class between an "old family upper-upper" and a "newer family lower-upper." Below the upper class level, each community has been described in terms of four social classes: two predominantly white-collar in occupational composition, and two predominantly blue-collar.

Table 14 compares the social classes across communities in terms of salient socioeconomic characteristics. Here the descriptions and the quantitative evidence provided by the original investigators have been carefully analyzed and equated with the data on Kansas City. The characteristics in the first two pages of the table are derived from the study of Kansas City but have been generalized to apply to a nationwide status system. Income figures are in 1954–55 dollars in Kansas City. To translate to 1970 equivalents applicable to average communities, add approximately 70 per cent. When comparing with any given community, take into account the local salary structure and cost of living.

Educational levels refer to men and women born in 1885–1914. The vertical bars on page 258 do not refer to percentages of persons included in each class but rather to the range of characteristics on pages 256–257. For example, the Jonesville upper class is given a large amount of space, not because a large percentage of Jonesville residents were upper class but because that group included some people with characteristics like Kansas City's upper-middle-elite and others like those in Kansas City's upper class. Dotted lines within the vertical bars suggest the presence of substrata within the class. Within each vertical bar the left side represents persons whose status depends primarily upon educational qualifications and family background, and the right side represents persons whose status depends primarily upon their economic achievements.

Table 14.   COMPARISON OF STATUS GROUPS IN EIGHT CITIES[a]

Characteristics Associated with Each Status Level, Kansas City, 1954–1955

Upper Class:

Capital S Society

Wealthy descendants of men who achieved renown; usually above $35,000 in annual income.

Men, "prestige" college backgrounds; women, "fashionably" educated.

Non-Capital S Society

First-generation elite—executives, owners, professionals, at least $25,000; moderately well-to-do descendants of renowned families.

Men, college graduates; women "semi-fashionably" educated.

Upper-Middle Class:

Upper-middle-elite

Semi-executives or professional men, $18,000–$24,000; well-to-do governmental, educational leaders, $15,000–$20,000; business operators, 25–30 employees.

Men, 2–4 years college; women, "good" college, sorority backgrounds.

Upper-middle-core

Managers, professionals, $12,000–$17,000; governmental, educational, religious functionaries, $10,800–$14,700; business owners, 10–18 employees.

Men, 2–4 years college; women, college, art, music school.

Upper-middle-marginals

Semi-managerial personnel in business, government, $9,600–$11,700; status-conscious teachers, ministers, other professionals, small-business owners.

Men, 1–4 years of college; women, college, art, music school.

Lower-Middle Class:

Lower-middle-elite

White-collar workers, $7,200–$9,300; teachers, ministers, less successful professionals; businessmen with 4–8 employees.

Men and women, high school graduates or attendance at low-ranking colleges.

[a] Descriptions in this table correspond to breakdown on p. 258.

Table 14. COMPARISON OF STATUS GROUPS
IN EIGHT CITIES (Cont.)

Characteristics Associated with Each Status Level, Kansas City, 1954–1955

Lower-middle-core

White-collar workers, $5,400–$6,900; small business owners, contractors, neighborhood merchants, highly-paid technicians, gray-collar civil servants.

Men and women, usually high school graduates.

Lower-middle-marginals

White-collar workers, $4,200–$5,100; foremen, skilled craftsmen, usually $5,400 and above; technicians, gray-collar workers, $4,800–$6,000.

Women, usually high school graduates; men, 2–3 years of high school.

Working Class:

Working-class-elite

Foremen, craftsmen, contractors, $6,000 and up; union leaders, politicians, small businessmen living in working class neighborhoods.

Men, possibly beyond 8th grade; women 8th grade or less.

Working-class-core

Blue-collar workers, $4,200–$5,400—assembly line workers, craftsmen, service workers; white-collar workers, $3,300–$3,900.

Men and women, typically 8th grade graduates.

Working-class-marginals

Blue-collar, typically semi-skilled, $3,300–$4,050; factory, service workers, occasional unemployment; thriftiest unskilled laborers.

Men and women, typically 8th grade graduates, possibly less.

Lower Class:

Not quite the lowest

Semi-skilled or unskilled, below $4,500 plus poor housing or identification wih disparaged ethnic groups; *not* slumdwellers.

Men and women, less than 8th grade.

"Slumdwellers"

Low incomes, chronic unemployment, unskilled jobs. "Slumdwellers," skid row habituees, visibly poverty stricken.

Men and women, less than 8th grade.

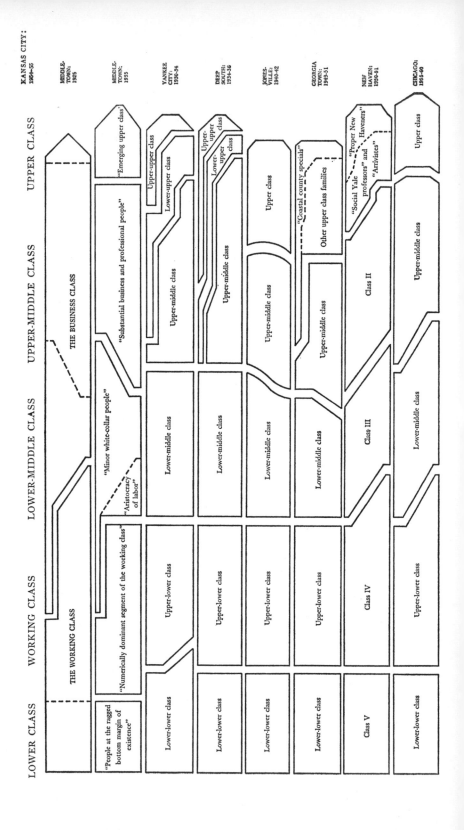

Dividing lines between classes have been drawn on the basis of occupational composition and income levels, modified by data on education, housing, and ethnicity, and at upper levels by data on genealogy. Data regarding club and association memberships and political and civic leadership have not been utilized in drawing the table, because these dimensions of status vary considerably from community to community. (For example, unlike the situation in Kansas City, investigators in Georgia Town, Jonesville, Yankee City, and Deep South all described the upper class as exerting behind-the-scenes controls, while it was upper-middle men and women who filled the visible leadership roles. Specifically, in Jonesville in 1941, 77 per cent of the leadership positions in civic organizations were concentrated in the hands of upper-middle men and women— this is about the same proportion that was concentrated in the hands of upper-class men and women of Kansas City in 1955.)

Size of Classes: Table 15 shows, for those communities in which the data are available, the proportion of the population assigned to each of the five major social classes by the original investigators. The differences between communities with regard to the relative size of each social class are to be attributed to at least four sources: First, real differences exist in occupational distribution and ethnic composition of various American towns and cities. Second, these eight communities were studied at somewhat different points in time. A third factor is related to the differences in overall social organization that inevitably accompany differences in size of community. In small towns, careful analysis of the eight studies has shown that more fallen aristocrats maintain their social ties with persons in the top status group than is true in large cities, probably a reflection of the fact that old families maintain their visibility, and loss of prestige follows more slowly upon loss of wealth. At the same time, relatively more nouveau riche participate in the top status group, perhaps because informal criteria for acceptance are less stringent when there are fewer persons from whom to choose one's associates and when standards may be less definitive than in more urbane communities. In small towns, furthermore, there seems to be less differentiation in patterns of participation between upper-middle and lower-middle classes, perhaps for the reasons just stated. A small town provides neither the diversity of settings nor the num-

Table 15. SOCIAL CLASS DISTRIBUTIONS IN SIX AMERICAN COMMUNITIES[a]

Social Classes[b]	Adults at Each Social Level Per Cent					
	Kansas City (Mid-1950s)	Yankee City (Early 1930s)	Jonesville (Early 1940s)	Georgia Town (Early 1950s)	New Haven (Early 1950s)	Chicago[c] (1956, 1960)
Upper Class	1.8	3.0	2.7	3.2	2.7	2.1
Upper Middle	11.6	10.1	12.0	15.7	9.8	8.1
Lower Middle	33.3	28.3	32.2	27.3	21.4	21.6
Working Class	40.2	33.3	41.0	27.4	48.5	43.6
Lower Class	13.1	25.3	12.1	26.4	17.6	24.6
TOTAL	100	100	100	100	100	100

[a] Deep South and Middletown are not included because the investigators did not report the numbers of families assigned to each social class.

[b] In the New Haven Study, the classes were referred to by Roman numerals, I through V; in Yankee City, Jonesville, and Georgia Town the Working class was called Upper-Lower, and the Lower Class, Lower-Lower.

[c] The percentages for Chicago are averages, based on two different studies, Martineau (1957) and Simmons and Associates (1960). For the Martineau study based on 3,600 households, a modified version of the Warner I. S. C. was used, producing the following class distribution: 0.9 per cent Upper, 7.2 per cent Upper-Middle, 28.4 per cent Lower-Middle, 44.0 per cent Working Class, and 19.5 per cent Lower Class. The second study was conducted by W. R. Simmons and Associates, a New York research firm, in a study of the Chicago area market for the Chicago Sun-Times and Chicago Daily News newspapers. It was based on a sample of 4,374 Chicago area residents, classified by the Hollingshead two-factor Index of Status Position. The class distribution of metropolitan Chicago estimated by Simmons and Associates was: 3.3 per cent Upper, 8.9 per cent Upper-Middle, 14.8 per cent Lower-Middle, 43.2 per cent Working Class, and 29.8 per cent Lower Class.

bers of people conducive to differentiated participation patterns (Lasswell, 1959).

A fourth factor relates to the differences in the methods and the indices of status used by different investigators. In the studies of New Haven and Chicago, status was measured primarily by occupation and education. Many highly educated people were placed in the upper and upper-middle classes who would not have been placed there were an observational analysis made of their community participation. Similarly, on this basis, only a tiny fraction of blue-collar workers were placed in the lower-middle class, contrary to studies based on analysis of participation patterns. In those, as in Kansas City, some 25 per cent to 38 per cent of the lower-middle class were blue-collar workers. The fourth factor can be illustrated further. In the Chicago study by Simmons (1960), the use of a two-factor index (head's occupation and education) had the effect of placing all persons with advanced college degrees and with at least moderate professional or occupational success in the upper class, and of omitting persons who, like those in Kansas City, had reached the top in the occupational and social status world without benefit of higher education. A similar effect was produced at the upper-middle level, where, as seen in the Kansas City data, a college education was not necessarily characteristic of adults over age forty, and where degree of occupational success was evaluated differently for persons under age thirty-five than for persons over forty. The result is that perhaps as many as one-third of the families who have been described as upper-middle class in Kansas City would have been placed into the lower-middle class by the methods of both Chicago investigators.

Five Basic Status Positions: More striking than the differences just described are the similarities across social class groups as these similarities emerge from the analyses made by different investigators studying different communities. Examination of Table 14 shows that the characteristics of the social classes are much the same in the several communities. For instance, with regard to occupations, income, and education, the people designated as working class in Kansas City are identical to those designated upper-lower in Jonesville or Georgia Town. (Although not shown in Table 14, comparison of the published descriptions shows also that the associational patterns of members of the working class are much the same from community to community.) If persons assigned to working-class status in one community were to meet their peers from another community, it is likely they would recognize each other as social equals. So too with the lower class: while differences exist between communities in the relative numbers who are Negro or Mexican or Italian or "hillbilly," the groups are almost identical with regard to housing level, occupations, and education.

The upper class is something of an exception. The people who are at the top of Chicago's status structure are different from those at the top in Jonesville or Georgia Town—different in degree of wealth, occupational status, cultural interests and sophistication, and in terms of national visibility, a point to which we shall return presently.

Overall, families who are very nearly identical in occupation, educational background, and other salient socioeconomic characteristics have been placed by successive social scientists at the same social class level. This fact supports the proposition that the five core groups can be viewed as the main convergence points in the social status system in America, and that people of similar characteristics are perceived, both by their fellow citizens and by the social scientist, as equal to each other in status from community to community. Thus we can speak meaningfully of a nationwide status system.

Five basic status groups constitute that system. An *upper class* forms around the executive, professional, and capitalist elite. Its top is the old, fashionably educated, socially august families who constitute the Capital S or *Social Register* circles in America's largest cities. This class probably includes only 1 per cent, or 2 per cent at most, of families. Next, an *upper-middle class* forms around the college educated, managerial level businessmen and successful professionals. In large cities managers and professionals are the archetypes; but in smaller communities, and among the older generation especially, the independent businessman is more nearly the typical man of this class. Including elite and marginal members, the upper-middle class likely totals 10 per cent of the population, probably somewhat more in large cities, and less, in small towns.

A *lower-middle class* forms around families in the white-collar world who will never reach full-fledged managerial status in their respective corporate or governmental bureaucracies. Increasingly this class is shifting away from its historic definition as the class of clerks, salesmen, and small businessmen, and is coming to include both the blue-collar technician and the well-housed, well-educated, gray-collar service worker. Among older members of this class but not among younger, a high school education was considered an important mark of differentiation from the working class. The lower-middle class, including elite and marginal members, embraces approximately one-third of adult America.

A *working class* forms around families of unionized blue-collar workers. In the first half of this century, the typical man or woman of this class was handicapped by lack of a high school diploma; but more recently, the handicap is defined as lack of junior college or post-high school training in a business school or technical institute. Approximately 40 per cent of urban families have been identified with this class.

A *lower class* of unskilled workers historically has been derogated by the rest of America because they live in poverty, are disreputable, or are identified with the most unfavored minority groups. They have not established themselves as average working-class people. In cities this group has constituted about 16 per cent of the population, but including the rural areas, perhaps as much as 18 to 20 per cent.

Status Equivalence

To reiterate, a social class as defined here means a group of persons who are judged, by members of the wider community as well as by themselves, as equal to one another in social status. As a group, they are believed to be superior or inferior in prestige to other groups of people who constitute the social classes above or below them. Is this concept meaningful when generalized across communities? Within a given town or city, social classes are primarily differentiated in terms of occupational and related economic differences; but it is clear from everything Americans say and do that social status and occupation are not perfectly correlated, and that many other factors, such as education, housing, club and association memberships, and ethnicity, are recognized as modifiers.

Americans do not require face-to-face contact to judge social prestige. Their images about social classes and about the characteristics of people with whom they feel equal are based upon abstractions as well as upon concrete and personal experiences. We have already said that city dwellers do not view the status system of their community in the same way as do residents of small towns. City people do not proceed, like small town people, to build whatever status system they imagine around the differing reputations of particular fellow townsmen with whom they are personally acquainted. Instead, they speak of abstract categories of people in terms of occupational, income, and residential groupings—in short, in terms of particular characteristics. Much the same is true at a national level.

Americans in both large and small cities are conscious of a social prestige hierarchy existing in their home communities; they tend to project this hierarchy upon other towns and cities and, at the same time, to generalize the bases of status to wide groups of people across the country. On the basis of salient social characteristics, Americans render quick estimates of the place of persons whom they happen to meet or read about in the newspaper. In different words, people who live in Kansas City or Chicago (and also people who live in Jonesville or Yankee City) assume that their community is a microcosm of the status system prevailing over the United States. Time and again Kansas City informants prefaced their observations with the comment, "Well, Kansas City is just like any place. . . ."

This is not to say that the status system which exists in the minds of Americans is a five-class (or a thirteen-stratum) system, or that the existence of classes as entities is recognized by most citizens. Such conceptions are obviously created by social scientists. The individual citizen recognizes another person, known or unknown, as equal, inferior, or superior to himself in terms of information he picks up about the characteristics of that person. He creates equivalences from community to community on this basis. In short, he translates social status in his local community into social characteristics; then he observes equivalence of social characteristics across communities; and then he retranslates into presumed equivalence of status across communities—a process, incidentally, not unlike that which the social scientist himself follows. In generalizing from the local to the national level, the social characteristics by which status is evaluated change somewhat in their relative importance.

Occupation and Education: Occupation, while of great

importance within the local community, becomes even more significant across communities. In part this follows from the fact that occupational status does not vary from city to city and from the fact, reflected in Table 14, that the occupational core is the same from city to city for each of the five class levels. This emphasizes that occupational-economic status is the basis of the class structure, and it is also the factor which equates people from one community to the next. Because educational levels associated with successive occupational levels also are the same from city to city, education becomes the second most important factor in creating social status equivalences across communities.[1]

Participation: An index which varies from community to community is the type of social participation and club membership which typifies the various class levels. While certain types of civic leadership roles may be crucial indicators of status in any community, the same rules cannot be applied from city to city regarding the status significance of membership in the Rotary Club, Chamber of Commerce, Junior League, Lions Club, Elks Club, or an expensive country club. These organizations all derive their status from their history on the local scene and from their size as compared to

---

[1] Proceeding on this basis, the senior author has developed a formula for estimating the class distribution in different metropolitan areas. This formula was developed primarily on the findings from Kansas City on the relationship between occupational categories of the U.S. Bureau of the Census and social class distribution, and on the relationship between social class and years of schooling.

Application of this formula to 1960 census data suggests that in some of the 212 metropolitan areas as high as 55 per cent of the population are of lower-middle status or above while, in others, no more than 30 per cent or 35 per cent. Cities with the highest percentage of middle-class population are governmental and educational centers such as Madison, Wisconsin, Lincoln, Nebraska, and Raleigh, North Carolina; and those with the lowest percentage are older manufacturing or mining communities such as Fall River and New Bedford in Massachusetts and Wilkes-Barre and Scranton in Pennsylvania. The largest cities usually do not approach these extremes, except that in the Washington, D.C. metropolitan area the population is at least 54 per cent middle class and above. Otherwise, the range for large cities is from 48 per cent in greater Los Angeles to 44 per cent in greater New York City to 40 per cent in Detroit.

Predictions of status distributions based on this formula have proved useful to political scientists and market researchers in studying voting behavior and consumption patterns and in explaining differences from one city to another in such things as preferences for television programs. Details of these procedures and city-by-city estimates can be obtained from the senior author.

the size of the population; and their memberships are not to be equated across cities. For example, the Rotary Club in Kansas City was 60 per cent upper class and 40 per cent upper-middle, while in Jonesville it was 19 per cent upper class, 78 per cent upper-middle, and 3 per cent lower-middle in membership (Meeker, 1947). Even the Junior League, which is considered synonymous with high status for young women throughout the United States, varies from city to city in the degree of its exclusiveness.

Similarly, the sources of civic leadership vary from community to community. If the eight communities compared here are representative, then it appears that the larger the city the more exclusively are leadership roles concentrated in the hands of upper-class persons, except perhaps in political organizations and in government organizations in which leaders must be drawn from various ethnic groups, labor groups, and other lower-status sectors of the community.[2] As already mentioned, in the small towns of Yankee City, Georgia Town, Jonesville, and Deep South the upper class was described as exerting behind-the-scenes control, while the upper-middle class was described as providing the official front. Middletown, as described by Lynd, was different, for in 1935 the big business interests and the upper class interests had already taken over the Chamber of Commerce, while the real estate board and the retail merchants' association were still run by established middle-class merchants. Even the latter, however, is in contrast to Kansas City, where the real estate board and the retail merchants were observed to be controlled both covertly and overtly by members of the upper class.

There is one more significant difference between large cities such as Kansas City and the small towns studied in the 1930s and 1940s. The lower-middle class in each of the smaller towns was usually described as linking the community together, because many of its members were in the same clubs with upper-middle and upper class people, and others were in fraternal orders which combined

[2] The relationship between political leadership and social or economic leadership varies from one community to the next, depending on factors other than size of community. Furthermore, political leadership and socioeconomic leadership almost always represent intersecting, not identical, elites. See, for example, Hunter (1953); Dahl (1961); Banfield and Wilson (1963); Polsby (1963); Thometz (1963); Jennings (1964); Presthus (1964); and Wildavsky (1964).

upper-middle, lower-middle, and working class people into large multiclass social units. In contrast, in Kansas City very few lower-middles were in any club or association with either upper-middles or working class men and women. The churches, Boy Scout troops, PTAs, Masonic lodge units, and American Legion posts to which lower-middles belonged tended to be one-class in membership. Thus, in Kansas City the lower-middle class tended to be a more distinct and independent social world; it was not made up of leaders within the common man's world nor of followers of the upper-middle class.

Religion, Ethnicity, and Race: It cannot be expected that religious preferences would have the same status significance from community to community. The distribution of Protestants, Catholics, and Jews at each social class level depends on the ethnic and racial distribution in the city. The status of various Protestant denominations depends upon ethnic backgrounds and also upon regional and local history. Lutherans, for example, are found in considerable numbers at all class levels, including the highest, in areas settled mainly by Scandinavians; Methodists are found at higher status levels in the lower Midwest, border states, and Southwest; Baptists constitute a sizable segment in the upper-middle and upper classes of many Southern communities, particularly those which have been populated mainly by migration from the rural parts of the South. One relatively regular phenomenon among Protestants from city to city is the definite status advantage associated with membership in Episcopalian or Presbyterian congregations and the marked disadvantage associated with memberships in fundamentalist sects. Similarly, in cities in which the Jewish population is large enough to have become segmented into reform, conservative, and orthodox groups, those affiliated with reform temples gain and those affiliated with orthodox temples lose somewhat in status. The disadvantage of being Catholic varies from region to region, depending on the proportion of Catholics in the total population, the ethnic source of the Catholic population, and factors of local history. During the Catholic influx into Boston in the mid-nineteenth century, the Irish came in such great numbers that formal barriers were erected against their social acceptance. In cities settled early by Catholics of French descent, such as New Orleans and St. Louis, there has been no social stigma attached to being Catholic, even at the very highest levels of the status hierarchy. At the three higher class levels the proportion of white Protestants varies from community to community. Historically, however, middle-class and upper-class America has been predominantly white Protestant.[3]

The working class has been more diverse in ethnic and racial character, from city to city and region to region, than has the middle class. On the eastern seaboard it is mainly southeastern European Catholic plus Irish; so, too, in industrial cities of the Midwest, which experienced their main growth in the thirty years prior to World War I. In the less industrialized and slower growing cities of the Midwest and West, the working class is mainly Protestant and northern European or old-line American. In the South the white working class is also old-line American of English, Scotch, northern Irish, and German background, but in most Southern cities almost half the working class is Negro.

The lower class differs from place to place around the country, mainly according to whether the principal group is Negro (as in most of the South, and increasingly in industrial cities of the North), Mexican (as in many Southwestern and Pacific coast communities), "hillbilly" (as in smaller towns of the lower Midwest and border states), southern European (as in most Eastern seaboard communities), or French Canadian (as in upper New England and parts of Louisiana). Whatever the major ethnic component of the lower class, however, there has always been a certain number of old-line Americans of northern European and English descent in the lower class, many of whom have remained at that level from generation to generation at the same time that the children of more recent immigrant groups have moved up into higher levels of the status hierarchy.

From the preceding discussion we conclude that a view of a nationwide status structure is meaningful, a view in which status rests primarily upon occupation, income, and education. Persons may be placed in one of the major social class groups regardless of the size or geographical location of their community, although in

[3] The importance of church participation in the social life and status definitions of Americans has been described by Dillingham (1965), and by Goode (1966). See also Baltzell (1964) and Demerath (1965).

any given community, the status structure may be somewhat simpler or more elaborate than in others. In some communities the indices of status will be considerably modified by indices of participation, lineage, ethnicity, religious preference, and so on, and the relationships between indices will vary; but occupation, income, and education are likely to remain the best predictors of social status for the country as a whole, and they will continue to provide the basis for equivalence of status from community to community.

The Problem of Upper Class Equivalence

Most students of social stratification have found it difficult to draw a line distinguishing an upper class group from the upper-middle group. The large number of socially mobile families at the higher levels of the social structure make it difficult to decide which of the upper-middle-elite families have moved into the lower echelons of the upper class. The line is also difficult to draw because upper-class people enjoy mingling with persons of special intellectual or creative talents and with people who occupy functionally important community roles; it is not always possible to determine whether these latter persons are truly accepted as status equals by upper-class people or are looked upon merely as the most interesting upper-middles. Finally, participation in the top-set clubs and organizations varies with size of community; generally the smaller the city, the larger the percentage of residents who are regarded as part of the top crowd.

The data on participation patterns of high-status families in Kansas City, together with data from other sources such as Baltzell's study of *Social Register* and *Who's Who in America* listees in Philadelphia, lead to the view of a national upper class consisting of two layers (Baltzell, 1958; Amory, 1947). The first layer is a Capital S and *Social Register* group drawn mainly from the larger cities. The second layer is a less clearly differentiated group composed of people from the larger cities who are comparable to the Kansas Citians of upper class Levels III and IV and to those at the top in small towns.

In this view, it is likely that some small towns contain no families who are at the Capital S level in the nationwide sense of the term. That is, these towns have no families whose wealth, lineage, educational level and urbanity are equal to Kansas City's Capital S Society or to the families listed in the *Social Register* in America's largest cities. In turn, not even Kansas City's Bradshaws or Galbraiths rank with the prestigious families of Chicago, Boston, New York, Baltimore, or San Francisco. The Bradshaws and Galbraiths and high status families in Chicago who are not quite clique members with the McCormicks and Fields are no less to be regarded as Capital S however, for this social group nationwide is steeply and infinitely graded.

The core of Capital S Society in the United States is, broadly speaking, those families in large cities who have consolidated at least second-generation inherited wealth or political or civic prominence into visible social leadership, and who are regarded in their respective communities as the best families. They are linked together nationally through common associations in women's colleges and finishing schools and through men's Eastern college club and prep school ties. This group represents only a thin sliver of the population, probably no more than four-tenths of one per cent in large cities, and even a smaller proportion in smaller communities (Wecter, 1937).

The rest of the upper class—probably no more than 1.2 per cent of the total population of the United States—is an amalgam of small town aristocrats and the more socially successful of the nouveau riche in larger cities. To some extent they are linked together nationally through financial and business enterprises or governmental and military ties; on a statewide basis, they are joined together through the establishment—bankers, lawyers, and manufacturers who constitute the leadership in particular communities (see Mills, 1956).

Many families who associate with the top group in their particular localities do not qualify for upper-class status on the national scene. They are more like the upper-middle-elite of Kansas City in their social characteristics, as is suggested by the evidence from Jonesville and Georgia Town, and to a lesser degree, from Yankee City and Deep South. In every city there are probably persons who maintain membership in the Capital S world only as long as they remain in their home towns. Others, who are more widely well-connected economically and socially, can transfer their high positions to almost any other community. Compared to other social classes, this difference probably exists only at the upper-class level where local position is idiosyncratic for some families—in other words, upper-class position is rooted deeply in the local community and its history, whereas other class positions are likely to be interchangeable in different communities.

Chapter **13**

ᴬ Changing Class Structure?

In the preceding chapter we related our findings from Kansas City to findings from other community studies and described a nationwide status structure in terms of the characteristics of each of five social classes. The evidence suggests that from the 1920s, and possibly back to the turn of the century, up through the mid-1960s social scientists perceived the structure in much the same outlines: as a five-class hierarchy in the shape of a pyramid on an inverted base, with the classes differentiated primarily by occupation and income. The close relationships between status on the one hand, and occupation and income on the other, appear to have been relatively stable. The distribution of the population among the five classes varied from community to community, and probably became somewhat altered over the decades as the nation became more industrialized and more urbanized. With changes in the economic and technological base, there was continuing increase in the proportion of urban men engaged in white-collar, managerial, and professional occupations as compared with the proportion employed in manual and service occupations, changes which affected the shape of the status structure. Still, the overall picture was much the same in the views of successive observers.

We have maintained throughout this book that occupation is

an inadequate single index of social status. Yet in estimating the changes in class distribution over the past half-century, occupational data are the best that are available. Accordingly, using census data on distribution of occupations in successive decades for both rural and urban men, we estimate that the percentage of the total population that can be described as middle class or higher increased from some 32 per cent in 1900 to some 43 per cent in 1960.[1]

More specifically, we estimate that the group regarded as upper class has stayed approximately the same in size and has constituted little more than 1 per cent; the group regarded as upper-middle increased from approximately 5 per cent to 10 per cent; the lower-middle group increased from 26 per cent to 32 per cent; the working class decreased somewhat from 42 per cent to 39 per cent; and the lower class decreased from some 26 per cent to 18 per cent. These estimates are gross, and the evidence on which they rest leaves much to be desired. Yet they at least have the advantage of viewing various occupations in terms of their status significance, and in so doing, of proceeding on the consensus of a number of different investigators.

In considering the ways in which the national status structure may have changed since the mid-1950s and how it is likely to change in the next few decades, we can only speculate. For one thing, there have been no new studies of whole communities like those described earlier, nor other studies which would shed light on the question of whether Americans attach the same relative significance as before to the various dimensions of status and whether they make the same distinctions among their fellow citizens.[2] This is

[1] In making these estimates on changes in middle class size, we have made use of various community studies (in addition to those described in Chapter Twelve), studies of occupational prestige, income distribution, and related types of evidence. We have included a small proportion of wage workers in the middle class; but we have not included all white-collar, professional, or self-employed. Further, we have assumed that no more than 60 per cent of farm owners have been middle class. C. Wright Mills (1951) has presented a somewhat different picture of change through the years, but his class groupings are based on occupation alone, without modification for their status significance. Included in Mills' concept of middle class are all farm owners, all business proprietors, all professionals, managers, salespeople, and office workers. Using those criteria, he placed 45 per cent of employed American men in the middle class (or higher) in 1940, as compared with 39 per cent in 1870.

[2] The study by Hodge, Siegel, and Rossi (1964) has shown that the

due in part to the fact that with the growth of metropolitan centers it becomes increasingly less feasible to carry out relevant community studies, in part to the fact that students of social stratification have shifted their attention to other types of problems and to units other than single communities. Whether new community studies have much or little to recommend them, the concepts and the terminology of social class are as prevalent as ever in the sociological literature, and single socioeconomic indices like occupation, income, or education are increasingly being used as synonyms for social class without the necessary accompanying studies of the status significance of these indices.

In any case, without new empirical studies on the bases of status in a changing America, the discussion to follow draws attention to changes in residential patterns, in the distribution of income by occupational groups, in the distribution of education, in patterns of social participation, in ethnic and social patterns, and in certain other factors that are presumably operating to produce changes in the status structure. As part of this discussion, we will look briefly at Kansas City as it appeared in the late 1960s. Although we lack a systematic follow-up study of the community, our impressions are based upon subsequent visits, regular perusal of Kansas City newspapers, and our continued contacts with residents of the city.

Impressions of Kansas City, Late 1960s

Probably the most dramatic change one notices in Kansas City is that its social geography, never as simple as popularly imagined, has become much more complex. Kansas Citians are aware that they can no longer divide the city into a working class wrong side of town and a middle class right side. Suburban developments of middle-status housing have grown up to the north, to the east, to the south, and to the southwest, where white-collar workers of relatively lower income levels and blue-collar workers of relatively higher income levels are intermingled. Meanwhile in the older parts of the city, almost all neighborhoods have deteriorated to a certain extent, except that programs of urban renewal and superhighways

---

prestige of various occupations has remained virtually the same in the period from 1925 to 1963, but that study does not shed light on the relation of occupation to other status dimensions, nor on the question of the number and size of various social class groups.

have eliminated some of the most deteriorated portions and in some cases replaced them with new public housing or new middle-income apartments near the downtown area. The heartland of Kansas City's lower-middle class on the southeast side has been occupied by the burgeoning Negro population, although old working-class areas to the north and northeast have been less affected.

The result is that in many respects the dimension of old versus new neighborhoods is crosscutting status lines. At each class level the new neighborhoods are more desirable than the old, and many of the old neighborhoods are described as being in some sort of peril even if they are not already greatly devalued from their former status. At the same time new neighborhoods are even more homogeneous with regard to income (if not occupation) than old neighborhoods were perceived to be in the early 1950s.

There remains a large area in the Southwest and in Johnson County that is unquestionably regarded as a right place to live, but other areas which are widely acceptable to middle-class people are divided into many different high school districts of mixed social characteristics. These are regarded as acceptable residential areas on grounds of availability of housing and their distance from the deteriorating old city, rather than in terms of their social desirability or status reputation per se. Thus, perceptions of the status hierarchy are probably no longer closely related to perceptions of social geography.

It is our impression, also, that at all social class levels, neighborhoods have become increasingly age-graded. In some instances, areas of high-rise apartment buildings are occupied primarily by middle-aged and older people, areas of single houses, primarily by families with young children. In other instances, older neighborhoods are occupied by older people who evidently have chosen to remain despite the deterioration going on around them, while newer—especially newer suburban—neighborhoods are occupied by the young. To this extent, old-young occupancy is a dimension which, like old-new housing, crosscuts earlier social status lines.

A second trend which is evident in Kansas City is the depolarization of attitudes with regard to city politics and the feelings of Kansas Citians toward national political parties. With Pendergastism now thirty years gone, and with the citizens reform group no longer as powerful a force, the issues of topdog versus underdog and decency versus corruption—and the division between Republicans and Democrats that accompanied these issues in the early 1950s—are no longer central. In particular, the 1964 presidential campaign reduced some of the feeling that the Democratic party was the party of the underprivileged and the Republican party the party of the overprivileged. The Kansas City *Star* supported Lyndon B. Johnson, for instance, a fact which further blunted the old political division. The result is that the lower-middle and working class groups in Kansas City do not see themselves as split as earlier by political party affiliation. Negro rights, the Vietnam war, and other problems have arisen to create divisions that cut across social class lines.

Thus, just as residential redistribution of people in Kansas City has blunted the perception of a division between working class and middle class, so the diminution of hostility between the two political parties and the blunting of the *Star*-and-reform versus Pendergast issue seem to have washed away some of the division between the two classes, producing a large group of swing voters from both classes whose votes are influenced by other issues besides that of siding with the haves or have-nots.

At the upper levels of the Kansas City status hierarchy, certain other changes are becoming apparent. For one, there appear to be fewer new, big fortunes being made in Kansas City these days than in the two preceding decades. At the same time, many local business firms have been sold into national and international corporations. Kansas City is becoming more a branch office, branch plant city than it was fifteen years ago. Many business executives are less local in their orientations and concerns; many more are transient executives. Perhaps some of these changes are related to the age of the city itself, or to the growth of the big corporation in American business; or they may be products of what is generally perceived by Kansas Citians as a period in which the city has not grown or changed as much as other cities. In any case, it seems that there are fewer newly visible families participating at the lower levels of upper-class Society, and fewer nouveau riche who attract the attention of Kansas Citians. While these impressions rest upon insufficient data, it nevertheless appears that the importance of nouveau riche families in Kansas City's leadership is diminishing. A certain amount of bureaucratization is occurring in cultural and educational institutions as well as in business. Many formerly separate institutions such as the Art Institute, the Conservatory, and Kansas City University have in the 1960s become part of one large educational organization: the University of Missouri in Kansas City. These institutions formerly were heavily supported by individual families, many of lower rank upper class status; now that the patronage of private donors is needed less, the opportunities for and influence of such families are diminished.

The lower level of the upper class is increasingly composed of second and third generation families holding on to their memberships in the exclusive country clubs. However, there is no evidence that as the city gets older the Capital S group is becoming more closed off from the groups below; perhaps, to the contrary, the distinction between Capital S and the lower ranks of the upper class is more blurred than before—or less relevant. The separation between lower rank upper class Kansas Citians and the upper-middle-elite also seems more blurred, and perhaps less relevant. A large number of family-style country clubs have grown up to accommodate people at these levels, and formal and informal participation among persons of relative affluence seems to overlap more than in the 1950s.

These are a few of the changes that appear to be occurring in the status structure of Kansas City, changes which may have a particular local flavor not generalizable to the nation as a whole. Many other changes are more clearly the reflections of national trends, and as such can be discussed within the broader perspective.

In interpreting the discussion which follows, the reader must keep two cautions in mind. One is the danger of reifying social classes and speaking of them as real entities rather than as conceptualizations useful to social scientists. The second is the danger of assuming that dimensions of status—prestige, reputation, patterns of informal participation—continue to bear the same relationships to dimensions of income, occupation, and education as they did in the past; this is an assumption which needs to be confirmed by new empirical evidence.

The Nationwide Structure

A commonly expressed point of view among sociologists, business analysts, government officials, and other observers of the

American scene is that a five-class status structure is no longer accurate. Economic and technological changes are producing not only raised standards of living but changed relationships between various classes. Some of the differences between classes are becoming obliterated. The lines between upper class and upper-middle class, for example, seem to be less clearly delineated, with less emphasis being placed on lineage in most communities and upper-middle class people assuming active leadership roles in a wide range of community affairs. The line between white-collar and blue-collar is also believed to be disappearing as more and more blue-collar workers have entered the middle income group. Some differences are perhaps becoming sharper—for instance, between the group who are dependent upon various forms of public assistance and all the rest of the population.

The American status structure appears to some observers as one in which only three major divisions are apparent: on top, an amalgamation of the upper-middle and upper classes into what might be called above the middle-majority, a group that represents some 12 to 15 per cent of the total population; a huge, increasingly undifferentiated middle-majority composed of both white-collar and blue-collar families; and a small lower or below the middle-majority group composed of public assistance families, unemployables, and the unskilled—sometimes referred to as the underclass or even the hopeless class. Mayer (1963) is one of those who describe the changing outline of the status structure as approximating a diamond in which there are small groups of nonmobile people at top and bottom, with all the rest of the population in between, and where gradations in the middle are so numerous and so gradual that class lines are relatively imperceptible.

Changing Significance of Occupation and Income: The three socioeconomic indices most widely accepted as the bases of the social class hierarchy in America—occupation, income, and education—may be changing in their relative significance. As already mentioned, income levels no longer differentiate between white-collar and blue-collar occupations. One observer has written,

> The wage earner's way of life is well nigh indistinguishable from that of his salaried co-citizens. Their homes, their cars, their babysitters, the style of the clothes their wives and children

wear, the food they eat, the bank or lending institution where they establish credit, their days off, the education of their children, their church—all of these are alike and are becoming more nearly identical. . . . The typical wage earner no longer lives in an identifiably "working class" neighborhood. . . . (All told) there has been a rapid fading in the distinctive coloration of the working class. . . . The adoption of middle-class attitudes, the change in what workers have come to expect, even more than the greatly augmented real family income, points to this great revolution in class relations (Seligman, 1959).

While this view has been challenged by other investigators who doubt that the attitudes and values of the working class follow directly upon changes in relative income, the important question in the present context is whether income itself is coming to have greater significance than type of occupation as the underlying dimension of social status. In other words, is it warranted to assume all blue-collar workers with middle-class incomes are now regarded as middle class in the eyes of their fellow citizens, and that they participate as full social equals with white-collar middle class people?

If the assumption is warranted, then it might be said, from the perspective of a five-class structure, that the lower-middle class is growing larger. Or it might be said, from a different perspective, that the two class groups, lower middle and working class, are drawing closer together in status and are forming a single middle-majority world. In either instance, income rather than occupation could be said to be the more significant dimension of status at this level in the social structure.

Changes in occupational patterns may be producing other shifts in the status structure: the appearance of new occupations as the outgrowth of technological advances; the multiplication of medium-salaried positions in the expanding educational, governmental, and corporate bureaucracies; the decline in certain highly-skilled crafts; and the decline in the role of the individual entrepreneur.

Education as Status Variable: The changes in the occupational base of the society mentioned above are intricately intertwined with changing educational levels, as will be indicated again below in reference to particular levels of the status hierarchy. Meanwhile, education itself as a dimension of status may be taking on more significance than occupation.

The increasing years of schooling that characterize successive generations of Americans may be having a generalized effect up and down the whole structure, so that each social class maintains its relative position. In this case, the upper-middle will become increasingly a select college graduate group with an increasing proportion who hold advanced academic degrees, the lower-middle, a group who have some college or technical education beyond high school, and so on. A second possibility, depending again upon the perspective of the observer, is that the higher social classes will be regarded as expanding in size, and the lower classes, contracting. In this view, the percentage of upper-middle and upper class Americans could rise to 18 per cent or 20 per cent, as increasing proportions of each age group graduate from college. At present, in the age group fifty-five and over, the percentage who are college graduates corresponds with the size of the upper-middle class; the percentage who are high school graduates corresponds with the size of the lower-middle class; and the percentage who have less than eight years of schooling corresponds with the size of the lower class. With the generations born from 1915 to 1940, dramatic changes have occurred in the proportions reaching higher educational levels. The percentage of college graduates has doubled, and the percentage who completed high school has advanced from under 50 per cent to nearly 75 per cent. Thus, no longer is there the clear-cut relationship between number of people at each educational level and size of class.

From the perspective of a three-level structure, educational differences may be sharpening the distinctions between an above middle-majority group of persons with college and postgraduate degrees, the vast middle-majority group of persons who range from high school graduates to those with junior college or technical school training, and a below middle-majority group of high school dropouts. The latter view of the social structure presumes that educational background will be of increasing importance in determining occupational levels and in setting ceilings on achievement. Furthermore, to the extent that a majority of adults can expect to change occupations at various points in their work lives, then both high school and college educations become less specialized in terms of preparation for specific occupations, and a given level of education will provide entry into a relatively wide range of occupations. Thus, it may be that education will become a more significant dimension of status than occupation. In other words, in the status system of the future, social divisions are likely to be based even more upon differences in educational background than has been true in the past.

Overall, if the five-class structure which prevailed in the first half of this century is becoming transformed into a three-class structure, it is likely that the new structure is organized around educational differentiation with its subsequent impact upon careers at the upper end, and around economic differentiation (income) at the lower end. In this sense, the three dimensions of status—occupation, income, and education—may be changing with regard to their relative importance as dimensions of status.

Above the Middle Majority

As stated earlier, the line between upper and upper-middle classes is becoming increasingly vague. There is emerging a larger group like that which we described in Kansas City in the mid-1950s as upper-middle-elite, now drawing from both above and below. This group is composed of people of relative affluence, seemingly more interested in career, in cultural and civic affairs, and in creative achievements than in the amassing of wealth or in memberships in the most exclusive country clubs.

Occupationally this group is more varied than before, an amalgam of corporate executives, expert consultants to business, highly paid researchers, professors at large universities, high ranking officials in government and education, physicians, lawyers, and other professionals. An increasing proportion, especially in the larger cities, are creative writers, editors, artists, musicians, television personalities. Managerial and executive positions in government, education, and other nonprofit institutions had become more respected in the America of the late 1960s. As a whole, this upper-middle-elite group is composed more than before of intellectuals rather than big business executives, although the two are by no means separable.

In Kansas City in the 1950s persons who occupied positions as school officials, personnel managers, and planning directors—

even those who held fairly important public roles and were frequently mentioned in the newspapers—did not participate socially with persons at higher status levels, as they seem now to be doing. Similarly, persons in the creative arts, in education, in research, and in the mass media, once considered the interesting minority of upper-middle-elites, seem now to occupy a more central position. As their incomes catch up with their prominence and their civic contributions, these people are now participating in circles which a decade ago were relatively closed to them. Much the same changes seem to be occurring at higher status levels in other American cities.

At the same time the characteristics which earlier distinguished Society from non-Society seem less valued. Old families are less visible; many second- and third-generation children of such families move to new cities in pursuit of careers, with the effect that the percentage of heirs to high status who stay in their home communities diminishes and the percentage who lose visibility by moving to another city becomes greater. Simultaneously there are changes in the educational system, which is not operating as before to maintain distinctions between upper and upper-middle groups. The most prestigious colleges, like the others, now recruit bright students from a wide range of social classes, and so attendance at such schools is no longer a differentiating mark of upper-class status.

Perhaps these factors will lead some observers to draw the line between upper and upper-middle class ever higher in the structure so that only those dramatically successful families or those of the most impeccable credentials as inheritors of aristocratic positions will be seen to qualify for top-class status. This will have the effect of making the upper class an ever smaller segment of the population. It is more likely, however, the old differentiations among high status groups will become increasingly blurred as the indicators of status change from lineage and wealth to occupational and civic achievement, making it not only more difficult but also less valid to distinguish between upper and upper-middle levels.

If we move one step down the status hierarchy but remain still within the upper-middle class, the line of demarcation between the upper-middle-core and the upper-middle-marginal—as these groups were described in Kansas City in the 1950s—is probably losing significance, certainly as compared with the line between the upper-middle class as a whole and the middle majority of non-college graduates. The whole group of self-employed professionals, middle management executives, and salaried professionals is perhaps becoming one orbit, more age-graded than differentiated by family background, educational level, or patterns of social participation.

Perhaps this group can be called the new *organization man* group, since an increasing proportion are salaried employees, not likely to rise to positions of prominence in their organizations. Within the bureaucracies of government, industry, and education, certain changes are nevertheless taking place at this level. In the mid-1950s the dominant type was the salesmanager or the man who occupied the center-line position, like the head of accounting or of production. Now it is the expert in research, in marketing, in personnel, or in product development; these are the fields in which young men are making their mark and in which older men are being sent by their companies to postgraduate institutes for further training. In company after company, there has been a reversal of salary policies which favored the line manager over the specialist. Now the man with expert knowledge is receiving more pay than the manager whose skills are in the areas of organization, efficiency, or managing other people—or, if not more pay, then more prestige and more easy access to top management.

A second difference at this level is the decreasing proportion of independent entrepreneurs, a point once made by Ralph McGill, late publisher of the *Atlanta Constitution,* in his syndicated column: "Two Americas are emerging, one a society protected by the corporate umbrella, and the other a society whose members have failed to affiliate themselves with the dominant institutions. . . . In part, this latter will consist of small businessmen and other independent spirits who manage to do well without corporate attachments." McGill goes on to observe that no longer is the independent enterpriser in the mainstream of developing America. Our own observations are congruent with those made by many others, namely that the entrepreneur is becoming less frequent in the upper-middle class as a whole, and that this type of man is perhaps not as admired now by higher status people as by those of the middle-majority. Meanwhile, under the corporation-government-education-military hegemony, status distinctions are not clear-cut in the community at large, but are limited primarily to distinctions within the organization itself.

The Middle-Majority

In the vast group that is clearly neither at the top nor at the bottom of the status hierarchy, the earlier dimensions of status are becoming less differentiating than before, and reputational differences less easily delineated. As a total group, the middle-majority encompasses a wide range of blue-, gray-, and white-collar occupations, with the large mass of office workers making room for an ever-increasing proportion of technicians—computer programmers, metallurgists, and technical assistants to research directors in both industrial laboratories and government agencies.

At the upper end in this range of occupations are an increasing number of teachers, ministers and others who, although college educated, remain part of the middle-majority because—in terms of their social origins, their life goals, their attitudes and customs— they relate more comfortably to other people at this level than to people in the upper-middle world above.

A sizable proportion are small businessmen—flooring and roofing contractors, proprietors of bakeries, barber shops, service stations—and a sizable proportion are gray-collar postal employees, policemen, expressmen, shipping clerks, barbers, milk route drivers. The largest group are the relatively well-paid blue-collar railroad section foremen, cross-country bus drivers, engine overhaul foremen for airline companies, electricians, linotype operators, assembly line workers, mechanics, and others in the wide range of skilled labor.

Income levels, while they vary from one end of the range to the other, overlap occupational groups. What is more important, perhaps, than the income differences is the rise in real income that has characterized all the groups. In the 1940s and 1950s, the skilled blue-collar occupations gained markedly in income in comparison to white-collar, a trend by no means as clear-cut in the decade from 1955 to 1965. (In the period between 1955 and 1964, census data show that median income for professionals rose 59 per cent, managerial occupations, 49 per cent, clerical, 58 per cent, and sales, 55 per cent; in the same period, the income of skilled craftsmen rose 49 per cent, and operatives, 55 per cent—about the same as the white-collar groups. It was in the categories of service workers and laborers, with increases of 60 per cent and 73 per cent, that the gains were most marked, a fact which blurs the distinction in income between skilled and unskilled blue-collar just as it has already been blurred between blue-collar and white-collar.)

With such income gains, the middle-majority are well housed and, for the most part, live in neighborhoods located away from deteriorating or slum areas, in respectable neighborhoods in the city or in suburban areas. While some suburbs across the country have been described as working class and others as lower-middle, most such suburbs are homogeneous not only with regard to cost of housing, but also—now that working class men and women are also high school graduates—with regard to educational levels (Gans, 1967). With the general rise in income has come, also, widespread purchasing of all material goods of life by both white-collar and blue-collar groups—houses that are largely indistinguishable inside and out, with the same cars, television sets, and backyard barbecue equipment. With the shortened working day which characterizes both white-collar and blue-collar groups have come also shared patterns of leisure time activities, leading to the phenomenon so often described as the mass culture of America.

As is true in Kansas City, so in other cities changes in urban politics seem to be obliterating the lines between lower-middle and working classes. Neither group identifies with the Republican Party when that party is seen to promote programs that favor the rich too much, and both groups are ambivalent about identifying with the Democratic party when that party is seen to promote programs that favor the Negro or the welfare class too much. The have versus have-not issue is watered down not only by the eradication of economic differences within the middle-majority but also by the fact that, with the movement upward of so many ethnic groups, a larger proportion of this middle status world contains persons who retain certain kinds of sympathy for the underdog.

This latter point is also important in other ways: increasing numbers of people with Italian, Slovak, Polish, or Greek names, second- and third-generation American-born, are moving into the middle class both occupationally and socially. Although in the mid-1950s the working class was still distinctively an "old country" group in many large American cities, this is no longer so, given the

social mobility rates described in Chapter Eleven of this book. In
many cities the old ethnic neighborhoods have been broken up by
urban renewal or by new immigrations of Negroes, Puerto Ricans,
and "hillbillies," with third- and fourth-generation ethnic families
dispersing themselves throughout the cities and suburbs according
to their income levels. The result may be that ethnicity is no longer
as significant as a differentiating factor between working class and
lower-middle class as it was even a decade ago.

Given these changes, it is likely that the lower-middle class—
instead of identifying psychologically with the upper-middle class
above it—is becoming more closely linked with the working class and
is becoming the higher echelon of the vast middle-majority world.
This group is less clearly delineated than before, less a self-contained
interactional system, and less the buffer class between those who
work with their hands and those who work with their brains, as the
old distinction would have it.[3]

The Underclass

The social distance between the working class and the lower
class—or between the middle-majority and those below middle-
majority—is now perhaps the greatest of all. Many observers describe it as increasing rather than decreasing. The change in attitudes toward the lower class on the part of other citizens is perhaps
greater than any changes going on within the lower class: the view
that to be poverty stricken is less a sign of personal failure than a
sign of failure in the socioeconomic system. At the same time, the
increased visibility of the urban Negro ghetto, and of the Puerto
Rican, American Indian, and "hillbilly" people who have changed
the face of the American city, has made the status differentiation
perhaps sharper than ever before. Although various ethnic groups
differed in the rates at which they moved up the social scale, upward mobility out of the lower class was relatively easy in earlier
periods of American history when the class was composed mainly of
European ethnic groups who were newcomers to America.

Upward mobility now appears to be far more difficult: The
lower class is more heavily people who bear the stigma of skin

[3] The view that the lower-middle and working classes are merging
into one is expressed in Hamilton (1960) and in Bonjean (1966). The
opposite point of view, namely that the working class is retaining a distinctive
life style and value structure, is expressed in Miller and Reissman (1960)
and in Handel and Rainwater (1964).

color, and the special history of the Negro in America—with slavery, and then newer forms of racial discrimination, at its foundation— creates distinctive problems. Differences in rates of mobility depend on several factors. One is the extent to which the group possesses work skills that are valuable in the economy; another is the degree to which the dominant groups are willing to permit equal access to jobs, housing, and schooling. On both scores, the lower class of the late 1960s and early 1970s is more disadvantaged. (That skin color itself is an insufficient factor to account for the differences in mobility is reflected in the following data: In the period from 1940 to 1960, employment in white-collar jobs rose from 45 per cent to 56 per cent for Japanese in United States, and from 35 per cent to 51 per cent for Chinese; but from 9 per cent to 14 per cent for Negroes. In the same period, the percentage of males with four years of high school or more rose from 34 per cent to 69 per cent for Japanese, and from 11 per cent to 40 per cent for Chinese, but from only 7 per cent to 18 per cent for Negroes.)

With the elimination of poverty and the improvement of relations between Negroes and whites as our present most important domestic issues, it is hazardous to make predictions regarding changes in status distinctions that can be anticipated in the next decade or two. Some observers believe that the increased opportunities for Negroes in education, housing, and jobs will provide continued impetus for the upward mobility that has been so striking for Negroes in the decade just past. Others fear that changes in technology and the lessened demand for unskilled labor may make the gap between the lower class and the rest of society larger rather than smaller. In this latter view, larger numbers of Americans will be relegated to a spectator class, a permanent nonworking group whose children, like themselves, will be unable to perform meaningful functions in the society.

In the present context—whether a larger proportion of the lower class can be provided with steady employment and will move up into the middle majority, or whether a larger proportion will remain unemployed and supported by one or another form of government subsidy—the visible signs of poverty will probably diminish. The question then arises: with improvements for lower class people in housing, education, and incomes, will other dimensions of status continue to produce the same degree of social distance as presently exists, or will America move toward becoming a classless society at its bottom levels—that is, with no discernible under-class?

In summary, there are many signs that the status structure in America is changing from a five-class to a three-class configuration, with the rate of change possibly becoming greater in the last third of the twentieth century than before. With a rapidly altering technological and economic base, and with continuing high rates of upward mobility—to say nothing of the many other currents of social change that are influential—the dimensions of status are shifting, but in ways which are not altogether clear. It has been suggested by some observers that the most significant social revolution now in process is one based not on social class distinctions nor even on racial distinctions but on age-group distinctions. What are needed now are major new studies to provide an empirical base for social scientists as they continue to probe the nature of social organization.

Brief Economic History of Kansas City

$\mathcal{K}$ansas City is variously described as an urban center, as a standard metropolitan area, and as a conglomeration of cities of varying size. As an urban center, in 1955 it had a population of nine hundred thousand people who lived and worked in an area of 308 square miles extending into two states and five counties. As defined in the 1950 census, the standard metropolitan area was composed of three Missouri and two Kansas counties. Approximately eighty incorporated cities extended their jurisdictions over the urban population, varying in size from Kansas City, Missouri with 465,000 citizens and Kansas City, Kansas with 130,000, to the smallest town with several hundred families.

  Although Kansas City is situated on the eastern fringe of the great plains area, its topography more nearly resembles the Ozark Mountain region to the south and east. The most rugged terrain is found near the center of the urbanized area and gradually smooths out into rolling hills at the periphery. Three rivers meet near this point: the Missouri and Kansas (Kaw) rivers which join at the Missouri and Kansas state border, and the Blue River which flows into the Missouri eight miles to the east. The flat bottom land along these rivers is utilized largely by heavy industry and railroads,

This chapter written by William D. Bryant.

while the high or top-of-bluff areas have been developed by light industry, trade, and residential housing. Although flood protection now exists in all major industrial districts, at infrequent intervals in the past the flood crests of the Missouri and the Kansas rivers have met at their confluence, causing extensive flooding and property damage.

The land-use pattern of Kansas City is in many respects similar to that of other large urban centers when the major topographic features are considered. There is an inner hub known as the downtown area which is the central shopping district for clothing, furniture, jewelry and department stores; the work center for banks and offices of various kinds, for the city hall, the federal and county courthouses and for the federal offices; and the location of hotels and major cultural and recreational facilities. Secondary shopping centers are spaced at several miles distance from the central hub. Major industrial districts include two well-planned and controlled river bottom areas and several much older and unplanned areas along the Kansas River, at the confluence of the Missouri and Kansas rivers, and along the Blue River. Others include a large partly planned district along the Missouri and lighter industry surrounding the downtown center.

The three rivers divide Kansas City into four sections that may be used in describing the residential areas. The section lying north of the Missouri River had not yet received substantial residential development in the 1950s, although it has since become the most rapidly growing area of single family homes. The western segment formed by the joining of the Kansas and Missouri rivers includes most of Kansas City, Kansas, and Wyandotte County. The eastern segment formed by the confluence of the Blue and Missouri rivers includes Independence on the north and a mixture of new developments and small cities to the south. The fourth segment lies between the Blue and Kansas rivers and south of the Missouri. It includes most of Kansas City, Missouri and extends southwestward into Johnson County, Kansas.

The economic base of Kansas City is rather diversified. It is the regional trade center for the state of Kansas and the western half of Missouri. Thus its major competing centers are Omaha on the north, St. Louis on the east, Dallas and Fort Worth on the south, and Denver on the west. Nearer at hand are such expanding centers as Wichita, Oklahoma City, Springfield, and Des Moines. In servicing this region, Kansas City has become a transportation center of considerable importance. It processes agricultural products of the region, manufactures and wholesales goods, provides hospital and specialized medical care, makes available cultural, educational, and recreational services, accommodates conventions, and finances and serves as the regional center for federal offices. It is the metropolis of its agricultural and small-trading-centers region. Of course, portions of the economy are not restricted to the regional trade area. Many manufacturing firms sell on the national and international markets.

Kansas City began as four small competing centers that today form segments of the metropolitan complex. Independence was laid out in 1827 and for a period of years was the principal point of departure from the Midwest for the Santa Fe Trail. Westport—established about 1833—catered originally to the Indian trade, then became an oufitting center during the California Gold Rush, and received a big impetus from the Mexican War in 1846. Westport Landing, now downtown Kansas City, was the site of a fur warehouse in 1826. It was laid out as a town in 1838 and rapidly supplanted Independence as the place where wagons were outfitted and supplied for the overland trip to Santa Fe. The town of Wyandotte, now Kansas City, Kansas, incorporated in 1858, was originally established by Wyandot Indians.

Kansas City's role as point of departure for the Santa Fe Trail reached its peak in 1857. During that year three hundred local merchants and freighters were thus engaged, and some ten thousand wagons left for New Mexico hauling fifty-nine million pounds of freight. In the same year there were 725 arrivals and departures of steamboats that traveled between Kansas City and St. Louis. With the opening of the Kansas and Nebraska Territory to settlement in 1854, the tide of migration began to roll through the Kansas City gateway. By 1860 wholesaling had become an important activity as manufactured goods were dispersed to an ever widening agricultural region.

A destructive flood had occurred in 1844, washing away all but one of the business establishments; in 1850 a cholera outbreak killed many people and caused others to leave the city; by 1851 the resident population was not over three hundred persons. Yet by

1860, the census counted 4,418 persons in Kansas City and 3,164 in Independence. By 1870 the Kansas City population had risen to 32,260, although Independence had gained only twenty persons. The town of Wyandotte was not listed by the census until 1880, when it had a population of 3,200. Westport, which reached its maximum prosperity before the Civil War, lost heavily thereafter to Kansas City.

The period between the Civil War and World War I was a time of great growth when the controlling factors of location were structuring the city's future. The resident population in the Kansas City area reached 375,000 by 1914. This growth was made possible by the tremendous expansion of the city's economic base. At this time, the two-way trade system that has been the heart of Kansas City's economy had been developed. Raw materials collected from the farms, ranches, mines, and oil fields of the west flowed into the city over a network of rail lines. There they were processed and then shipped to consumers concentrated in the large eastern centers. Back from these eastern industrial cities came manufactured articles, which moved through Kansas City to the farms and smaller towns to the west, south, and north. Thus, Kansas City became the major jobbing and wholesale center for a vast region.

This jobbing and wholesale trade came first. Only later, when the potentialities of processing the raw materials flowing through its markets were realized, did manufacturing become important. The livestock markets led to meat packing, and the grain elevators led to milling. Industrial areas made their appearance: Armourdale, Rosedale, North Kansas City, Blue River Valley. Freight rates were vital, sometimes helping, sometimes preventing economic growth, but always a matter of concern. River transport was tried, off and on, to keep rail rates down. Disastrous floods in 1903 and 1904 brought up the problem of flood control that was to plague the city for many years. The first organizations were created to advance the interests of Kansas City through publicity, creating adequate local financing, developing a local attitude that encourages manufacturing, and fighting freight and insurance rates that were considered injurious.

During this period, Kansas City attained national prominence in several economic areas. It became the largest stocker and feeder cattle market in the world. The market for yellow pine,

Mexican oranges, and salted beef and the primary wheat markets were the nation's largest. In manufacturing, Kansas City had the world's largest walnut veneer company, the two largest cracker and biscuit companies, and the biggest and most perfectly equipped metallurgical works. It also was the second-largest portland cement producing area in the United States.

During these years Kansas City also became the big city for a huge population spread over a wide area, offering many attractions to visitors as well as pleasure spots that became notorious. Culture was brought in from the East in the form of plays, musicals, and lectures. And Kansas City became a style center of sorts for a large feminine population. It was also viewed as the wicked city by a sizable portion of the residents of the surrounding Bible Belt.

Another factor was of great importance to the city. In the 1890s an imaginative city architect named Kessler secured the adoption of a comprehensive plan for boulevards and parkways which provided the backbone of Kansas City's trafficway system. The boulevards, tying together the major parks and stimulating an elm tree planting program, created a city of trees that became a matter of pride to local residents and subsequently made comprehensive city planning a somewhat easier task.

By World War I, Kansas City was well established as a regional trade and manufacturing center and as a significant component in the evolving national economy. Thus it was subjected to the strains and stresses engendered by the nation's dynamic growth. First, World War I demanded production of war matériel, and Kansas City business expanded to meet the challenge. During and after the war, food in sizable quantities was funneled through the city in an ever-increasing stream. The period of the 1920s was one of growth and prosperity as Kansas City participated in the nation's upward surge. Then the economic depression of the 1930s occurred, and Kansas City was crushed between the national decline and a long-term serious drought in the surrounding agricultural areas. These rapid fluctuations were unsettling for the young urban center, but out of these problems grew a relatively sound economy that was to serve as a base for the World War II and postwar expansions.

Within the larger movements of the Kansas City economy there were several components that should be noted. One of these was the general decline of wholesaling. Some of this occurred because chain stores, department stores, and direct purchasing were bypassing the wholesaling function. But a significant factor was the relative increase in importance of manufacturing. Indicative of this trend was the city's position in 1923 in certain manufacturing areas: first in manufacturing black walnut woods, first in manufacturing livestock serums, first in manufacturing work clothing, second in meat packing, third in milling, third in manufacturing soap, third in manufacturing crackers and confections, and tenth in value of manufacturing. By 1928 Kansas City factories employed 88 per cent more persons and produced 70 per cent more goods than they had in 1921 and were far ahead of the national average.

Meat packing and livestock receipts, which had expanded considerably during World War I, declined to prewar levels during the 1920s, then decreased further in the depression years. Flour milling, however, registered a large increase during the twenties and held relatively stable throughout the thirties. About 1920 the large amounts of scrap iron and steel in the surrounding territory made feasible the location of several open hearth furnaces and rolling mills that led to the development of a considerable metal fabricating industry. By 1930 all major industrial districts had been formed and their economic characteristics established. By 1940 Kansas City had evolved from a trading center to a metropolis of over half a million population, with a diversified economy substantially based upon manufacturing, and functioning as an interdependent segment of the national economy. However, its economy was still based on the agriculture of the West.

During this period between the wars, Kansas City became known as an open city for various forms of urban and municipal vice. Kansas City, Missouri, had adopted the city manager form of government so that its municipal affairs might be conducted justly and efficiently. However, this soon began to serve as a device for perpetuating in power a political machine that appeared to have somewhat lower ideals. This machine ran the city government from the mid-1920s until it was ousted in 1940 by a reform movement. Thus, by 1940 Kansas City had weathered a world war, a period of major economic growth, a major depression, and a decade or so of corrupt government.

By the time the United States entered World War II, the industrial base of Kansas City had been developed to the point where major war contracts could be assumed. During World War I Kansas City had filled the world's bread basket, but during World War II it produced bombers, ammunition, rocket powder, aircraft engines, landing craft, communication equipment, and other weaponry. Six major government war plants operated in the area throughout the war. Flour milling and meat packing again operated at full capacity, but were definitely in a subsidiary position.

The tremendous expansion in manufacturing activity coincided with a period of high farm yield, so that an abnormal amount of consumer and producer purchasing power awaited the termination of war. This postwar demand supported a sizable growth period that placed the Kansas City economy on a firm and diversified industrial base. The wave of new manufacturing activity initiated by the war successfully adjusted itself to peacetime demands and went on to develop new products and new markets.

The evolution was now complete. Born as a small fur-trading center in a wilderness economy, Kansas City had performed the functions of a service center to the developing agricultural region, had assembled products of the farms and wholesaled manufactured goods, and then with increasing speed had turned to manufacturing. Thus Kansas City in the postwar period became a full-fledged metropolitan area with a population approaching one million persons, beset with all the problems common to metropolitan areas, and in other fundamental respects similar to most other large urban centers in the United States.

By the 1950s, all of the forces tending to homogenize urban populations were operating in Kansas City. National mass media were looked at, read, and listened to and probably exercised the same degree of influence over people's lives as in other cities. Students attended nonlocal colleges, families went on vacations to distant areas, businessmen traveled widely, junior executives were moved through branch offices in Kansas City and on to central posts, national and sectional conventions were held in the city, and the resident population was constantly changing as large numbers left and were replaced by immigrants each year.

In other ways, too, Kansas City constituted an environment for its citizens which was quite similar to other urban centers. There was an art gallery housed in a palatial building, visited mainly by school children and tourists. A symphony orchestra played to a limited audience and struggled to meet its budget. Local theater groups produced plays of varying quality. Lecturers, plays, and musical productions came to the city as they toured the national circuits. An open-air musical theater operated during the summer months. An art institute and conservatory of music drew students from the nearby towns. There were several small colleges in the immediate area, a junior college, and an underfinanced university. And major league baseball had come to Kansas City.

The distinctive images of Kansas City found in the minds of its native sons were no longer sharp and proudly held, yet some of these images persisted. They are of interest as pictures of Kansas City in another era, of a value system long accepted, or of a desired position for Kansas City in the contemporary world.

Several such images focused on geographical location. Kansas City is situated near the geographic center of the nation and hence was often referred to as the heart of America. It was easy to move from geography to other characteristics, and some citizens in the 1950s considered Kansas City representative of the nation at its best. A related image was a holdover from the past—in it Kansas City, at the edge of the great plains, was seen as the last bastion before the western wilderness. In other images, Kansas City was described as a northern city with a southern exposure, a throwback to Civil War days, and as the place where East and West meet, a picture stemming from early frontier days.

Another set of images centered on the theme that Kansas City was vigorous, modern, and up to date. The city had adopted science and research as the means of solving its business and community problems; its city government was perhaps more efficiently operated than any other in the United States; it was an industrial city with modern production methods and wide markets. It had a major league ball team, a philharmonic orchestra, and other cultural assets which established it as major league, if not another Athens. These images were largely inspired by Kansas City's desire to be a big modern urban center and to divest itself of the crudeness, naivete, and general backwardness commonly associated with frontier cities.

A third set of images described Kansas City as extraordinarily beautiful. These were based on its heavy blanket of trees, its large parks and extensive boulevard system, its huge areas of fine homes, its rolling terrain, and the fact that many visitors so described it in well-publicized press releases. It was a matter of much pride to the city resident to witness a visitor's pleasure when he discovered the interestingly rugged terrain in place of the flat, treeless city he had expected.

A fourth set of images centered around the leadership of Kansas City as vigorous, farsighted, community-minded, and action-oriented. When a major problem arose, it was faced squarely; an action program would be developed without delay. These images also looked backward to the frontier days of quick and ready action, and to the time when major business activities had been developed locally and were operated by their original owners. Other images held in lesser degree were still to be found. One described Kansas City as a religious center and as part of the Bible Belt; another described it as a friendly city; another saw its people as unfettered by customs and outmoded social values. There was also the image of the big city (Kansas City, Missouri) dominating and engulfing the remainder of the metropolitan area. All of these images had some, although varying, bases in fact. Some stemmed quite directly from the first history of the area.

Appendix ***B***

The Study Populations

*T*his study is based on sets of data concerning two large groups of persons residing in the Kansas City metropolitan area: Interview data were obtained from a cross-sectional sample of men and women in the age range forty to sixty-nine, and data were gathered from various sources on the several thousand families who constituted the top three of the thirteen substrata. In the first instance, the study population is a systematic probability sample; in the second, the study population is the universe of families that fit the criteria.

Cross-Sectional Sample

As indicated in the preface, this study of urban social structure formed part of two interrelated sets of investigations that have come to be called the Kansas City Studies of Adult Life. The respondents were selected in accordance with the sampling plan designed for the first set of studies.

The area to be sampled was that defined by the U.S. Bureau of the Census as the Kansas City Metropolitan Area, and consisted of Jackson, Platte, and Clay Counties in Missouri, and of Johnson and Wyandotte Counties in Kansas. These five counties contained the two Kansas Cities which in 1954 were practically contiguous;

298

they also contained rapidly growing suburbs to the north, south, southeast and southwest, and in addition a few small towns and some open farm country. The total population of the metropolitan area was approximately 880,000 at the time of interviewing. Kansas City, Missouri, and the suburbs in its orbit represented about 590,000 of this total; Kansas City, Kansas, and the other satellite towns and rural areas accounted for the remaining 290,000.

The sample was designed to be representative of noninstitutionalized persons and was drawn to be a subsample of persons aged forty to sixty-nine from a larger cross-sectional sample containing adults of all ages. There were 2,392 households in the larger sample.

Selection of Dwelling Units: A two-stage stratified systematic probability sample was drawn. (The field work was carried out by Community Studies, Inc., a nonprofit research agency which had been conducting research in Kansas City for civic and welfare agencies for many years.)

The first stage was to designate a representative sample of blocks in the metropolitan area. Representativeness was assured by guaranteeing that every block had a chance of being included in the sample. The reports of the 1950 U.S. Census of Housing for the two Kansas Cities listed all blocks that contained dwelling units. These tables were supplemented by lists of blocks taken from the latest maps. For the area outside of the central cities, large scale maps were obtained and blocks were numbered serially within administrative areas. In the urbanized area as designated by the 1950 census, including the closely settled areas that comprise the urban fringe of the central cities, blocks were numbered within incorporated places or townships. In the rural districts, where blocks in the usual sense are nonexistent, the boundaries of census enumeration districts were drawn on county highway maps and these were subdivided into "blocks" and numbered. The primary sample of blocks was selected from these lists by designating certain blocks at regular intervals (every nth block).

The second stage of the sampling operation called for a systematic subsample of dwelling units (DUs) to be drawn from the primary sample of blocks. Field workers visited each of the sample blocks and noted the address or description of each DU on a form prepared for this purpose. The lists were then arranged by strata and block number. Dwelling units were marked off at regular intervals (nth household in nth block).

The intervals used to draw the sample blocks and DUs were derived from the ratio of the number of DUs in the area to the number desired in the sample. Since there were an estimated 290,000 DUs in the area and it was estimated that a pool of 2,300 were needed for the study sample, this ratio was 126 to 1.

Although a sample could have been drawn from a complete list of DUs in the metropolitan area, the time and cost of compiling such a list would have been prohibitive. The purpose of using a two-stage sample of blocks and DUs was to cluster the sample of DUs in a limited number of blocks so that the cost of listing and of interviewer travel could be reduced without an appreciable loss of reliability. However, because the presence of a few blocks containing very large numbers of DUs could distort the sample, all blocks that contained one hundred or more DUs were placed in a separate list. Thus the blocks were stratified by size (large and ordinary) as well as by geographic areas (Kansas City, Missouri; urban fringe; and rural). Since there were no large blocks in the urban fringe, there were five strata in all. The sampling ratios are shown in Table 16.

Interviewers were then sent to each of the 2,392 DUs to obtain initial information about the members of the household (including age, sex, color, occupation, income, and number of persons per room). If no personal contact was made on the first visit, additional calls were made up to a maximum of four. No substitutions were permitted. From this round of interviews, usable schedules were obtained from 1,889 persons aged forty to sixty-nine.

Initial Groupings: Because the investigators wished to study approximately equal numbers of persons at various social class levels, this initial sample was stratified further. On the basis of the preliminary information, the sample was divided into four groups representing first approximations to social class groups.

Placement was determined by rating each household on a scale from 1 (high) to 7 (low) on each of the following variables: prestige of occupation of the head of household, number of persons per room, amount of income per family, and residential area. The derived score is known as the Index of Economic Status (IES). A rating of 4 (the midpoint on each scale) was made equivalent to the medians of family income and number of persons per room as

Table 16. THE INITIAL SAMPLE OF DWELLING UNITS:
SAMPLING RATIO

| | Blocks | | Dwelling Units | |
Stratum	Sampling Ratio[a]	No.	Sampling Ratio[a]	No.
Ordinary blocks in Kansas City, Mo.	27.3	210	4.6	1,058
Large blocks in Kansas City, Mo.	9.2	20	13.0	224
Urban fringe	41.0	108	2.4	712
Ordinary rural blocks	24.5	14	5.0	219
Large rural blocks	10.0	13	13.0	179
Total number		365		2,392

[a] The considerations used in determining the sampling ratios were (with slight modifications) as follows: (1) The standard of 5 *DU*s were drawn from the ordinary-sized blocks containing less than 100 *DU*s. (2) The necessity of weighting the data from the different strata was avoided by requiring that the product of the block and *DU* sampling ratios within each stratum equal the overall sampling ratio. (3) Large blocks were selected at smaller intervals than ordinary blocks in the same area, and *DU*s were selected at correspondingly wider intervals. (4) Blocks outside urban centers were selected at larger intervals than those inside the city, and *DU*s were selected at correspondingly smaller intervals.

known from other data on Kansas City. Ratings of residential areas were made on the basis of judgments of real estate salesmen and others who knew property values and neighborhood prestige factors. The occupational prestige ratings were based on those made earlier by Warner (Warner, Meeker, and Eells, 1949), but the list of occupations was enlarged to suit the complexity of occupations in a metropolitan area.

The IES scores ranged from 4 (a score of 1 on each scale) to 28. This range was broken into four segments corresponding roughly to the social class division made by Warner: upper and upper-middle, lower-middle, upper-lower or working class, and lower class. Accuracy of these groupings was not expected to be high at this point because the data were gross, but more refined determinations of social status were to be made on the basis of information obtained in the follow-up interviews.

Each estimated social class group was then subdivided by sex and by five-year age groups. By this procedure the 1,889 persons were placed in forty-eight cells by age, sex, and estimated social class.

Subsamples: By the time this stage in the sampling had been reached, another decision had been made: to carry out separate but parallel studies with comparable subsamples of Kansas City men and women. Each subsample was designed to total 240 cases, to contain equal numbers of men and women in the four social class groups, but with age distribution approximating that of the total Kansas City population (that is, successively fewer persons in each higher five-year age group from forty–to–forty-four to sixty-five–to–sixty-nine). The actual number of individuals in each forty–to–forty-four year-old cell was seven; then six, five, five, four, with three in each sixty-five–to–sixty-nine year-old cell.

From the population of 1,889 individuals, names were drawn at random within age, sex, and social class cells to establish the study populations for each of four parallel studies. The pool provided enough cases for three studies, but there were insufficient upper-middle and lower-class cases for the fourth, a study of social mobility in men. In 1954, when Community Studies, Inc., drew a new master sample of the Kansas City metropolitan area in connection with a different research project, that sample was drawn upon to provide additional cases for the Study of Adult Life. In this instance, the names of 127 men were drawn, constituting subsample C in Table 17. (The 1954 master sample followed the same general procedures used in 1953.)

Thus the study population for the present study of social status is composed of three subsamples, two from the master sample of 1953 and a small one from the master sample of 1954. Combining cases from two master samples is, of course, open to objection from the point of view of sampling theory, but it does not raise as serious an objection to the quality of the final sample as does the fact that not all the people drawn for the original subsamples were actually interviewed. The numbers of interview completions are shown in Table 17. Inevitable variations developed between the

Table 17. Summary of Interviewing Experience

	Subsample A		Subsample B		Subsample C[a]	
	Number	Per Cent	Number	Per Cent	Number	Per Cent
Assignments	451	100.0	443	100.0	127	100.0
Completions	242[c]	53.7	234[c]	52.8	87	68.5
Refusals	98	21.7	111	25.1	26	20.5
Moved-untraced	36	8.0	27	6.1	—	—
Moved out of city	14	3.1	11	2.5	—	—
Unable to contact[b]	35	7.8	34	7.7	8	6.3
Deceased	2	0.4	8	1.8	1	0.8
Incomplete record	24	5.3	18	4.0	5	4.0

[a] Subsamples A and B were parts of the 1953 sample of the Kansas City metropolitan area; subsample C was part of the 1954 sample.

[b] Persons who were not at home, who failed to keep appointments, who were away for duration of interviewing, or who were seriously ill.

[c] Of the 476 completions shown in subsamples A and B, a few persons were causes of overlap: that is, in addition to questions pertaining to social status, they were asked the questions relating to both studies A and B. (This constitutes a slight inflation of the completion rate.) In several other instances, a husband was interviewed for Study A, and a wife, for Study B.

standard design and the distribution of those actually interviewed, not only because of losses due to moves and refusals but also because of revisions in social class placement in certain cases following the research interview.

Intensive efforts were made to secure interviews. Interviewers were trained at length by the professional staff members, all interviews were read as they came in, and interviewing assignments were carefully monitored. Special efforts were made to match interviewer and interviewee. With the highest status respondents, a letter of explanation was sent out, then a telephone call was made asking to set a time for an interview, and in many cases the professional staff of the study conducted the interview. Special efforts were employed also in the interviews with the lowest status group. Negro interviewers were used with Negro respondents.

Generalizing from all four parallel studies, the male interviewers were more successful with male respondents; female interviewers were almost equally successful with both sexes. The higher status respondents gave more refusals than other groups, and women were more likely to refuse than men. The refusals were about evenly distributed by age, but with somewhat fewer refusals in the forty-five to forty-nine group and somewhat more in the fifty-five to fifty-nine group.

Altogether, of the completed interviews indicated in Table 17, relevant data were obtained on 462 family units (as reported in Table 2, Chapter Four), and relevant data were obtained on larger numbers of individual men and women (as reported in Chapter Eleven and elsewhere).

It is clear that the final sample is not strictly representative of the Kansas City population in the age range. The primary shortcomings of the final sample are: (1) It is biased in favor of geographically stable residents. The group interviewed did not include an appropriate number of people (primarily of lower status) who move frequently and do not leave forwarding addresses. (2) The sample did not include people living in institutions, in hotels, or in rooming houses. (3) Some 20 per cent of the original sample refused to be interviewed. These people are most difficult to characterize. Undoubtedly some did not have time for an interview some two hours in length. Others may have had personality characteristics which made them significantly different from the persons who co-operated. The effects of such bias are unknown.

Upper-Status Families

Field work aspects of the study of upper-status families were carried out by the senior author in the three years from 1952 to 1955; additional data were gathered from 1955 to 1962. Some one hundred Kansas City men and women, themselves at upper levels of the social structure, were used as informants regarding the relative status of persons in the upper strata, the subtle differentiations that characterized the social interaction patterns, and the symbols associated with differences in social position.

In addition to lengthy interviews with informants, other research procedures were followed. The initial step was to assemble a file of names of prominent citizens. Into this file went the names of all Kansas Citians who: were members of one or more of the private clubs identified as socially prominent; served on a civic board or committee that was generally considered prestigeful; were listed in *Who's Who in America* or *Who's Who in Commerce and Industry;* were listed in *Poor's Register of Executives and Directors;* were mentioned on the business and financial pages of the Kansas City newspapers as officials, directors, or owners of large industrial firms in the area; were listed in Polk's *Kansas City Directory* as residing in the Gold Coast Ward Parkway and Mission Hills neighborhoods; or were mentioned in one or more issues of *The Chatterbox,* a weekly magazine devoted to reporting the activities of high-status Kansas Citians. Other names were placed in the file if an obituary story appeared in the Kansas City *Star* or *Times* which suggested that the individual had at some time in the past been an active member of Kansas City's upper class.

Data on social characteristics were then assembled for some six thousand families and individuals whose names entered the file. These data were obtained in a variety of formal and informal ways: newspaper accounts, historical records, association records, and so on. Information included all club memberships and civic participation, quality of housing, location of house, educational background, religious affiliation, occupational role, estimated assets and income.

In addition, when available, information regarding previous areas of residence, children's educations, children's marriages and present activities, parental generation, names and social characteristics of siblings were all recorded.

Information regarding informal clique behavior was assembled from the society columns of the Kansas City newspapers and *The Chatterbox*. People who vacationed together were noted, as well as persons who attended one another's parties. During a two year period over fifteen hundred lists of party hosts and guests were accumulated, as well as an uncounted number of references to pairs of families who were friends. Analysis of this information on clique behavior was important in delineating the various "crowds" that Kansas Citians talked about.

Historical data were acquired on family social participation and club memberships in previous years and in previous generations. Every copy of *The Chatterbox* dating back to 1918 was examined. Also scrutinized was a locally published *Kansas City Social Register,* which had appeared sporadically since 1899. (This *Register* was not affiliated with the Social Register Association of New York City.)

As a separate research step, a representative group of thirty high-status men and women were asked to rank some of the families listed in the file. The names were grouped by age and each rater was asked about persons of his own age group. The rater was asked if he agreed with the tentative placements made by the investigator, why or why not, and for his own views of the top rungs of the Kansas City social ladder.

Each family's social placement was determined as of January, 1955. Finally, from 1955 to 1962, changes in club memberships, clique groupings, and civic participation were recorded by the continuous monitoring of the two Kansas City newspapers and *The Chatterbox*. While a few persons may have escaped the investigators' net, these procedures yielded data on what we regard as the universe of upper-status families in Kansas City.

Appendix C

Social Characteristics of People at or Near the Top

Table 18. LINEAGE, SOCIAL AFFILIATIONS, CIVIC PARTICIPATION

	Capital S Society		Non-Capital S Uppers		The "Non-U Rich"	Upper-Middle Elite
	Level I (N = 158)	Level II (N = 350)	Level III (N = 669)	Level IV (N = 1,092)	(N = 285)	(N = 1,240)
Class of Origin: Families in which husband or wife inherited status in[a]						
(1) Capital S Society or equivalent elsewhere	74	45	3	3	—	2
(2) Upper class, but not Capital S level	26	48	45	29	—	14
(3) Upper-middle class	—	6	43	50	9	58
(4) Lower-middle class	—	1	7	15	55	21
(5) Working class or lower	—	—	2	3	36	5
Club Memberships:						
Families with one or more elite country club memberships	99	66	70	37	—	17
Men with one or more elite downtown private club memberships	97	59	54	46	—	30
Women in Junior League	71	49	6	2	—	—
Civic Leadership: Families represented by husband or wife, or both, in the following roles:						
(a) director of a cultural institution (Nelson Gallery, Art Institute, Philharmonic, Conservatory, Historical Museum, area colleges)	44	20	14	4	—	1
(b) director of a welfare agency (Community Chest, Red Cross, YMCA, Boys Club, etc.)	53	27	29	20	1	3
(c) director or officer of Chamber of Commerce, American Royal, Starlight Theater, other promotional organizations	27	18	24	9	1	2
(d) member of official board or commission of the city, county, and state government	10	6	6	4	1	1

[a] Families are classified here by family origin of the more highly-placed member of the couple. For method of judging "inherited status," see Chapter Eleven on Social Mobility. These class judgments here apply to origin in other communities as well as Kansas City. When parents rose in status to Capital S or to upper class after their children had reached adulthood, the children were counted as inheriting the new status at this class level, even though they had not invariably shared in the parent's rise.

Bibliography

ALLINGHAM, J. D. "Class Regression as Aspect of the Social Stratification Process." *American Sociological Review*, 1967, *32*, 442–449.

AMORY, C. *The Proper Bostonians*. New York: Dutton, 1947.

BAILEY, W. C. "The Status System of a Texas Panhandle Community." *Texas Journal of Science*, 1953, *5*, 316–331.

BALTZELL, E. D. *Philadelphia Gentlemen*. New York: Free Press, 1958.

BALTZELL, E. D. *The Protestant Establishment*. New York: Random House, 1964.

BANFIELD, E. C., AND WILSON, J. Q. *City Politics*. Cambridge, Mass.: Harvard University Press, 1963.

BARBER, B. *Social Stratification*. New York: Harcourt Brace Jovanovich, 1957.

BARKER, R. G., AND WRIGHT, H. F. *Midwest and Its Children: The Psychological Ecology of an American Town*. New York: Harper and Row, 1954.

BENDIX, R., AND LIPSET, S. M. (Eds.) *Class, Status and Power: A Reader in Social Stratification*. (1st ed.) New York: Free Press, 1953.

BENDIX, R., AND LIPSET, S. M. (Eds.) *Class, Status and Power: Social Stratification in Comparative Perspective*. (2nd ed.) New York: Free Press, 1966.

BERGER, B. M. *Working Class Suburb*. Berkeley and Los Angeles: University of California Press, 1960.

BESHERS, J. M. *Urban Social Structure*. New York: Free Press, 1962.

BILLINGSLEY, A. *Black Families in White America*. Englewood Cliffs, N.J.: Prentice-Hall, 1968.

BLAU, P. M., AND DUNCAN, O. D. *The American Occupational Structure*. New York: Wiley, 1967.

BLOOMBAUM, M. "The Mobility Dimension in Status Consistency," *Sociology and Social Research*, 1964, *48*, 340–347.

BOGUE, D. J. *The Population of the United States*. New York: Free Press, 1959.

309

BONJEAN, C. "Mass, Class, and the Industrial Community: A Comparative Analysis of Managers, Businessmen and Workers." *American Journal of Sociology,* 1966, *72,* 149–162.

BUCKLEY, W. "Social Stratification and Social Differentiation." *American Sociological Review,* 1958, *23,* 369–375.

BURCHARD, W. "The Status of Status." *Sociology and Social Research,* 1960, *44,* 417–423.

CHAPIN, F. S. *The Measurement of Social Status by the Use of the Social Status Scale.* Minneapolis: University of Minnesota Press, 1933.

CENTERS, R. *The Psychology of Social Classes.* Princeton: Princeton University Press, 1949.

CHINOY, E. *Automobile Workers and the American Dream.* New York: Doubleday, 1955.

COLEMAN, R. P. "The Significance of Social Stratification in Selling." *Proceedings of the Forty-Third National Conference of the American Marketing Association,* 1960, 171–184.

CUBER, J. F., AND KENKEL, W. F. *Social Stratification in the United States.* New York: Appleton-Century-Crofts, 1954.

DAHL, R. A. *Who Governs? Democracy and Power in an American City.* New Haven, Conn.: Yale University Press, 1961.

DAVIDSON, P. E., AND ANDERSON, H. D. *Occupational Mobility in an American Community.* Stanford, Calif.: Stanford University Press, 1937.

DAVIS, A., GARDNER, B. B., AND GARDNER, M. R. *Deep South.* Chicago: University of Chicago Press, 1941.

DAVIS, K., AND MOORE, W. F. "Some Principles of Stratification." *American Sociological Review,* 1945, *10,* 242–249.

DEMERATH, N. J., III, *Social Class in American Protestantism.* Chicago: Rand McNally, 1965.

DILLINGHAM, H. C. "Protestant Religion and Social Status." *American Journal of Sociology,* 1965, *71,* 416–422.

DOBRINER, W. M. *Class in Suburbia.* Englewood Cliffs, N.J.: Prentice-Hall, 1963.

DOLLARD, J. *Caste and Class in a Southern Town.* Garden City, N.Y.: Doubleday, 1949.

DRAKE, ST. C., AND CAYTON, H. R. *Black Metropolis.* New York: Harcourt, Brace, and Jovanovich, 1945.

DUNCAN, O. D. "The Trend of Occupational Mobility in the United States." *American Sociological Review,* 1965, *30,* 491–498.

DUNCAN, O. D., AND ARTIS, J. W. *Social Stratification in a Pennsylvania Rural Community,* Bulletin 543. State College, Pa. Pennsylvania State College of Agriculture, 1951.

EDWARDS, A. E. *Comparative Occupation Statistics for the United States: 1870–1940.* Washington, D.C.: U.S. Government Printing Office, 1943.

EELLS, K., et al. *Intelligence and Cultural Differences*. Chicago: University of Chicago Press, 1951.

ELLIS, R. A. "The Continuum Theory of Social Stratification: A Critical Note." *Sociology and Social Research*, 1958, *42*, 269–273.

ELLIS, R. A., AND LANE, W. C. "Structural Supports for Upward Mobility." *American Sociological Review*, 1963, *28*, 743–756.

FERMAN, L. L., KORNBLUH, J. L., AND HABER, A. (Eds.) *Poverty in America: A Book of Readings*. Ann Arbor, Mich.: University of Michigan Press, 1965.

FORM, W. H. "Status Stratification in a Planned Community." *American Sociological Review*, 1945, *10*, 605–613.

FRAZIER, E. F. *Black Bourgeoisie: The Rise of a New Middle Class in the United States*. New York: Collier, 1962.

GALLAHER, A., JR. *Plainville: Fifteen Years Later*. New York: Columbia University Press, 1961.

GANS, H. J. *The Levittowners: Ways of Life and Politics in a New Suburban Community*. New York: Pantheon, 1967.

GANS, H. J. *The Urban Villagers*. New York: Free Press, 1963.

GLAZER, N., AND MOYNIHAN, D. P. *Beyond the Melting Pot: the Negroes, Puerto Ricans, Jews, Italians and Irish of New York City*. Cambridge, Mass.: Harvard University Press, 1963.

GOODE, E. "Social Class and Church Participation." *American Journal of Sociology*, 1966, *72*, 102–111.

GORDON, M. S. (Ed.) *Poverty in America:* Proceedings of a National Conference held at the University of California, Berkeley, Feb. 26–28, 1965. San Francisco: Chandler, 1965.

GORDON, M. M. *Social Class in American Sociology*. Durham, N.C.: Duke University Press, 1958.

GROSS, L. "The Use of Class Concepts in Sociological Research." *American Journal of Sociology*, 1949, *54*, 409–421.

GROSS, N. "Social Class Identification in the Urban Community." *American Sociological Review*, 1953, *18*, 398–404.

HAMILTON, R. F. "The Marginal Middle Class: A Reconsideration." *American Sociological Review*, 1960, *31*, 192–199.

HANDEL, G., AND RAINWATER, L. "Persistence and Change in Working Class Life Style." In Shostak and Gomberg, *Blue-Collar World* (1964), pp. 36–41.

HARRINGTON, M. *The Other America: Poverty in the United States*. New York: Macmillan, 1962.

HATT, P. K., AND NORTH, C. C. "Jobs and Occupations: A Popular Evaluation." In Bendix and Lipset, *Class, Status and Power* (1953), pp. 411–425.

HILL, M. C., AND MC CALL, B. C. "Social Stratification in Georgia Town." *American Sociological Review*, 1950, *15*, 721–729.

HODGE, R. W., SIEGEL, P. M., AND ROSSI, P. H. "Occupational Prestige in the United States, 1925–1963." *American Journal of Sociology,* 1964, *70,* 286–302.

HODGE, R. W., AND TREIMAN, D. J. "Class Identification in the United States." *American Journal of Sociology,* 1968, *73,* 535–547.

HODGES, H. M., JR. "Peninsula People: Social Stratification in a Metropolitan Complex." In W. W. Kallenbach and H. M. Hodges, Jr. (Eds.), *Education and Society.* Columbus, Ohio: Merrill, 1963.

HODGES, H. M., JR. *Social Stratification: Class in America.* Cambridge, Mass.: Schenkman, 1964.

HOLLINGSHEAD, A. B. "Cultural Factors in the Selection of Marriage Mates." *American Sociological Review,* 1950, *15,* 619–627.

HOLLINGSHEAD, A. B. *Elmtown's Youth.* New York: Wiley, 1949.

HOLLINGSHEAD, A. B., AND REDLICH, F. C. *Social Class and Mental Illness: A Community Study.* New York: Wiley, 1958.

HUNTER, F. *Community Power Structure.* Chapel Hill, N.C.: University of North Carolina Press, 1953.

HYMAN, H. H. "The Value Systems of Different Classes: A Social Psychological Contribution to the Analysis of Stratification." In Bendix and Lipset, *Class, Status and Power* (2nd ed.), pp. 426–442.

JACKSON, E. F., AND CROCKETT, H. J., JR. "Occupational Mobility in the United States: A Point Estimate and Trend Comparison." *American Sociological Review,* 1964, *29,* 5–15.

JENNINGS, M. K. *Community Influentials: The Elites of Atlanta.* New York: Free Press, 1964.

JONES, A. W. *Life, Liberty and Property.* New York, Octagon, 1964. Originally published in 1941.

KAHL, J. A. *The American Class Structure.* New York: Rinehart, 1957.

KAHL, J. A., AND DAVIS, J. A. "A Comparison of Indexes of Socioeconomic Status." *American Sociological Review,* 1955, *20,* 317–325.

KAUFMAN, H. *Prestige Classes in a New York Rural Community,* Memoir 260. Ithaca, N.Y.: Cornell University Agricultural Station, 1964. Reprinted with minor adaptions in Bendix and Lipset, *Class, Status and Power* (1st ed.), pp. 190–203.

KNUPFER, G. "Indices of Socioeconomic Status: A Study of Some Problems of Measurement." (Doctoral dissertation, Columbia University, 1946.)

KOMAROVSKY, M. *Blue Collar Marriage.* New York: Random House, 1964.

KORNHAUSER, R. R. "The Warner Approach to Social Stratification." In Bendix and Lipset, *Class, Status and Power* (1st ed.), pp. 224–254.

LASSWELL, T. E. *Class and Stratum.* Boston: Houghton Mifflin, 1965.

LASSWELL, T. E. "Social Class and Size of Community." *American Journal of Sociology,* 1959, *64,* 505–508.

LASSWELL, T. E. "Status Stratification in a Selected Community." (Unpublished doctoral dissertation, University of Southern California, 1952.)

LAUMANN, E. O. *Prestige and Association in an Urban Community: An Analysis of an Urban Stratification System.* Indianapolis: Bobbs Merrill, 1967.

LENSKI, G. E. "American Social Classes: Statistical Strata or Social Groups?" *American Journal of Sociology,* 1952, *58,* 139–144.

LENSKI, G. E. *Power and Privilege: A Theory of Social Stratification.* New York: McGraw-Hill, 1967.

LENSKI, G. E. "Status Crystalization: A Nonvertical Dimension of Social Status." *American Sociological Review,* 1954, *19,* 405–413.

LEWIS, O. *Children of Sanchez.* New York: Random House, 1961.

LEWIS, O. *Five Families.* New York: Basic Books, 1959.

LIPSET, S. M., AND BENDIX, R. *Social Mobility in an Industrial Society.* Berkeley and Los Angeles: University of California Press, 1959.

LYND, R. S., AND LYND, H. M. *Middletown in Transition.* New York: Harcourt, Brace, and Jovanovich, 1937.

LYND, R. S., AND LYND, H. M. *Middletown: A Study in American Culture.* New York: Harcourt, Brace, and Jovanovich, 1929.

MC CALL, B. C. "Georgia Town and Cracker Culture: A Sociological Study." (Unpublished doctoral dissertation, University of Chicago, 1954.)

MAC DONALD, D. "Our Invisible Poor." *The New Yorker,* January 19, 1963.

MARTINEAU, P. *Motivation in Advertising.* New York: McGraw-Hill, 1957.

MAYER, K. B. "The Changing Shape of the American Class Structure." *Social Research,* 1963, *30,* 458–468.

MAYER, K. B. *Class and Society.* New York: Random House, 1955.

MEEKER, M. L. "A Study of Associations and Their Relationship to the Class System of a Midwestern Community." (Unpublished master's thesis, University of Chicago, 1947.)

MEISSNER, H. H. (Ed.) *Poverty in the Affluent Society.* New York: Harper and Row, 1966.

MILLER, H. P. *Rich Man, Poor Man.* New York: Thomas Y. Crowell, 1964.

MILLER, S. M. "The American Lower Class: A Typological Approach," *Social Research,* 1964, *31,* 1–22.

MILLER, S. M., AND REISSMAN, F. "The Working Class Subculture: A New View." *Social Problems,* 1960, *9,* 86–97.

MILLS, C. W. *The Power Elite.* New York: Oxford University, 1956.

MITFORD, N. (Ed.) *Noblesse Oblige: An Inquiry into the Identifiable*

Characteristics of the English Aristocracy. New York: Harper, 1956.

MONTAGUE, J. B., JR. "Class or Status Society." *Sociology and Social Research,* 1956, *40,* 333–338.

PARSONS, T. "A Revised Analytical Approach to the Theory of Social Stratification." In Bendix and Lipset, *Class, Status and Power* (1st ed.), pp. 92–128.

PFAUTZ, H. W. "The Current Literature on Social Stratification: A Critique and Bibliography." *American Journal of Sociology,* 1953, *58,* 395–398.

PFAUTZ, H. W., AND DUNCAN, O. D. "A Critical Evaluation of Warner's Work in Community Stratification." *American Sociological Review,* 1950, *15,* 205–215.

POLSBY, N. W. *Community Power and Political Theory.* New Haven: Yale University Press, 1963.

PRESTHUS, R. *Men at the Top: A Study in Community Power.* New York: Oxford University Press, 1964.

RAINWATER, L., COLEMAN, R. P., AND HANDEL, G. W. *Workingman's Wife: Her Personality, World, and Life Style.* New York: Oceana Publications, 1959.

REISS, A. J., JR. "Change in the Occupational Structure of the United States, 1910–1950." In Paul K. Hatt and Albert J. Reiss, Jr., Eds., *Cities and Society: The Revised Reader in Urban Sociology.* New York: Free Press, 1957.

REISS, A. J., JR., DUNCAN, O. D., HATT, P. K., AND NORTH, C. C. *Occupations and Social Status.* New York: Free Press, 1961.

REISSMAN, L. *Class in American Society.* New York: Free Press, 1959.

ROACH, J. L., GROSS, L., AND GURSSLIN, O. (Eds.) *Social Stratification in the United States.* Englewood Cliffs, N.J.: Prentice-Hall, 1969.

ROACH, J. L. "Sociological Analysis and Poverty," *American Journal of Sociology,* 1962, *71,* 68–77.

ROGOFF, N. *Recent Trends in Occupational Mobility.* New York: Free Press, 1953.

SCHULZE, R. O. "Economic Dominance and Public Leadership: A Study of the Structure and Process in Power in an Urban Community." (Doctoral dissertation, University of Michigan, 1959.)

SELIGMAN, D. "The New Masses." *Fortune,* May 1959, pp. 106–107.

SHOSTAK, A. B., AND GOMBERG, W. (Eds.) *Blue Collar World: Studies of the American Worker.* Englewood Cliffs, N.J.: Prentice-Hall, Inc., 1964.

SIEGLE, P. E. "The Social Life of a Jewish Community." (Doctoral dissertation, University of Chicago, 1958.)

SIMMONS AND ASSOCIATES, private communication to the Chicago *Sun-Times,* 1960.

SOCIAL SCIENCE RESEARCH COMMITTEE FROM THE UNIVERSITY OF CHIcago, *Rotary: A University Group Looks at the Rotary Club of Chicago.* Chicago: University of Chicago Press, 1934.

STENDLER, C. B. *Children of Brasstown.* Urbana, Ill.: University of Illinois Press, 1949.

STONE, G. P., AND FORM, W. H. "Instabilities in Status: The Problem of Hierarchy in the Community Study of Status Arrangements." *American Sociological Review,* 1953, *18,* 149–162.

TAUSSIG, F. W., AND JOSLYN, C. S. *American Business Leaders.* New York: Macmillan, 1932.

THERNSTROM, S. *Poverty and Progress: Social Mobility in a Nineteenth-Century City.* Cambridge, Mass.: Harvard University Press, 1964.

THERNSTROM, S. "'Yankee City' Revisited: The Perils of Historical Naivete." *American Sociological Review,* 1965, *30,* 234–242.

THOMETZ, C. *The Decision Makers: The Power Structure of Dallas.* Dallas: Southern Methodist University Press, 1963.

TUMIN, M. M. *Social Stratification: The Forms and Functions of Inequality.* Englewood Cliffs, N.J.: Prentice-Hall, 1967.

TUMIN, M. M. "Some Principles of Stratification: A Critical Analysis." *American Sociological Review,* 1953, *18,* 387–397.

USEEM, J., TANGENT, P., AND USEEM, R. "Stratification in a Prairie Town." *American Sociological Review,* 1942, *7,* 331–342.

VIDICH, A. J., AND BENSMAN, J. *Small Town in Mass Society: Class, Power, and Religion in a Rural Community.* Princeton, N.J.: Princeton University Press, 1958.

VIDICH, A. J., BENSMAN, J., AND STEIN, M. R. (Eds.) *Reflections on Community Studies.* New York: Wiley, 1964.

VOLLMER, H., AND MILLS, D. L. (Eds.) *Professionalization.* Englewood Cliffs, N.J.: Prentice-Hall, 1966.

WARNER, W. L., et al. *Democracy in Jonesville.* New York: Harper, 1949.

WARNER, W. L., AND ABEGGLEN, J. *Occupational Mobility in Business and Industry.* Minneapolis: University of Minnesota Press, 1955.

WARNER, W. L., AND LOW, J. O. *The Status System of the Modern Factory.* New Haven: Yale University Press, 1947.

WARNER, W. L., AND LUNT, P. S. *The Social Life of the Modern Community.* New Haven: Yale University Press, 1941.

WARNER, W. L., AND LUNT, P. S. *The Status System of the Modern Community.* New Haven: Yale University Press, 1942.

WARNER, W. L., MEEKER, M. L., AND EELLS, K. *Social Class in America.* Chicago: Science Research Associates, 1949.

WATSON, W. B., AND BARTH, E. A. T. "Questionable Assumptions in the Theory of Social Stratification." *Pacific Sociological Review,* 1964, *7,* 10–16.

WECTER, D. *The Saga of American Society*. New York: Charles Scribner's Sons, 1937.

WEST, J. *Plainville, U.S.A.* New York: Columbia Univ. Press, 1945.

WHEELER, W. *Social Stratification in a Plains Community*. Minneapolis: Minnesota, privately published, 1949.

WHYTE, W. H., JR. *The Organization Man*. New York: Simon and Schuster, 1956.

WILDAVSKY, A. *Leadership in a Small Town*. Totawa, N.J.: Bedminster Press, 1964.

WRONG, D. H. "The Functional Theory of Stratification: Some Neglected Considerations." *American Sociological Review*, 1959, 24, 777–782.

ZICK, R. "Do American Women Marry Up?" *American Sociological Review*, 1968, 33, 750–759.

Index

A

Age and status, 136–137, 152–154
ALLINGHAM, J. D., 220n
AMORY, C., 269
Association status scale, 106–108

B

BAILEY, W. C., 4n
BALTZELL, E. D., 268n, 269
BANFIELD, E. C., 266n
BENDIX, R., 4n, 220
BENSMAN, J., 4n
BERGER, B. M., 176n
BILLINGSLEY, A., 66n, 67n
BLAU, P. M., 84n
BLOOMBAUM, M., 220n
BOGUE, D. J., 84n
BONJEAN, C., 286n

C

CAYTON, H. R., 66n., 67n
Civic leadership, 139, 154–155, 266
Class consciousness, 11–29; and city line, 26–29; and collar color, 18–19; and ethnic groups, 22–26; and political parties, 19–21; and skin color, 21–22
Class structure. See Status structure
Club membership: and association status scale, 106–108; as dimension of status, 41–43, 75; in Negro status structure, 68–69

COLEMAN

COLEMAN, R. P., 110, 176n
Collar color, 18–19, 158–159, 191–193
CROCKETT, H. J., JR., 220

D

DAHL, R. A., 266n
DAVIS, A., 34, 66n, 80, 254
DEMERATH, N. J., III, 268n
DILLINGHAM, H. C., 268n
DOBRINER, W. M., 4n
DOLLARD, J., 4n, 66n
DRAKE, ST. C., 66n, 67n
DUNCAN, O. D., 4n, 84n, 220

E

Education: as dimension of status, 51–53, 77–79, 264–265, 279–281; intergeneration differences in, 223; of Negroes, 68; and status scale, 96–103; in upper class, 139–140; of wives, 99
EDWARDS, A. E., 84n
EELLS, K., 80, 82, 90, 97, 254, 301
ELLIS, R. A., 248n
Ethnic and racial groups, 12–13, 21–25, 197–198, 200–202, 206–210, 267–268; American Indians, 206–208; Arkies, 25; Italians, 22–24; leaders of, 179–181; Mexicans, 24–25, 208–210; Negroes, 21–22
Evaluated participation, 6–7, 253